Mary Baker Eddy

Mary Baker Eddy

An Interpretive Biography of the Founder of Christian Science

Julius Silberger, Jr., M.D.

Little, Brown and Company   Boston · Toronto

FIRST EDITION

Library of Congress Cataloging in Publication Data

Silberger, Julius.
  Mary Baker Eddy, an interpretive biography of the founder of Christian Science.

  Includes bibliographical references and index.
    1. Eddy, Mary Baker, 1821–1910.   2.   Christian Scientists—United States—Biography.   I.   Title.
  BX6995.S513   289.5′092′4   [B]   .80–11098
  ISBN 0–316–79090–7

Quotes from *The Life of Mary Baker G. Eddy and the History of Christian Science* by Georgine Milmine, reprinted 1971 by Baker Book House and used by permission.

The permission of The Christian Science Board of Directors to quote from the copyrighted works of Mary Baker Eddy, including the first edition of *Science and Health*, should not be construed by the reader as implying that Board's knowledge, responsibility, or approval of the way in which these selections are interpreted or used in this book.

MV

Designed by Janis Capone

*Published simultaneously in Canada
by Little, Brown & Company (Canada) Limited*

In memory of
Morris Adler,
Beata Rank,
and
Elvin Semrad

Preface

The clinical practice of psychoanalysis and the writing of historical biography are naturally complementary aspects of my daily work. However much they differ as activities, each offers something to the other.

A patient's life can be known only up to the moment of inquiry — we cannot know what he is to become; the life of a subject of biography can be known as a whole, but in less detail and texture. The patient in psychoanalysis is an active participant in the process, taking a comment, modifying it, bringing new information to bear, and transforming it into a statement more precisely expressive of his own experience; the subject of our historical inquiry cannot participate in this way and, more often than not, might not want to. Here, the author depends more on his own experience, on as broad a range of information as he can have access to, and on whatever capacity he might have to read himself into the subject's life in a way that offers the least possible distortion to the subject's own frame of reference. Beyond that, a biographer exercises much greater initiative in the choice of his subject than the psychoanalyst does, and has a broader choice in the questions to which he may address himself.

In effect, the psychoanalyst can show the biographer how to integrate apparently disparate details of a person's life into a coherent whole, and the biographer can remind the psychoanalyst that the facts of a patient's life are not yet known at the moment of analytic study; much remains for the future. One cannot know what a patient will do with what he has; people find ways of using their griefs and discontents to generate creative lives that transcend psychopathological inquiry.

There is one recurrent problem in biographical writing for which the practice of psychoanalysis has a built-in corrective — the attitude of the author toward his subject, which in the psychoanalytic situation is called the problem of Counter-transference. This term relates to the attitudes and biases that arise within the analyst in response to his patient, biases that can tell him something about himself and, often, a great deal about his patient. A systematic attention to these attitudes is part of the analyst's activity that keeps the analysis moving along properly. In the writing of biography, however, the author is not required to monitor his reactions to his subject. Indeed, he often approaches his subject with a predetermined bias that may account for his selection of the subject in the first place and that may define in advance the kind of biography he is going to write. This is at least one reason for the tendency of biographical studies either to adulate or to depreciate their subject. The biographer becomes caught up in his own subjective reactions.

In certain instances other considerations may motivate the decision to produce a slanted product; the wish to compose an object lesson is the most common of these justifications, and I suppose no great harm is done if the reader knows the author's intention or if the practice is so transparent as to be readily discernable.

My own interest in Mrs. Eddy was stimulated when, by chance, I came across a biography written by someone who admired her very much. I was browsing in the library when I should have been doing something else. But there were at least three other immediate reasons for my sudden interest. First, at that moment of my life I was particularly awake to the charm often exerted by impressive, sometimes inconsistent, but intuitively gifted elderly women. Second, I thought I perceived in the book evidence that Mrs. Eddy's creation of Christian Science followed a period of grief in her middle years, a grief that arose from the loss of two men who were very important to her. But it seemed that the author, who provided the suggestive evidence, read between the lines, was not consciously aware of this time in Mrs. Eddy's life as a period of mourning, nor of how it arose in relation to her personal losses.

The third reason for my interest was that my own field of professional study, psychoanalysis, like Christian Science, had its origins in mesmerism, with alliances in mental healing, and if it differed radically from Christian Science by looking into the psychology of the individual for the keys to understanding symptoms, rather than outwardly into notions of divine order and universal harmony, yet both psychoanalysis and Christian Science were perceived by their contemporaries as revolutionary and even subversive activities, and each took on in its organizational aspects some of the defensiveness that characterizes revolutionary movements, with struggles over orthodoxy and tests of devotion and of commitment.

Once you begin a piece of work, you hope that its scope will grow beyond the immediate restricted interests that moved you to undertake it. Writing this book has been an educational experience for me, not only in learning to put pen to paper, though that, too, but also in trying to understand what Mrs. Eddy was trying to accomplish from her own point of view, or from as close a version to her own point of view as I could bring myself to imagine. This made it possible for me to think that I understood obscure passages in her letters and more public writings and even, at times, to decipher words in manuscripts of her letters which one might otherwise have passed over with a shrug of incomprehension. Whether my optimism is justified is for the reader to decide.

I have by choice included quotations as much as possible, limiting them only by a wish not to distract the reader with excessive detail, but hoping by using the original words themselves to give to the reader some basis for assessing my own inferences as well as some of the texture of Mrs. Eddy's own real life and a small taste of the stylistic idiosyncrasies of her late-nineteenth-century environment.

One may object that I have not speculated on subjects about which I have no data, on specific aspects, for example, of Mrs. Eddy's intimate relationships. I can plead only that I have preferred to confine my speculations to subjects about which I felt I had more adequate information. Similarly, it may be found disappointing that I do not use psychiatric and psychoanalytic terms and that I do not attempt to make diagnoses. To this objection the reply is one of judgment rather than of ignorance. My experience has been that such a practice, rather than enhancing understanding, reduces it. The reader tends to see the person as a patient in a restricted sense, as someone suffering from X, Y, or Z, whereas I prefer to hope that I'm writing about a person who was complex, interesting, and impressive in her own way.

This is naturally a Boston book, about a New England person, much of whose life was centered in Boston. I had to my advantage the use of the Boston Public Library and the Harvard College libraries, to whose staffs I want to give my thanks. They were unfailingly courteous to someone they didn't know; their considerateness is the more impressive for being routine. It is a great pleasure to have as my publisher Little, Brown and Company, a Boston firm. Let me express my particular thanks to Richard McDonough for his confidence in my work and for his enlightened and judicious advice. Betsy Pitha was a source of scholarly information, offered tactfully, with a keen sense of style, coherence, and economy. I thank my family and friends for their continual encouragement of my project. Finally and most particularly, let me thank Evelyn Stone for her wise counsel and unfailing optimism, and let me thank Joyce Olesen for her expert introduction, volunteered in a friendly and unreserved spirit, to the fine art of pruning and shaping.

Mary Baker Eddy

Introduction

Mary Baker Eddy was, improbably, one of the most influential women of her age. She was born into unpromising circumstances. She never mastered the limited education that was available to her. She lacked a literary talent and any real vocation for family life. She struggled against a social order and a century that permitted women only the narrowest range of life choices. And yet, having decided at an early age that she would become a successful author, rich and respected, she succeeded, despite all of the improbabilities, and even though her first real chance didn't come until she was forty-five. Then she seized upon the little pebble of opportunity that life dropped in her path, developed it with single-minded insistence, and made the best possible use of its every aspect. She succeeded not only in becoming rich and respected for what she had written, but she became as well the founder, architect, and builder of a burgeoning church and the discoverer of an enormously successful way of integrating mental healing with religion.

Success brought its detractors, and in the last years of her life Mrs. Eddy and Christian Science became the objects of attack from at least three different sources — the other Protestant clergy, the medical profession, and those who shared various aspects of her own beliefs but objected to the way she used them in the development of Christian Science.

The clergy were threatened by the dramatic increase in the numbers of her followers. While they undoubtedly had doubts about her theology, there was enough pluralism in formal Protestant organized worship to permit the presence of yet another sect. But Christian Science was growing too large, too fast. The dedication of Mrs. Eddy's First Church of Christ, Scientist, in Boston, The Mother Church, in 1895 brought nearly six thousand worshipers from all over the country. Only eleven years later, the completion of the many-times larger Excelsior Extension of The Mother Church brought at least twenty thousand people into Boston for six dedicatory services. They were good, prosperous people, most of whom came to Christian Science from active participation in other churches, which regretted their defection. The converts themselves often felt that the people with whom they had formerly worshiped resented their departure and wished them harm, which, in the mythology of Christian Science, could cause misfortune to befall them, so their transition from the older congregations to the new one was accompanied by open and mutual acrimony. The striking growth of Christian Science led some observers to fear that if it continued, Christian Science would soon become the dominant Protestant religious congregation in the world.[1]

The medical profession, no more united than the Protestant clergy, offered a spectrum of resistance, from those at one extreme who greeted every misfortune attending Christian Science healing as occasion for an attack upon the Church itself, to those like Dr. Richard Cabot of the Massachusetts General Hospital, a more temperate and secure critic. While he felt that most Christian Science cures represented the treatment of illnesses that proceeded from a psychological cause, he expressed the opinion

. . . that many patients have been driven into Christian Science by a multitude of shifting and mistaken diagnoses, by the gross abuse of drugs, especially of morphine, and by

4

the total neglect of rational psychotherapy on the part of many physicians. . . . the success of the Christian Science movement is due largely to the ignorance and narrow-mindedness of a certain proportion of the medical profession. . . .[2]

The most intense attacks upon Mrs. Eddy and Christian Science, however, came from people who had been closely associated with her. In the early days, before 1885, it was she, more often than not, who instigated publicity about conflicts within Christian Science. For example, in a spate of lawsuits in 1877–1879 she attacked former associates either for refusing to pay her sums of money that they had promised in anticipation of being taught a new technique of mental healing, or, more worthy of attention in the newspapers, of having attacked her or various others of her students and disciples by practicing the art of mesmerism from a distance — that is, by thinking bad thoughts about her or people close to her and thereby causing them great suffering. She publicly accused another former disciple of plagiarism and pronounced yet others guilty of gross immorality for having defected from Christian Science.

Certain of these people proved themselves enterprising enough to retort by accusing Mrs. Eddy herself of plagiarism, of usurping ideas and priorities that really should be attributed to someone else, and of flagrant falsification of her own life story and experience in healing. And they submitted as documentary evidence letters and newspaper articles that she herself had written years before.

Nothing is as tantalizing to the public as the accusation of dishonesty directed against a successful, controversial moralist, so that from the very beginning, full-scale attempts to examine Mrs. Eddy and Christian Science fell into two groups: those which purported to tell the "real truth," exposing the middle-class mythologizing with which Mrs. Eddy tried to legitimize Christian Science; and those "lives" written by her disciples and apologists, some more sophisticated than others but all of them permeated by a defensive need to ignore or to explain away those eccentric and unusual details of her life and personality and behavior which, suitably elaborated, gave such comfort to her enemies.

In all of this chaos of charge and countercharge, what was most often ignored was that Christian Science was a most remarkable event in American social history and that Mary Baker Eddy, its discoverer and founder, was a most remarkable, talented, and individualistic woman.

Because the early controversies were so passionate, investigators were stimulated to undertake the serious search for historical evidence when people involved in the events of Mrs. Eddy's life were still alive and able to give personal testimony. Sometimes the significance and reliability of these witnesses were uncertain, and sometimes the investigators were themselves biased, but their prejudices, however transparent or however subtle, do not completely distort the historical record, and enough information is included in what they wrote to permit later readers to achieve a more balanced view.

The Christian Science Church attempted to deal with attacks on Mrs. Eddy and on its own legitimacy by collecting as much as it could of original source material and sealing it up in its own Archives, to which it allowed only very carefully limited and scrutinized access. The Church seemed to be trying to deal with controversy by avoiding it, but learned that its ability to still dissent by discouraging publicity was only partially successful and often engendered intense counterreaction.

If the Church itself or one of its associated institutions held copyright to a book, circulation could be carefully curtailed.[3] On one occasion, an injunction was obtained against a book because it contained letters written by Mrs. Eddy whose publication had not been authorized by the inheritors of her property. It seemed as if the Church was motivated more by a wish to avoid public acknowledgment of Mrs. Eddy's own attitudes at a certain period of her life, as revealed in her letters, than by the need to protect for her heirs the monetary value of her literary property. The book in question[4] was withdrawn from sale and a new edition prepared in which a narrative chapter, inserted in place of the letters, recounted in general terms the biographical information they contained. While controversy may have been muted, it was hardly suppressed.

All of the facts used in this book come from published sources, although very few copies of certain publications may exist. Several books in particular are compendious collections of information, some of them with histories of their own intertwined with that of Christian Science. A few preliminary notes may be useful here as a reference point for what is to follow.

The first serious attempt to marshal the facts of Mrs. Eddy's life and the history of Christian Science was published in a series of fourteen articles in *McClure's Magazine* in 1907–1908. *McClure's* was a popular general magazine with a wide circulation. A newspaper writer, Mrs. Georgine Milmine, approached the publisher with a proposal and preliminary documentation that promised an interesting series. He assigned several members of his staff to assist her, Willa Cather most prominently, along with Will Irwin, Burton Hendrick, and others. Specific testimony and documentation were obtained and published in detail to provide a store of data for the future. The series, somewhat revised and enlarged, was issued as a book in 1909, *The Life of Mary Baker G. Eddy and the History of Christian Science* by Georgine Milmine, and was for a long time very hard to find because of attempts made by Christian Scientists to suppress it. It was published in a new edition in 1971 by the Baker Book House of Grand Rapids, Michigan. Its tone is that of an attempt to set the record straight, so that it has a partisan oppositional bias expressed in as neutral a tone as the authors could muster. But the data are presented largely intact, references are reliable, and enough is told about witnesses to give some indication of their particular personal slant.[5]

At the same time as the Milmine series, an authorized version of Mrs. Eddy's life was being published in *Human Life* magazine by Sibyl Wilbur O'Brien, who issued *her* series as a book too, in 1908, under the title *The Life of Mary Baker Eddy*.[6] Mrs. O'Brien had been subsidized in her venture by John V. Dittemore, then a Director of The Mother Church. She attempted to explain away those facts about Mrs. Eddy's life that couldn't be ignored and to weave into an inspirational tapestry the stories that Mrs. Eddy told about herself. However contrived the story might appear to be, it yet conveys a sense of the gifted and unusual woman that Mrs. Eddy was, even as a mythmaker, and it has a more sprightly and engaging style than the later authorized biographies. Too, Mrs. O'Brien juxtaposed information about events in a way that suggests connections of which she might not have been consciously aware, so that it is a book which one can read between the lines.

Two years later, in 1910, just before Mrs. Eddy's death, Frederick W. Peabody published *The Religio-Medical Masquerade: A Complete Exposure of Christian Science*.[7] Peabody had been attorney for one of Mrs. Eddy's former lieutenants, Josephine Woodbury, who sued her for defamation of character in 1899. His experience with Christian Science so incensed him that he devoted an important part of his subsequent practice to legal attacks on the sect and on Mrs. Eddy herself. He worked for *McClure's Magazine* to obtain affidavits from people who gave testimony about earlier events. His book is a polemic, as one might expect from its title, but Peabody was an informed man and had much to report about certain events that might not have been otherwise available.

In 1921, *The Quimby Manuscripts* were published, edited by Horatio W. Dresser.[8] Phineas Quimby was a mental healer, a very unusual and natively intelligent man, who

8

had treated Mrs. Patterson (Mrs. Eddy's name in a former marriage) at an important time in her life, and about whose importance in the genesis of Mrs. Eddy's career there was lively controversy. Although she was unstinting in her loyalty to Quimby while he was alive and for a period after he died in 1866, she began after 1870 to minimize his importance to her own development and ended by disavowing him entirely. Others of his patients took the opposite view, and the controversy between the two camps became a matter of Mrs. Eddy's saying it was nothing and her opponents' saying that all that was good in Christian Science came from Quimby. His writings were in the possession of his son George, who refused to become actively engaged in the controversy, limiting himself to writing a short biography of his father in which he made no reference to Mrs. Eddy at all.[9] He refused to allow publication of his father's papers, which went to press only after his death. Horatio W. Dresser, the editor, was the son of Julius and Annetta Dresser, patients of Quimby who knew Mrs. Patterson when she first came to Quimby for treatment. The Dressers later became leaders in the development of a school of mental healing and life philosophy that became organized under the title of New Thought. Along with Quimby's writings, Dresser included fourteen letters to Quimby written by Mrs. Patterson during the years 1862 to 1865. Mrs. Eddy's heirs sued successfully for the suppression of those letters, and the book was withdrawn and reissued with a chapter in their place describing Mrs. Patterson's relationship to Quimby. In 1953 the Quimby material, including Mrs. Patterson's autograph letters to Quimby, was given to the Library of Congress, and in 1969 the Library of Congress Photoduplication Service issued microfilm copies of all of this material for distribution.

In the decade after the publication of Sibyl Wilbur O'Brien's book, John V. Dittemore, who had subsidized it, engaged in the labor of collecting letters written by Mrs. Eddy and other documents relating to her career for sequestration in the Archives of The Mother Church. He kept copies of much of this material for his own use. In addition, he was a friend of Calvin Frye, the man who was Mrs. Eddy's devoted assistant for the last thirty years of her life, and had access to Frye's private diaries of this period. During this decade after her death, Dittemore found himself increasingly at odds with the other members of the Board of Directors of The Mother Church and increasingly drawn to a dissident group. Finally, he was dismissed by the other directors.[10] He gave access to some of his data to Edwin Franden Dakin, whose book *Mrs. Eddy: The Biography of a Virginal Mind* was published in 1929.[11] It was a carefully written, full-scale biography, critical of Mrs. Eddy and her ideas. An immediate attempt at suppression by Christian Science was met with equal and insistent resistance by Dakin's publisher, Scribner's, and a second edition was issued in which Dittemore allowed Dakin to publish an appendix of excerpts from Frye's diaries.[12] Dittemore himself then proceeded, in collaboration with a historian, Ernest Sutherland Bates, to write his own biography, *Mary Baker Eddy: The Truth and the Tradition*, perhaps the most knowledgeable and temperate one yet.[13] There were disagreements between co-authors about how certain material should be treated, and sometimes the disagreement was made explicit. Many things are paraphrased that one wishes had been quoted directly in more detail, but, on the whole, the book achieves the best balance between narrative and respectful judgment.

Dittemore's subsequent history is of some interest. Dakin wrote later that Dittemore told him in the late 1930s, shortly before he died, that he had just sold all of his documents because he needed the money.[14] More recently, Robert Peel, in the third volume of his recent *Mary Baker Eddy* (1977), quoted a letter of recantation written by Dittemore to the Directors of The Mother Church, dated March 23, 1937, shortly before his death.[15]

Robert Peel is Counselor on Publications to the Committee on Publications of The Mother Church. He has written the most detailed biography of Mrs. Eddy, one that approaches her life and the history of Christian Science from the perspective of the history of ideas. It is natural that such a work, coming from such a source, should turn away from an interest in Mrs. Eddy's character and personal psychology. An inevitable result is that the ostensible subject of the book becomes lost in the remarkable texture of ideas and details in which she is embedded, a triumph of Principle over Personality, and an expression of what Mrs. Eddy herself tried to accomplish: that her book be given more attention than her person.

But Mrs. Eddy was a woman of great historical and psychological interest, and the purpose of this biography is to understand and to describe how it was that her ingenuity and strength, her capacity for innovation and boldness, her peculiarities, the very weaknesses which others could so easily document, were all intertwined, interrelated parts of a whole woman of unusual endowment. She was able to exemplify in her own personality the contradictions that characterized her era and to utilize those very contradictions in building her own success. As she herself wrote to one of her disciples:

Oh the marvel of my life! What would be thought of it, if it was known in a millionth of its detail. But this cannot be now. It will take centuries for this.[16]

Chapter One

Although the preoccupations of Mark Baker's family were bound and shaped by the society and general interests of rural New Hampshire in the first third of the nineteenth century, the special ambitions and intensities of that family as well as the unusual qualities, personalities, and achievements of the individual members must have been of at least equal importance. The yeomanry of that region and in that time, dating their traditions and their values back to the days of the Indian wars and the Revolution, took particular interest in their conservative religion and their conservative politics. They were serious about their education, such as it was, and they took for granted a social order in which each man and each woman had a foreordained place. Mark Baker's family, though, was considered always to be a little different, stamped perhaps by the character of Baker himself, intelligent, capable, ambitious, self-important, with a range of expectations that contrasted with the ordinariness of his beginnings.

Mark Baker had been the youngest of his family, the youngest of thirteen, and his mother's favorite. He had inherited about two hundred acres of farm, woodlot, and pasture from his father's estate and, as an extra share, on condition that he provide a place for his mother, the family homestead as well. His eldest brother had inherited the adjacent portion of land, but the two brothers had fallen out and they and their families had little contact. Mark Baker farmed his inheritance in Bow without great acumen or enthusiasm and with no greater material success than his neighbors. His family and that of his wife, Abigail Ambrose, had a genealogy of reasonably respectable folk and a sprinkling of heroes from colonial days, but the same could be said of most of the other families living in the region too. And like the others, the Baker and Ambrose antecedents were largely English and Scots, some having arrived earlier and some later. After Mrs. Eddy became famous and revered, there were persistent attempts to make something special of her ancestry. Her biographies gave great attention to these matters, but they reveal only about as much distinction as one might have found among any of her early neighbors, none of whom, however, was ever to begin to make as big a mark in the world as she did.

In the early years of this century, when Georgine Milmine went back to the New Hampshire countryside to find witnesses still living who could tell about those early times, she was able to collect a number of reminiscences and anecdotes about Mark Baker and his family and about Mary in particular, which, though they may have been more mythical than accurate and colored by envy or outrage or respect for celebrity, nevertheless gave a consistent, impressionistic portrait of both the father and the daughter.

Baker was a rigid, narrow, inflexible, grudging, controlling, litigious, and angry man, obsessed with his granitic religious beliefs, austere and scrupulously moral in his own personal conduct, imposing a harsh consistency of observance on his family, and able to soften only when his fondness for his children was touched by their helplessness or by his ambition for them. Mrs. Eddy was consistently sparing and vague about her family and her early life, except when she could compose an anecdote that would frame her life within a biblical context. She said of her father only that he "possessed a strong intellect and an iron will."[1] That economy of observation was to be supplemented by the

MARK BAKER

Mrs. Eddy's father

15

more generous reminiscence of others. Georgine Milmine, for example, told a story that she said had become a neighborhood tradition, that on one occasion Baker had lost track of the days and labored on the Sabbath, arising the next day to dress in his Sunday black to go to church. His neighbors along the way attempted to convince him that the day was Monday. It was not until he arrived at the church itself and found the doors closed that he was forced to believe. He went to the preacher, who verified his error and prayed with him.

As Milmine tells the story:

> . . . Back to his home went the old man, the godly part of him purged. But the old Adam remained, and as he strode up the hill he trembled with excitement. A tame crow, a pet of the children of the neighborhood, hopped on a bush in front of him, cawing loudly. In his perturbed condition, the sight of the bird made Mark angrier than ever, and raising his stick, he struck the crow dead. "Take that," he said in a passion, "for hoppin' about on the Sabbath," and he stormed on up the hill. At home he kept the day strictly as Sunday to atone for his worldliness of the previous day.[2]

This story is more likely to be a reflection of attitudes than a memoir of a real event. But if Baker was known for his stubbornness, he was also respected for his talents. When he was living in Bow, he served the village in a number of official capacities, planning a new one-room schoolhouse of twenty-two feet square, surveying the roads, serving a term as county coroner, as member of the school board, as town moderator, and as selectman. He also served for a time as clerk of the Bow Meeting House. In later years, at least, when he was older and perhaps softer, and when he had made some money in railroad investments, his neighbors called him Squire Baker and Uncle Baker. One of his grandsons said of him that "although he was as set as the hills on politics and religion, he was as kindhearted a man as ever lived. He never turned anyone from his door hungry. If there wasn't anything handy in the house, he would give them money to get something at the Tavern."[3] But, however much softened, he remained an ardent proslavery advocate before and during the Civil War, made vigorous attempts to have the minister, the Reverend Corban Curtice, removed from his pulpit for his antislavery preachings, and is said to have rejoiced on hearing the news of Lincoln's assassination. And he would bring his doctrinal quarrels with his neighbors up before the church membership for judgment, insistently, year after year, even though the general opinion was against him. He believed firmly in the doctrine of predestination, was opposed to notions of salvation through faith, and certainly through works, and imposed rigidities of observance on his family that were to inspire in them urges to ardent rebellion and to escape.

Thus we have some general picture of Mark Baker's character and temperament and some sense that he had broader talents. There is almost no information to be found of his wife. Mrs. Eddy herself was characteristically reticent:

Of my mother I cannot speak as I would, for memory recalls qualities to which the pen can never do justice.[4]

She then offered an extract from a eulogy said by the minister at her mother's funeral, which describes her generally saintly qualities, her placidity, self-denial, elevating moral standards, and lively sense of parental responsibility. It is an ideal portrait and not very personal. In her later years, Mrs. Eddy was to tell and tell again a small number of anecdotes about her childhood, all worn smooth, refined, freed of details, and shaped toward a moral, like biblical parables. In those in which her mother appears she takes on a scrupulously pious and unassertive character.

A more specific impression of her thoughts and interests can be gleaned from letters that Mrs. Baker wrote to her children during the years 1844 to 1849. In these well-written letters, she is preoccupied with illness: the health and illness of the daughter or the son she is writing to, her own health, and that of those of her neighbors whom she has talked to or heard of or whom she has nursed. She is filled with concern for others, always, despite the vagaries of her own physical condition, and absorbed in what she can *do* for them, particularly in the concrete way of nursing and caring for their bodily needs. Then there are exhortations to piety and goodness and, particularly to her son George Sullivan, some concern that he not be surrounded by bad influences that might tempt him to dissipation. She refers to her husband in two ways, either with an uncritical comment on one of his quarrels with a neighbor or to reassure the child she's writing to that despite Father's angry words, he's really loving at heart. She excuses and explains away whatever feelings she might have that her children don't write to her as often as they might or that Sullivan has, for example, made a botch of a business venture in New York, or that his wife-to-be, Martha Rand, has slighted her. She calls herself a drudge, overly fond and devoted to her family, and having an exaggerated devotion to the memories or mementos of her absent ones, treating Sullivan's picture as an icon, loving Mary with an intensity that should be reserved for God. She is so acquiescent and self-abnegating that one senses a feeling of implicit dissatisfaction that her children don't think of her often enough, don't write enough, and don't appreciate her devotion.[5]

The contrast in the temperaments of Mark and Abigail Baker is but an extreme example of what one might find in many couples, in people of today as well as in people of that earlier time: the father aggressive, insisting on his self-assertion, preoccupied with his own special interests, tending not to express feelings except within that narrow range of anger and ambition, and assuming that he has the right to have things very much his own way; the mother acquiescent, showing easily only the tender emotions, devoted to her children with little thought for herself, and likely to feel that it was not within her prerogative to expect something for herself. What is unusual is not the *trend* toward parceling out feelings and attributes in this way, but that the trend in this family seems to have been expressed in the most rigid and unmitigated way. The father could express little but resentful, narrow self-interest, and the mother couldn't be directly discontented at all. The father could not relapse into a moment of tender fondness, the mother could express little else. One wonders what place there might have been for common understanding, each of the other, and how much pressure the children were under, given these examples, to parcel out their own feelings and attitudes in the same extreme ways. How much difficulty must they have had in bringing together degrees of self-assertion and degrees of tenderness into whole, relatively peaceful personalities?

On the other hand, one could also wonder how another woman, different from Abigail Ambrose, could ever have lived with a man like Mark Baker, tolerated him, even. But he certainly gave her ample daily opportunity for the continual exercise of her humility, and in that way, at least, they were well suited to each other.

She was his elder by two years and already twenty-five when they married, almost an age of spinsterhood in those days. Her daughters were to hasten to marry younger, when their time came. Her childbearing began promptly and continued at intervals of two and three years until Mary was born when her mother was thirty-eight. It was considered a great old age for motherhood, like that of Sarah, the wife of Abraham, who conceived her child when she was already past mid-life, Mrs. Eddy would say later.

All of the children suffered from the need either to pattern themselves on one parent and repudiate the other or, not being able to do that comfortably, to live out their lives with the disparate elements of both parents warring within. The first was Samuel Dow, born in 1808. He could not ally himself with either parent and left home for Boston in his early teens to apprentice himself as a mason and to embark on what his family considered an alcoholic and dissipated life. He married a local girl but was soon widowed, and married later a woman who had been a missionary among the Indians and who caused him to take the pledge and reform, and to pass over into sobriety and melancholy.

The next was Albert, born in 1810. Albert was the one formally educated member of the family, the one who showed some promise of playing a part in life on the greater stage of the world. He left home to teach school in Concord when he was sixteen, attended Dartmouth with a fine record, and then practiced law with Franklin Pierce's firm in Hillsborough, New Hampshire, after 1834. He became a member of the New Hampshire legislature in 1839 and received the Democratic nomination to Congress in 1841, tantamount to an assured election. His career after 1836, however, was interrupted by episodes of a serious illness, and he died, apparently quite suddenly, on October 21, 1841, just before the congressional election. In contrast to Samuel, he remained interested and involved in his family. He spent the periods of his ill health at home, and in his letters one detects that he felt a detached affection for his father. He didn't seem to seek romantic involvements and he never married, perhaps in part because of his poor health. Looking backward, Mrs. Eddy would say that her brother Albert had taught her the classical languages and that he gave her the benefit of his Dartmouth education. There's no evidence for it, but even at the time she must have been proud of his growing influence in the world, and his ambition may have served as a support for her own.

The youngest of the boys, George Sullivan, was born in 1812. He was his father's favorite, the youngest son of a youngest son, and was to be almost the sole heir to his father's estate, for Mark Baker was to leave his three daughters one dollar each, nothing to Samuel Dow, and all the rest to Sullivan. He left home suddenly when he was twenty-three, hurriedly and in secret, pursued by a romantic embarrassment, not even telling his father that he was abandoning him to work the land alone, and hoping to enjoy what his mother and sisters called the "healthier climate" of Connecticut. Attractive but impulsive, he was later to be marked by failure in business, unhappy marriage, blindness, and early death. His mother's letters to him imply reproach and forgiveness, but also that he was her spoiled youngest son.

The daughters' lives, too, were marked by unhappiness and bitter disappointment, although Abigail, the eldest, and Mary, the youngest, were each to persevere to solid worldly success. Abigail was the fourth child, born in 1816. She was sturdy, single-minded, with much of her father's dominating spirit; rather more practical-minded than he, she was already off teaching school in her late teens. When the family moved to Sanbornton Bridge in 1836, after Grandmother Baker died, she set about successfully to capture the most eligible young man in town, Alexander Hamilton Tilton, who owned the woolen mills. She was to outlive her husband and both of her children and to become the local grande dame, increasingly dogmatic and successful and intolerant of the idiosyncrasies of others as she became encased in her solitary wealth and social position. So important were the woolen mills to the economy of the town that in 1869 it changed its name from Sanbornton Bridge to Tilton.

Martha, the fifth child, born in 1819, like her mother remained unobtrusive, helpful when she could be, and not markedly ambitious for herself. She was widowed at an early age and lived in Sanbornton Bridge until her later years, when she moved to the Midwest with her daughter and son-in-law. She would give support and concrete material help to her sister Mary at times, but eventually they were to become unfriendly and she was to withdraw or — like so many others — to be pushed away.

Mary, born July 16, 1821, was the youngest of the family, spoiled, petted, and much valued. If we are to believe Mrs. Eddy's own reminiscence, her mother anticipated the birth of her last child with awe. As the story was told:

Mrs. Eddy's mother, Mrs. Mark Baker, had a neighbor who was a most devout and pious woman. Her name was Sarah Gault and she and Mrs. Baker used frequently and regularly to meet and talk over religious matters and pray together audibly. During these meetings Mrs. Baker many times told her neighbor, Mrs. Gault, that she felt herself to be a most wicked woman, because of the strange thoughts she had regarding her youngest child, which was yet unborn. She told Mrs. Gault that she could not keep her thought away from the strange conviction that this child was holy and consecrated and set apart for wonderful achievements, even before her birth. She said, "I know these are sinful thoughts for me to entertain, but I cannot shake them off." Then these two devout women would talk the question over and pray together, asking God's direction and blessing on this subject.[6]

Abigail Ambrose did indeed think in religious terms and did idealize her daughter Mary. For example, in a letter which she wrote to her on May 6, 1844, she says, ". . . and sometimes I fear I worship mary instead of the great jehovah. . . ."[7] Thus, whatever Mrs. Eddy's tendency may have been to construct parables that would enhance her religious stature, she had encouragement for it from her mother and clearly occupied as youngest child a very special place in the family.

She was named after her father's mother, Mary Anne Moore Baker, seventy-six at the time of Mary's birth, who lived with the family in the crowded little farmhouse. Coming last into the family, never having to give up the position of youngest child, Mary was permitted and even encouraged to develop qualities of willfulness, imaginativeness, and seductiveness. She believed that she had the right to have her own way, that others would take care of her, and that she was beautiful, talented, and free from the need to struggle. On the other hand, she learned very quickly never to express direct anger and seemed unable to be consistently forceful and productive. That some such latent urges were present and struggling for expression within her can be surmised from the startling physical symptoms that appeared early in her childhood and remained with her until her last days, pursuing their own changing but ever-colorful course, year by year. These symptoms were of two main forms: abiding illnesses and paroxysmal attacks. She was thought to be of delicate constitution from early childhood. It is not clear how much of this invalidism grew out of organic illness — the infectious diseases of childhood, for example — and how much expressed a very early tendency to lean heavily on languishing as a form of self-expression.

Symptoms of illness were particularly acceptable to her family. They emphasized helplessness, a suitable state for a youngest child, and provided the occasion for her mother's continuing tender care. Her illnesses offered an excuse for whatever she wished to avoid, especially in the way of achievement or of competition with her slightly older sisters and, in effect, they kept her at home and out of school much of the time and served as a convenient explanation for her failure to master the rudiments of a formal education. In later times, when she was a success in the genteel Victorian world, she would insist that she had been exposed to the breadth of a classical training through the influence of her brother Albert but that with her spiritual enlightenment these husks of worldly learning had dropped away. This pretension would expose her to all kinds of ridicule, not least from Mark Twain, who had certain credentials as both literary critic and harpooner of puffed pretensions, but in fact she never really assimilated spelling or punctuation and had only impressionistic acquaintance with syntax. In style, her writing was much like her mother's and probably learned from her. The local schools themselves were good enough. At least four of her siblings had mastered the technique of writing correct, expressive English, and three of them — Albert, Abigail, and Martha — taught school at one time or another. Mary was heedless of detail, relying on a kind of intuitive approximation, but, as her writings reveal, she was able to communicate a sharp sense of what she felt, although expressed in an idiosyncratic way.

Her letters to her brother Sullivan, written in the years 1835 to 1837, when she was between fourteen and sixteen years old, show her concern about illness, expressed in her own very special style:

> . . . I must extend the thought of benevolence farther than selfishness would permit and only add my health at presant is improveing slowly and I hope by dieting and being careful to sometime regain it. . . .[8]

In another letter, written a year and a half later, she tells Sullivan:

> . . . I have been studying evry leisure moment this winter I shal attend school this summer if I possiblely can as my health is extremely poor occasioned by a cold I hope as almost everry won is complaining of some disseas occasioned undoubtedly by our severe seasons. Martha has been verry ill since our return from Concord. I should think her in a confirmed consumption *if I would admit the idea*, but it may not be so, at least I hope not. . . . We have not received any written communication from Brother Albert this long time, but heard verbally from him by way of a Mr. Glidden who returned from Boston that he was verry sick, we have since written a letter to him and hope that it may find him enjoying those blessings that an indulgent providence has been lavish to bestow uppon others but has been rather penurious of his bounty uppon him and me. . . .[9]

Her more chronic kinds of indispositions, then, which were to come and go in various guises throughout her life and were to afflict her even in her successful old age, were already a part of her way of being as a young adolescent. She was thought to be a helpless invalid, at times unable even to walk.

For sheer drama, however, these chronic complaints were

as nothing compared to her paroxysmal attacks, which were said to have begun in the midst of theological disputes with her father. The situation in which these symptoms arose was described by Sibyl Wilbur, who leaned heavily on Mrs. Eddy's own reminiscences:

> Her religious experience reached a grave crisis when she was twelve years of age, though she did not unite with the church until five years later at Sanbornton Bridge. While still in Bow, writing and studying, her father's relentless theology was alarmed at her frequent expression of confidence in God's love. He held to a hard and bitter doctrine of predestination and believed that a horrible decree of endless punishment awaited sinners on a final judgment day.
>
> Whether it was logic and moral science taught her by her brother, or the trusting love instilled by her mother who had guided her to yield herself to the voice of God within her, Mary resisted her father on the matter of "unconditional election." Beautiful in her serenity and immovable in her faith, the daughter sat before the stern father of the iron will. His sires had signed a covenant in blood and would he not wrestle with this child who dared the wrath of God?
>
> And well did he wrestle and the home was filled with his torrents of emotion. But though Mary might have quoted to him her own baby speech, she was too respectful and his "vociferations" went unrebuked. It is a remarkable thing to note, the conscience of a child in defense of its faith. Can anyone suppose it an easy thing to resist a father so convicted with belief in dogma, a father, too, whom all their world honored and heeded? We may be sure it was not easy; that, indeed, to do so tortured this little child's heart. But Mark Baker was acting according to his conscience, and the child knew it and respected him. She did not view this struggle of conscience as a quarrel, and repudiated all her life the idea that she ever quarreled with her father.

The notion went abroad, however, that Mark Baker and

his daughter Mary were at variance over religion. The silly gossip of their world reported that she would not study her catechism. They said that Mary had a high temper for all her learning, she of whom her mother had said, "When do you ever see Mary angry?" They even said that Mr. Baker had reported in his anguish to his clergyman, "If Mary Magdalene had seven devils, our Mary has ten." The struggle, it may be seen, was no casual argument, but a deep wrestle of souls. At last the child succumbed to an illness and the family doctor was summoned. When Mark Baker drove to fetch him his religious intemperance must have given way to paternal affection and fear. . . .

The physician declared Mary stricken with fever. He left medicines, recommending her to her mother's most watchful care and admonishing her father to desist from discussions. Mrs. Eddy has said of what followed:

"My mother, as she bathed my burning temples, bade me lean on God's love, which would give me rest if I went to Him in prayer, as I was wont to do, seeking His guidance. I prayed; and a soft glow of ineffable joy came over me. The fever was gone and I rose and dressed myself in a normal condition of health. Mother saw this and was glad. The physician marvelled; and the 'horrible decree' of Predestination — as John Calvin rightly called his own tenet — forever lost its power over me."[10]

I like the pious, enthusiastic tone of the biographer, a protection against taking too literally what she says. But I quote this passage at such length because Miss Wilbur brings the onset of these spells, and the onset of Mary Baker's intense wrestling with her father, down close to the age of early puberty, and suggests that the spells were the only acceptable way of bringing to conclusion a scene with her father that would not permit of the expression, frank and direct, of either open affection or open anger.

It is no longer considered daring speculation to observe that little girls and their fathers tend to have romantic attachments to each other and even flirtations, often particularly noticeable earlier in childhood and again in early adolescence. If the family is reasonably stable and the parents in good rapport, the mother's special place by the father's side serves to temper the child's love and to temper, too, whatever encouragement the father may give to the child's romantic fantasies. In family arrangements in which the father is particularly dominant and self-centered and the mother particularly self-effacing, this protection is withdrawn at some distance, and the relationship between a father and a daughter may become exceedingly intense, often requiring equally intense efforts from both daughter and father each to repudiate the other, pulling toward and pushing away. Miss Wilbur's description of a father and daughter wrestling together over a subject of intense mutual interest, but each holding firm to an opposing view, suggests to me just such a struggle, close but fearful of becoming too close, with the mother hovering anxiously at the periphery, fearful of the outcome.

Georgine Milmine discusses the same events from a different perspective and gives a description of the paroxysmal seizures themselves:

> . . . Mary Baker's "fits," as outsiders rather crudely called them, are still a household word among her old friends. They frequently came on without the slightest warning. At times the attack resembled a convulsion. Mary pitched headlong on the floor, and rolled and kicked, writhing and screaming in apparent agony. Again she dropped limp and lay motionless. At other times, like a cataleptic, she lay rigid, almost in a state of suspended animation. The family worked over her, but usually in vain. Mark Baker, standing upright in his wagon and lashing his horses, would drive for Dr. Ladd, the family physician. An old neighbor remembered him driving thus and shouting all the way: "Mary is dying!" The family actually believed that she was. For years they expected that Mary would end her days in one of her hysterical attacks, and went to every extreme to prevent them. As a precautionary measure they gave in to all the girl's whims. . . . Dr. Ladd occasionally

diagnosed them as "hysteria mingled with bad temper"; but at other times he took them seriously. He regarded the girl as an interesting pathological case. Becoming much interested in mesmerism at about that time, he practiced up on Mary Baker. He found her a sensitive subject. He discovered that, by mental suggestion, he could partly control her. "I can make that girl stop in the street any time, merely by thinking," he would tell his friends; and he frequently demonstrated that he could do this.[11]

Well, this description is dramatic, too, and shows how two descriptions of the same material, written in the same year but from different points of view, can supplement each other and permit a fuller understanding than either one taken alone or at face value. Mary Baker's theological disputations with her father may have represented the most acceptable outlet for all the energies and drives that are so intensified in puberty — sexual drives, ambitions, and urges toward independence, self-expression, and the exercise of some control in one's own life. Outright expression of anger in conflict was not acceptable for her and certainly would never have had a useful impact on an unbending father; the development of other methods of persuasion was necessary if she was to have her own way, which she had been brought up to believe was her birthright. She developed both the capacity to charm and the power to terrify, by making it appear that she was in imminent danger of losing her life and desperately in need of protection.

If her power to terrify was awesome, though, her ability to charm and to attract the interest of others was also most unusual. Georgine Milmine records the reminiscences of those who knew her at Sanbornton Bridge and remembered her attention to dress and manner, taken so seriously as to border on affectation and yet conveying an impression of delicacy and gentle grace. She aroused the attentions of a succession of suitors and the mild jealousy of a cluster of competitors, but although she was charming and flirtatious, she did not seem to direct her attention to any particular suitor for any long period of time with very much intensity. Her letters from her brothers Albert and particularly Sullivan advise her about this young man and that, and she herself, in her own letters, makes reference to a number of young men interested in her, but without suggesting that she is drawn to any of them very much.

The force of her feelings and some durability of attachment seemed at this time in her life to be reserved for men closer to home — her father and her brothers, and for those older men toward whom attachment and respect and admiration could be experienced without its passing over into the kind of fearful intensity that she felt with her father. We have already seen that Dr. Ladd had an unusual interest in her, justified, of course, by the medical problems that invited his attention but intensified by her especially appealing qualities. The Congregational minister, the Reverend Enoch Corser, also became much interested. Robert Peel quotes a letter, written sixty-five years later, from Corser's son:

> As Mrs. Eddy's pastor — and for a time teacher — my father held her in the highest esteem; in fact he considered her, even at an early age, superior both intellectually and spiritually to any other woman in Tilton, and greatly enjoyed talking with her. It was in 1837 when, if I remember rightly, Mrs. Eddy was about 15, that I first knew her, she being several years younger than myself. I well remember her gift of expression which was very marked, as girls of that time were not usually possessed of so large a vocabulary. She and my father used to converse on deep subjects frequently (as I recall to mind, from remarks made by my father) too deep for me. . . .[12]

Mrs. Eddy herself later memorialized her relationship to Corser as a struggle over beliefs, very much like a gentler version of what she is described as having experienced with her father; in all of these relationships, the pleasure in attachment is fused to and expressed in some kind of mutual attention to a topic of common interest — illness, learning, philosophical ideas, or theological inquiry.

Mary Baker had the ambition, from an early age, to be a writer. Sibyl Wilbur composed a touching scene between the little Mary and her brother Albert:

> "And I want very much to be a scholar, too," she said.
> "A scholar? and why, little sister?"
> "Because when I grow up I shall write a book; and I must be wise to do it. I must be as great a scholar as you or Mr. Franklin Pierce. Already I have read Young's *Night Thoughts*, and I understand it."[13]

She would represent herself as an authoress and take advantage of the incidents of her life to compose poems and commentaries that she would submit for publication to local and regional newspapers and magazines. Her interest in words, the style of her letters, her deep conversations with Corser — each reflected some facet of this ambition. But her ambition was not married to drive or to force of character. Her productions were diffuse, and the occasions for her publications were trivial, much like so many of those letters to the editor or poems submitted to a newspaper feature section today, whose appearance testifies to an unharnessed, undirected urge to see one's name in print. In that respect, her ambition to write was, like those other elements of her personality, subjected to her dependency, to her need to be taken care of by her family. She could be a precocious child, she couldn't be a purposeful mature woman. She never would have to struggle to perfect a technique. Spelling, syntax, care of construction, precision of expression were not necessary. Intuition, seizing a word, giving it wings, sending it on its way to friendly reception — that was the way it worked! Implicitly, her writing was restricted to the world of her family and small community, and she had no need to construct her craft to reach more distant shores.

Even had she been able, in those early years, to devote herself with serious intensity to the craft of writing, one wonders what real encouragement would have been available there to a young woman for such an enterprise. In rural New Hampshire, in those days, a respectable middle-class girl could be a wife or a teacher, and that was about all. In earlier, troubled times, a farm wife would have shared almost equally with her husband responsibility for running the farm, particularly if he was likely to be called away to the militia, and this bred a kind of equality that faded in the more peaceful years after the Revolution, but that was preserved to some degree in the rural community, where everyone participated actively in the business of living.

In town, this was much less the case, and in New England in the 1830s and 1840s further great changes in the nature of family life were wrought as a consequence of the construction of the Erie Canal. That waterway opened in 1825 an easy transportation route from the Great Lakes to the Hudson River and gave the potentially rich farmlands of western New York state and of the Midwest access to the eastern markets. Agriculture in New Hampshire had depended on proximity to the cities, despite the difficulties of cultivation in the region, and now the farms of the area became less profitable. Mark Baker had sold his farm in 1836, the year after his mother died, when he could still get a good price for it. He moved to Sanbornton Bridge, a real town in contrast to Bow, which was really a farmers' village. He no longer farmed intensively and ultimately invested his money in railroads, which were pushing westward and opening other new lands to production. The once-cultivated fields of New England, now abandoned, gradually grew up into great stands of white pine that half a century later would become the basis for a new thriving local industry, the manufacture of pine boxes. By then, the earlier history of the area would have been largely forgotten, so that a stray traveler might marvel to come upon an old stone fence in the middle of a forest. Many farmers were not so fortunate as Baker and left their land to migrate to the Midwest or to work in the mills, which now had a ready source of labor — the men who had left their farms and the men who might have worked for them. Women in this situation lost much of the feeling of participation in the productive work of the family and lost with it a sense of independence and usefulness. And men and women alike lost much of that feeling of community which has become memorialized in American myth as the golden age of the young republic. Those who sought these feelings went west, and the scene of heroic life shifted now to the Midwest and then to the Great Plains and the Rockies.

For Mary Baker, poorly educated, unprepared to struggle, with little sense of sustained initiative, the expectation was that she would marry. What else was there for her to do? But even the circumstances of her marriage reflected her attachment to her own family and her feeling that she needed the care of a mature person.

Her eldest brother, Samuel, had a friend who had gone with him to Boston when he went to begin his apprenticeship. This man, George Washington Glover, was eleven years older than Mary and became acquainted with her when Samuel married Glover's sister in 1832; Glover was then twenty-one and Mary ten. Five years later, he reappeared at Abigail Baker's wedding to Hamilton Tilton and chose that time to move to Charleston, South Carolina, to become a building contractor. His own testimony to his prosperity is contained in a letter to Samuel Baker dated April 20, 1841, when he was visiting in New Hampshire:

. . . I left Charleston last Tuesday every thing appers to be in a prosperous condition there. I come north for Stock and Trimings for thirteen Dwelling Houses that I am now Building. I should visit you If I had time but I must be in Charleston on tuesday next as my Buiseness Calls me there.

I should be pleased to hear from you will you write me soon tell me all about Abi's Boys and how they grow, tell her to name her first son for me and I will give it a negro servant worth one *thousand*. You may hold my respects forth to all young Lady's now in *market*. Give me respects to your Sisters and the rest of the familey Frend Baker you must visit me at Charleston, — You will find me in the heighth of prosperity — as I think I shall complete my comtrots [contracts] by the first of July and then I shall visit North and pass the Summar, unless some Buiseness starts that I am not yet aware of — ! . . .[14]

Apparently Glover did return that next summer, for among the Eddy papers John Dittemore discovered a phrenological analysis performed by one William B. Heberd of Charleston, who said that Glover was "Naturally cheerful and fond of enterprise, yet too cautious to venture much himself, without he is sure of success," to which Mary Baker had appended the droll notation, "in proof thereof Sept 5 — 1841," suggesting that he was already courting her then but in a manner somewhat less cocksure than his letter might have suggested him to be.

He resembled Sullivan in appearance, so much so, indeed, that on one of his visits to Sanbornton Bridge in 1843, the year they were to be married,

Mary, coming up behind him on the street, mistook him for her brother and slapped him on the back, saying, "Oh, you're dressed up!"[15]

He was as close to being a member of the family as one possibly could expect of a suitor, and finally the commitment to marriage was sealed and the ceremony performed by Dr. Corser on December 10, 1843. Mary and George left for Charleston by way of a visit to brother Samuel in Boston, carrying with them, sealed up, a copy of Mrs. Lydia Sigourney's *A Mother's Injunction*,[16] a gift from the bride's mother, telling the new husband to deal gently with his bride's frailty and inexperience.

33

Chapter Two

Six months later it was all over, the husband dead of a sudden fever and his young widow, pregnant, helpless, and penniless, escorted back to her family. If the personal details are obscure, hidden by romanticization, self-dramatization, and genteel revision, the bare externals of the matter at least are available.

It seems that Mark Baker, like many another possessive father, was not able to let his youngest girl go off in another man's arms without some harsh words. His wife, apologetic, admonished the newlyweds to ignore his words and to know that his heart was loving. Like many another bride, Mary Baker did not find marriage a cure for all her troubles, for her symptoms of illness persisted and the journey by ship to Charleston in winter and on high seas only added point to her chronic indisposition. She was already pregnant, although she may not have known it yet, and her pregnancy may have contributed nausea to her other miseries.

Although Glover considered Charleston to be his home, the couple stayed there in lodgings for only a few weeks, until late February, when they moved to Wilmington, North Carolina, in the pursuit of his business plans. Glover seems to have staked his whole future on a proposal to build a cathedral in Haiti and had begun to gather together at Wilmington the materials he would need for his venture.

His bride was busily engaged in writing poems and occasional pieces for the local newspaper, particularly pieces in support of Democratic candidates and in opposition to the Whigs. She professed to be an ardent Democrat like her father, whose politics were conservative and proslavery, and she felt in no conflict with the dominant political ethic of the South. Whatever her limitations of style, the sympathies her writings expressed made them perfectly acceptable locally.

In mid-June, after almost four months in Wilmington, Glover was stricken with what was called biliary fever, probably yellow fever, and died after an acute illness of a week and a half. Either before or during this illness, all of his stock of building materials disappeared from the Wilmington docks, variously reported as having been burned or stolen. His circumstances were so reduced that on the night before he died his brother Masons were called together to refer his case to their Charity Committee. It was they who arranged his funeral, paid the expenses of his illness and of his wife's lodging, and delegated one of their members, Mr. Cook, to conduct her safely to her family. Glover died on June 27, 1844, and was buried the next day. His wife left Wilmington on July 20, presumably having spent the interval gathering together some pitiful residue from her husband's estate and harboring her strength for the journey ahead. Her itinerary, described in detail on the basis of a diary she kept of that journey, offers a vignette of what it was like to travel in America then:

> From Wilmington, they went by rail to Weldon, North Carolina, where they changed cars for Portsmouth, Virginia; from Portsmouth they took a steamboat to Baltimore, where they changed to another steamboat for Frenchton; thence they traveled by rail across the state of Delaware to New Castle, where they took a boat to Philadelphia; then another boat to Bristol, Pennsylvania; then rail to Jersey City and ferry to New York, where, after some difficulty, they were met by George Sullivan Baker. According to Mrs. Eddy's statements, the Masons had instructed Mr. Cook to break the journey every night; when

he did not do so and Mrs. Glover became very ill in consequence, he begged her, she said, not to reveal the fact lest he be killed by the order on his return to Wilmington.[1]

Certainly the widow was not so abstracted in her grief but that she was able to make these observations and references to her immediate personal comfort.

The process of reworking and dramatizing her pitifully short marriage of six months appears to have begun almost immediately upon George Glover's death. Mrs. Glover's sense of self-importance drove her to puff up the facts to make them seem more becoming. George having been a major in the South Carolina Militia, she accorded him posthumous promotion to colonel. Charleston having had greater pretension to a genteel society than Wilmington, she presented herself as a resident of *that* town, although she had lived there only a few weeks, and said that she and her husband were on a short trip to Wilmington when he was taken ill. She inflated his fortune, saying that she had given his slaves their freedom, although there's no evidence he had slaves.

Had she nursed him in his last illness or not? She said that she was prohibited from doing so, but then, on another occasion, she told her brother that she *had* nursed him, after all. The question was even raised of whether he really had yellow fever. In those days, when transmission of yellow fever by mosquitoes was not known, many people thought that it was contagious. A pregnant wife might have been discouraged from nursing her husband because she had another life to consider besides her own. Just on the basis of pure probability, yellow fever was a good likelihood, for in coastal Carolina in the 1840s it caused almost twice as many deaths as all other fevers combined and broke out sporadically even in years in which it did not reach epidemic proportions.[2] If she hadn't nursed her husband or if she had, the matter could not be reduced to a simple question of selfishness or of devotion.

In her later retrospective campaign to tidy up the memories from this period of her life, Mrs. Eddy represented herself as having been an abolitionist, too, even though she had really been busy writing enthusiastic newspaper pieces supporting status quo candidates and would continue to do so in New Hampshire for the next decade. Another impression it seemed desirable to bolster was the assertion that George Washington Glover had died a man of means. It would have been useful to find a proper tombstone, erected by a widow who could afford to pay for such a monument, and in the 1890s two different Christian Scientists undertook separate and competing searches for this hypothetical grave marker. Mrs. Eddy in New Hampshire communicated with each separately, spurring each one on by elaborating from her memory convenient recollections to support their individual assumptions and stimulate their flagging enthusiasms. The marker in question was never found, for, in fact, Mrs. Glover had been in no position at the time to have one put into place.

Mary Baker was over and over again haunted by the fear that a plain story simply told would make her appear too ordinary and that a certain amount of embellishment would give it more style. In later years, this tendency would cause much discomfort to her followers, many of whom were people for whom embellishment had the moral taint of dishonesty. They were under the burden of justifying her every fantasy, both to reassure themselves and to withhold comfort from their many enemies, who already felt that they had ample rational ground for attack. And so the literature is full of claim and counterclaim, with heated argument about the validity of this fact or that, much like medieval controversies over the authenticity of venerated relics.

The widow was finally returned to her family where, shortly, she was delivered of her only child, a son, born on September 11, 1844. He had been conceived in the fortnight after his parents' marriage and was born two and a half months after his father's death. He was named George, probably George Washington, after his father, and so he was called in later years; but his grandmother, Abigail Baker, wrote her son George Sullivan that the boy was named after him. That may have been only her thought of the moment. So often, when writing to her children, she would be inspired by the need to inflate their pride and emphasize how important they were to her. Whatever his middle name, however, George was given to nurse to Mrs. Amos Morrison, the wife of a local mechanic, who had just lost one of her newborn twins.

His mother Mary was prostrate, both before and after the delivery, and is said to have been so sensitive and distraught that her father spread tanbark on the road outside to deaden the noise of carts rumbling by, a common practice in those days when there was severe illness in a house. Even about this point there was disagreement. Sibyl Wilbur mentioned it in her authorized biography, and so did Georgine Milmine, but Mrs. Eddy herself denied it.[3] Subject to even more vehement denial was the story that her father would take her into his arms and rock her like a baby to soothe her, and that at her sister Abigail's house the Tiltons had constructed for her a kind of cradle in which she would be rocked by the hired man, and had put a reclining swing in her bedroom in which, later on, she would be swung to and fro by her nephew or by other boys from the village, who would be paid a few pennies for the chore.

Then and later, Mary Glover was often angry with her father and often denied vehemently the feelings of closeness that lay between them, but that closeness was real and at times uncomfortably intense, and she derived great comfort from rocking herself and from being rocked, and would continue to enjoy that comfort into her old age. The persistence of the pleasures of infancy into mature years is no longer considered such an embarrassment as it once was. But for Mrs. Eddy, having been rocked in her father's arms and in the contrivances constructed for her at her sister's house was a reminder of a dependency and a closeness that she would take great pains later to deny and to erase if she could from the record of her life.

Rocking was not her only comfort. She used morphine too, to dull her pains and to put her into a state of equanimity. She used morphine at various times throughout her life, although it is not clear that she was ever seriously addicted. This matter has been a source of pain to Christian Scientists, who point out, quite correctly, that in the 1840s there was not the same stigma attached to the use of opiates — nor was there the same restriction — that there was to be later on, but Mrs. Glover was apologetic about her practice when she acknowledged it: ". . . My only relief is to take *Morphine* which I so much disapprove";[4] and it was always to be an embarrassing topic.

She was not able to care for her son, then or ever. This too would become a source of embarrassment later on, but the evidence bearing on the matter is unequivocal. Like many self-centered people who have a large tincture of the spoiled child in them, she had a romantic and somewhat abstract, distant affection for children and childhood, but she had little patience for the day-to-day demands of a real son. He may have had a good hour with her now and then, but most of the time he was felt to be more of a bother, a distraction when she was writing a letter or a poem, and his care could better be delegated to Mrs. Morrison or to Mahala Sanborn, the hired girl, or to his grandmother.

Once her health had reassumed its equilibrium of languishing invalidism, Mary Glover slipped into the routine of genteel postadolescent dalliance that she had enjoyed before her marriage. She wrote bad poetry and uninformed political polemic for the local press, entertained some vague relationship with various suitors, and dabbled in the intellectual interests and amusements of her small-town, middle-class society.

These amusements leaned heavily on the occult, on mysterious antirational mental phenomena, and on subjects of spiritual speculation, particularly phrenology, mesmerism,

39

and clairvoyance. Mrs. Glover was in the advance guard of her local society, for while she had as active an imagination as anyone, she had less worldly occupation. She was not emotionally suited to household interests, and wouldn't have been even had she been married. The options for useful and engrossing employment that were available to middle-class women in that small-town society were rigidly limited, mainly confined to managing a household and raising children, and Mrs. Glover's upbringing and personality did not support whatever native capacity she might have had for sustained creative work.

In those days, a woman who was to succeed as a writer required not only talent and artistic sensibility but great concentration and energetic application of the most sustained effort and, if her work was to enjoy appreciable sale, the most earnest cultivation of her channels of publication. Mrs. Lydia Sigourney, for example, the "sweet singer of Hartford," whose popular poetical effusion had been a gift to the newly wedded Glovers from the bride's mother, had started out in her adolescence to cultivate prospective patrons and never in her whole long life allowed herself to be distracted from a single-minded interest in appearing in print. Any topic that was of public interest, but particularly those designed to wring a tear from a tender reader, served as the inspiration for a series of poems, a cautionary essay, or an incident in a travel memoir. The energy that she devoted to her career was the greater because of the prejudice in the late eighteenth and early nineteenth centuries that a woman's place was to occupy herself with the needles and cooking pots and to subordinate herself to her husband's pride and interests. One cannot say that Mrs. Sigourney's innate talent surpassed that of Mrs. Glover; she may in part have molded Mrs. Glover's style, but the energy she brought to her task was of an entirely different range of magnitude.[5]

Louisa May Alcott and Emily Dickinson, both more nearly contemporaries of Mrs. Glover, displayed other aspects of the difficult discipline of writing. Alcott had no money and strove for financial independence and the means to help her family. She tried any honest job she could find, however menial, and resisted constantly the temptation to allow herself to become dependent on her wealthier relatives.[6] In her novel *Work*, largely autobiographical, she describes the limited range of possibilities for earning a living and the intense prejudices that any woman would have to overcome in the struggle for an independent life.[7]

Emily Dickinson, protected from the need to earn her own living but constrained from a public presence by her own internal conflicts, applied to the perfection of her craft an intensity of application and a crystalline artistic sensibility that went beyond the capacity of these other, more successful and worldly women.[8] But all three women realized their ambitions by applying a measure of energy, single-mindedness, and conviction far beyond what Mrs. Glover was able to muster at this time in her life.

A variety of stories are told as reminiscences by acquaintances from that time of Mrs. Glover's enthusiastic participation in trances and séances and in searches after buried treasure, but she engaged in these activities as amusements, without constancy or sustained productive effort. In later years, this period of pointless drift would be made to resemble the forty years that the children of Israel spent in the desert before entering into the promised land. Subsequent events of her life were to be so different that one would have liked to imagine that this was such a time of preparation. That is how myths are made. What was evident at the time, however, was a pretty, intelligent, self-indulgent woman who was unable to devote her attention to any serious purpose, frittering away those years that were, for others, the time of greatest creative and productive effort.

Once Mary had recovered from the acute illnesses that attended the loss of her husband and the birth of her son, she had no dearth of attentive male visitors. Among the first of those in regular attendance was the Reverend Richard S. Rust, principal of a Methodist academy that opened in Sanbornton in 1845. Rust was thought to be Mrs. Glover's suitor and invited her to serve as a substitute teacher for a time in his school. He seems also to have been influential in getting her to write for a magazine, the *Covenant*, which was published by his fraternal organization, the Independent Order of Odd Fellows. Mrs. Eddy denied that there was any particular emotional attachment between herself and Mr. Rust, at least she did later on, but in a letter to her sister-in-law-to-be, Martha Rand, she spoke in a tone of outraged possessiveness of another young woman who occupied center stage in one activity at Mr. Rust's seminary.

> . . . Little of real marvel has occured since you were an inhabitant of S.B. [Sanbornton Bridge]. The Sem. ladies are getting up a fare to defray the expense of *building* operations, such as fitting up an assembly room. Miss Lane is figurante and directress. Wonderful! that a girl of *twenty-two summers* can be so sage in counsel!!! I have an invite to join but *dis child* won't spend a whole *shilling* of *borrowed* money again on charitable occasions, I think.[9]

She claimed in later years that she had been offered $3,000 a year to serve as assistant editor of the *Covenant*, an enormous sum then. She was penniless and would be for years, so why she didn't accept that offer, if in fact it had ever been made, is hard to understand.

Mr. Rust was also said to have been the one to encourage Mrs. Glover to found what was called an "infant school," to which children of preschool age came and sang, at her behest, a paraphrase of a current song:

> *We will tell Mrs. Glover*
> *How much we love her;*
> *By the light of the moon*
> *We will come to her.*[10]

The school didn't last very long and she didn't achieve by it any kind of financial independence. Though the school building, which was on her sister's property, was free for her use, the schoolmistress was ill adapted to her task.

Mr. Rust was not her only suitor, of course. She was pretty and charming, delicate in constitution, inviting of the protection of manly strength, and undoubtedly cleverer and more intelligent than many of her literary and poetical effusions might have suggested. The irritated letter about the seminary ladies, quoted above, goes on about another beau:

> . . . John M. Burt has *paid* an annual visit to the homestead (not I) recently, and spoke of Miss Rand very kindly — wished me to send a little love to her. He now intends to go to Withsconsin after he graduates in August. I hope then people will mind their business about either of us, as I am getting a little *mad* at their *lies*, for such they are. . . .[11]

She was referring to John H. Bartlett, who was about to graduate from law school and whose home she had visited the year before. In a letter to her son Sullivan, Mrs. Baker commented that Mary had gone to Cambridge to see Mr. Bartlett take his degree and that Mrs. Baker thought Mary had decided to marry him. And so she had, apparently, for in her scrapbook Mary later wrote, ". . . He was engaged to marry Mrs. Glover when he left N.H."[12] But the engagement came to naught. Bartlett left New England shortly after his graduation to practice law not in "Withsconsin" but in California and died there suddenly in December 1849. Perhaps he was to have returned to marry Mrs. Glover when he was financially able. His death, coming so soon after he had left New England, was not Mary's only blow, as it followed by but three weeks the death of her mother. Pliant and accepting, Abigail Baker had been ill for some time but continued to perform her household chores even though they had become increasingly burdensome. Her husband, having become prosperous through the investments in railroads and real estate that he made under his son-in-law's guidance, was building a house in town where his wife might have an easier time of it. She did not live to enjoy her good fortune but died on November 21, 1849, at the age of sixty-five.

Mary Glover announced the news to her brother Sullivan in a letter written the next day:

> My Dear Bro':
> This morning looks on us bereft of a Mother! Yes, that angel on earth is now in Heaven! I have prayed for support to write this letter, but I find it impossible to tell you particulars at this time. She failed rapidly from the time you saw her, but her last struggles were most severe; her physician spoke of it as owing to so strong a constitution. Oh! George, what is left on earth to *me*! But oh, my Mother! She has *suffered long with me*; let me then be willing she should now *rejoice*, and I bear on till I follow her. I cannot write more. My grief overpowers me. Write to me.
> Your affec' Sister
Mary
> Died last night at half-past seven o'clock; will be buried next Saturday. I wish you could be here.[13]

She wrote a poem, "To My Mother in Heaven," which was published in the New Hampshire *Patriot*, December 20, 1849, of which this is one stanza:

> *The wild wind's trace, the stars which light*
> *Their shining lamps on high,*
> *Point to thy rest, thy being bright,*
> *Thy home beyond the sky!*
> *And all with mournful memories blent,*
> *No hopes of earth restore —*
> *Oh, winds and stars may wander by,*
> *Thy footsteps are no more!*[14]

Her brother was moved to respond in a poem, too, published in the Baltimore *Republican and Argus*:

> *Then patience, Mary, a few years,*
> *Or months, or weeks, — perhaps e'en days;*
> *Endure each pain, subdue each fear,*
> *The blessing's yours — "Who Christ obeys."*[15]

The report of Bartlett's death, following so closely upon her grief for her mother, threw her into dramatic mourning. Neighbors described her as having appeared at the memorial ceremony for Bartlett dressed in widow's weeds and of having wept such open and copious tears that many of those present were convinced that she and Bartlett had really secretly been married. She produced a poem, "The Meeting of the Two Spirits," bringing together the mother and the lover in heaven, in which the mother asks for news of her daughter:

> *Bear'st thou no tidings from my loved of earth,*
> *The desolate whose stricken joys have dearth*[16]

and the lover replies that though he's done with earthly passion now, he knows that the daughter will soon join them both.

Mary's father was not so inconsolable and by the following Thanksgiving was preparing to marry again. Mary, in a letter to her brother Sullivan, expressed her anger at having been moved from the center of his life:

> Father is to be married to Mrs. Duncan of Candia N.H. next Thurs week; her best carpets and goods have arrived. Last year a little later than this I went into that cold damp house with Father, helped cleanse and set it in order and lived alone with a little girl and him all winter; in the spring he told me if George was not sent away he would send him to the *Poor House* (after abusing him as he did through

45

the winter.) *Now* he comes to me to help arrange the things of his bride; but I will see them in the bottomless pit before doing it. Everything of our departed Mother's has to give place to them and Father is as happy as a schoolboy.[17]

It wasn't that the new Mrs. Baker was so difficult; indeed, she was generally agreed to be a kind, good-natured woman. Martha Pillsbury, Mary's next-older sister, who had lost her husband and come back with her children to live in her father's house, was able to share it comfortably with her new stepmother and to like her very well. But Mary would not — could not — and made plans to live with her eldest sister, Abigail.

But what of her son? He had, after all, been raised mostly by his grandmother and by Mahala Sanborn, the hired girl. His grandmother had died and Mahala had left to marry. George had been just five years old when he lost these two women. He had always been an active little boy. Now, inconsolable, he was hard to manage, especially for a mother whose attention to him had been only fitful up to that point. One solution, but only a temporary one, was to send him for long vacations with his father's relatives, but the best was to give him into the keeping of Mahala and her husband, Russell Cheney, who now lived in North Groton, forty miles away. They were glad to have him. George, at least, seems never to have felt ill served by this arrangement. He had in later years a correct, somewhat dutiful, rather uninvolved relationship with his mother. He did not appear to feel that she had treated him badly and, from the point of view of the six-year-old boy, the arrangement was the best one possible. Mahala was closer to his heart, and the loss of her was more intense than the separation from his mother.

All of this, of course, violated the conventions. Mrs. Glover wrote an elegy on the loss of her son but seems to have seen his departure as but one more pleasure removed, an arrangement that was made in his best interest. Later on, she could not allow it to rest at that. Mrs. Eddy had to justify her own conduct in a way that would satisfy the moral conventions of her followers and that would permit them to call her "Mother Mary" without having to suffer painful doubting second thoughts. As she explained these events later:

A few months before my father's second marriage to Mrs. Elizabeth Patterson Duncan, sister of Lieutenant-Governor George W. Patterson, of New York — my little son, about four years of age, was sent away from me, and put under the care of our family nurse, who had married, and resided in the northern part of New Hampshire. I had no training for self-support, and my health was regarded as precarious. The night before my child was taken from me, I knelt by his side throughout the dark hours, hoping for a vision of relief from this trial. The following lines are taken from my poem, "Mother's Darling," written after this separation:

> Thy smile through tears, as sunshine o'er the sea,
> Awoke new beauty in the surge's roll!
> Oh, life is dead, bereft of all, with thee, —
> Star of my earthly hope, babe of my soul.

The family to whose care my son was committed very soon removed to what was then regarded as the Far West, thus depriving me of the opportunity of having my son classically educated.

My second marriage was very unfortunate, and from it I was compelled to ask for a bill of divorce, which was granted me in the city of Salem, Massachusetts.

My dominant thought in marrying again was to get back my child. The disappointment which followed was terrible. His stepfather was envious; and although George was a tenderhearted and manly boy, he hated him as much as I loved him. A plot was consummated for keeping my son and myself apart; and after his removal to the West, I never saw him again until he reached the age of thirty-four and came to visit me in Boston. Meanwhile he had served as a volunteer throughout the War for the Union, at the expiration whereof he was appointed United States Marshall of the Territory of Dakota.[18]

She then revised this version. The amended passage softened her own angry reference to her husband, but expanded the accusation that unnamed others had plotted to keep her son from her:

> My dominant thought in marrying again was to get back my child, but after our marriage his stepfather was not willing he should have a home with me. A plot was consummated for keeping us apart. The family to whose care he was committed very soon removed to what was then regarded as the Far West.
>
> After his removal a letter was read to my little son informing him that his mother was dead and buried. Without my knowledge he was appointed a guardian, and I was then informed that my son was lost. Every means within my power was imployed to find him, but without success. We never met again until he had reached the age of thirty-four, had a wife and two children, and by a strange providence had learned that his mother still lived, and came to see me in Massachusetts. . . .[19]

Both versions are so inaccurate and so embarrassing with their talk of plots and letters that biographers committed to Mrs. Eddy have preferred to pass over them in silence, presenting the events of her separation from George as if they were engineered by her father and her sister Abigail primarily to absolve themselves of responsibility for the child, only incidentally out of consideration either for her or for the boy, and without her having had any real say in the matter. They say that Mrs. Glover was dominated by a repeatedly frustrated but continuing desire to recover the day-to-day motherly care of her son, but no evidence has been presented for that desire from among her many contemporaneous letters and scrapbooks or from letters of her relatives and friends. In a letter she herself wrote in April of 1851, just before George was sent off, she said that while she expected to miss him, she was anxious for him to get to the Cheneys in North Groton in time to begin attending school there.[20] By then he was almost seven years old.

She moved into her sister's house and was soon again thought to be dangerously ill. Perhaps one part of her renewed outbreak of symptoms was a reaction to the loss of her son. He was, after all, a part of herself, and she must have experienced some pain at the separation. But she had also been moved aside from the prime place in her father's house. She could no longer bear to live there and felt forced by her own need to submit herself to the household domination of her sister Abigail, in whose presence helplessness was more happily tolerated than was an independent competitive spirit.

The routine of rocking and soothing and comforting and encouraging had its customary partially good result. It was said later that she came into conflict with Abigail because she expressed anti-Democratic abolitionist notions in the Tiltons' proslavery, strongly Democratic household, and upset thereby the staid middle-class society of Sanbornton Bridge.[21] There is no truth to it. Mrs. Glover was her father's daughter in political matters and even wrote for publication an admiring sonnet in honor of Franklin Pierce, the Democratic candidate for President in 1852 and the man with whom her brother Albert had been associated in law practice a decade before. Though there must have been many occasions for friction between the sisters, neither her political beliefs nor the lush variety of her physical complaints were ever seriously perceived as a valid basis for her family's discontent.

In December of 1852 she had occasion to consult a new dentist, Mr. Daniel Patterson, who centered his practice in Franklin, a few miles from Sanbornton Bridge, but who supplemented his meager professional opportunities by traveling about the countryside with his horse and modest dental equipment. Mr. Patterson was the nephew of her father's new wife and it may be that his name was brought to her attention in that connection. Although her first known letter to him was dated December 12, 1852, by New Year's Day she was already sending him holiday greetings and a book that she liked and a poem, a modified version of one she'd written nine years before, which contained the lines,

Treacherous joy reveals the worthy crime
And gaping gums betray the tooth of time[22]

— certainly appropriate praise for a favorite dentist.

Mr. Patterson was a handsome man, something of a dandy, and by report a ladies' man. He had been born into a poor Maine farm family, had learned his dentistry by apprenticeship, and was not very successful. Mrs. Glover was a pretty, appealing, and coquettish woman of thirty-one. He was strongly attracted to her and admired her style and her sense of herself as a literary person. He proposed marriage. She hesitated, arguing that because she was Congregationalist and he Baptist, they had a religious incompatibility. Furthermore, she said, her father had raised doubts about his moral character. He protested in florid high style and threatened to accept her decision not to marry him. He sent her a lugubrious poem in sign of submission to her refusal. She relented. By late April, all was serene once again, he sending her dramatic descriptions of the countryside through which he passed as he pursued his career of wandering dentist, and she writing him of her physical complaints, for which morphine was the only relief, and signing her letter "thine forever, Mary."[23] They shared a tendency toward impulsive enthusiasms and an attraction to the dramatic. They were married on June 21, 1853. She was too ill to walk down the stairs to her wedding. He carried her down for the ceremony and then back up to bed.

Mr. Patterson returned alone to Franklin. It was not until some months later that the rocking bedroom furniture was removed from her sister's house and Mrs. Patterson brought it with her to join her husband in their modest quarters. Her situation in Franklin was very different from what it had been in Sanbornton Bridge. No longer was she a member of a prosperous household, with a social outlet immediately available for her wandering, undirected intelligence and with access to the "best people." A woman who later became a Christian Scientist reported a childhood memory of having been Dr. Patterson's dental patient in Franklin, and that while he worked on her teeth Mrs. Patterson sat in the window seat and read Ossian aloud. A mesmerist whom she had known in Sanbornton Bridge lived in Franklin, but there is no evidence that she was more interested in mesmerism than in any of the other occult phenomena, or in phrenology, homeopathy, or the other philosophical, spiritual, or healing interests of the day. She became increasingly confined to her couch, even by day, and would spend much of her time alone, reading the newspapers and a textbook of homeopathic medicine, ruminating upon transcendental issues, and bearing with whatever grace she could her husband's increasingly prolonged absences from home in pursuit of his practice. She kept scrapbooks in which she would paste selections from the various readings that caught her fancy. Later, when she had developed a focused purpose and interest, she would use bits and pieces of this omnium-gatherum in her own writings, sometimes without attributing them to their original sources, and would be accused of plagiarism when one or another of those sources became identified.

In March of 1855 the Pattersons moved to North Groton, where the Cheneys, caring for George Glover, already lived. Perhaps George's being there was one motive for the move. Mrs. Patterson hired as household help a blind girl, Myra Smith, who fifty years later signed a statement to the effect that Mrs. Patterson had come to North Groton with the purpose of educating George herself, for he was restless and shunned school and Russell Cheney was said to have discouraged his education. Myra said further that Patterson didn't like children and wouldn't allow George into the house.

Patterson has been presented by Mrs. Eddy's biographers as a mean-tempered, foolish man, and a rake. They follow Mrs. Eddy's lead, for she wrote him off in later years and justified her divorce from him by calling him an adulterer, although the proof for that is uncertain. A woman seeking a divorce in that period needed to justify her behavior by producing compelling reasons, lest she herself be considered immoral. This denigration of Patterson's character obscures what there was of strength in the relationship between husband and wife and serves to distract from what it was that led to their ultimate separation. Patterson was handsome, vain, self-centered, with a touchy, insecure pride. In a letter of courtship that he sent to Mrs. Glover he said, for example,

I will continue the same course with you that has always characterized my conduct in my acquaintance I take you as witness that my entire appearance before you has been open and frank, and without the least attempt to ingratiate myself in your good opinion by appearing better than I really was yes more I have taken great paines to exhibit the most objectionable characteristics, or at least that has been the case ever since our acquaintance assumed a character of seriousness, and have freely allowed you to put the worst constructions on every Idea or opinion advocated, I have allowed you to look the very extreme in the face as I am ultra in everything and wish to be prepared for the worst and also to have all connected with me prepared for the course I should persue in extreme cases and with myself so represented and truly represented to[o] I must confess I am not surprised that any lady should shrink from uniting themselves with me the only wonder is that you ever thought of such a thing — I know it must be love standing

52

at the very threshold of idolitry should induce such a woman as I should want to marry me, and that is the *only* live that will satisfy *me* — no ordinary commonplace love will ever answer my purpose — it must be stronger than love of life itself, and it would naturally be supposed that a woman would ask a guarantee of a suitable return which my caution must always prevent my giving — fearing I should raise hopes that would not be realized and I am resolved that my wife if I ever have one shall not have her hopes raised only to be dashed to the ground in a few months after marriage I have persued the cours I have because I have no guarantee of my own better feelings after matrimony and my worst feelings may predominate. . . .[24]

He certainly must have been jealous, the kind of man who would have found that children were an intrusion into his exclusive attachment to his wife. He was enough of a child himself to be able to understand and care for his wife in her childish helplessness and seems on the whole to have accepted what she had to offer with gratefulness and with continuing affection, punctuated perhaps by outbursts of disappointment when he felt slighted, but with enough caring to sustain their marriage. It continued firm despite their declining material circumstances. For example, in February of 1857 or 1859, he ends a newsy letter from Sanbornton Bridge,

. . . but I have written a murderously long letter and will close with a long embrace imaginary it is true but still I think I feel it with the warm kiss of unwavering love.

Husband
D. Patterson[25]

Daniel Patterson and Mary Baker Glover were married to images out of their own ideal conceptions: Patterson was marrying a cultivated, well-bred woman, an authoress, someone who loved him enough to give up the comforts of her sister's house to share his simple fortunes. Mrs. Glover was marrying a strong, warm, handsome bear of a man, a doctor, someone who could give her a home of her own and take care of her. Whatever the external circumstances, the dream of love could persist as long as neither of them changed enough to violate too forcefully the other's idealized expectations. It was a marriage in which neither partner quite touched the other as a real person and in which neither helped the other to change or to grow.

If Patterson was jealous and resented George Glover's presence in the house, he had at least been willing to make the move to North Groton knowing that George lived there. It was a small community and he had often to be away from home to earn his living. George and his mother could have visited together freely during his long absences if they had wanted to.

The Pattersons occupied a property that included a saw-mill, which Patterson himself operated to supplement his income from dentistry. Mrs. Patterson's sister Martha held the mortgage to the property. Although North Groton, in the southern foothills of the White Mountains, is a small village, now largely grown up in woods, in 1855 it was a likely enough town, just beginning to enter the decline that overtook so many of those New England communities when the economy shifted from agriculture to mill industry. The trend was to migrate westward. In 1856 the Cheneys, with George, moved to Enterprise, Minnesota, after a short visit with the relatives in Sanbornton Bridge. Mrs. Patterson was again separated from her son, after having lived near him for that first year in North Groton. There is no evidence that the Cheneys' move was motivated by a plot to separate mother and son, although Mrs. Eddy explained it so, many years later.

It is hard to know whether the loss of George brought any significant change to Mrs. Patterson's life. She continued to collect trivia from the newspapers, pasting them into her scrapbook, and still wrote occasional poems, mostly lugubrious, and still read over and over again the pages of

54

her textbook of homeopathy. She was taken with seizures occasionally. At first, the neighbors would send for her husband, who might be at his itinerant work, many miles away. As often as not, his wife would be recovered by the time he arrived, rocking serenely. The general impression spread that Mrs. Patterson's attacks were not so dangerous as they might seem. Indeed, Dr. Patterson, for he was by now called "doctor," was often confident enough of his wife's powers of recovery that he would finish his work in leisurely fashion before returning to rescue her.

To the people in North Groton, both Mrs. Patterson and the doctor were strange specimens; she was considered snobbish and pretentious, and he a man of uncertain temper. Their fortunes did not improve; they were unable to repay Mary Patterson's sister Martha the money she had lent them to buy their property. She needed the income from that money to support herself, and in the fall of 1859, she foreclosed her mortgage and sold their property at auction. The property was bought by a family named Wheet, who could not take possession until Dr. and Mrs. Patterson should vacate. Dr. Patterson was unable to bring himself to go. The Wheets lost patience and tried to drive him off. Mrs. Patterson rose from her couch of pain to rush to vigorous defense, an incident memorialized in the Nashua *Gazette* of March 15, 1860:

A North Groton (N.H.) correspondent of the Concord Patriot writes that on the 20th ult., Dr. Patterson, a dentist in that place, while employed in splitting wood before his door, was assailed by two men, father and son, named Wheet. The elder Wheet rushed upon him with a shovel, which the Doctor knocked from his hands with his axe, at the same time losing hold of the axe. The elder assailant then attempted to get him by the throat, but the Doctor knocked him down, when the young Wheet rushed upon the Doctor with the axe, and striking him upon the head, stunned and felled him to the ground. The father then seized him by the neck, and called upon his son to strike.

The son was about to comply with the murderous request, when the wife of Dr. Patterson, almost helpless by long disease, rushed from her bed to the rescue of her husband, and throwing herself before their intended victim, seized, with unwonted strength, the son who held the axe and prevented him from dealing the intended blow. Help soon came, the assailants fled, and the feeble but brave wife was carried back to her bed.[26]

I hope the reader can share with me the enjoyment of this workaday Victorian rhetoric. It seems to be compounded of careful attention to the weekly sermon and the Fourth of July oration, and of solid acquaintance with the Bible, *Pilgrim's Progress*, and *Paradise Lost*. At that time, before the invention of the telephone, radio, or television, people wrote letters and made speeches and seemed to cherish the written word and the art of composing fluent sentences.

The Wheets were tried for assault but succeeded in forcing the Pattersons to vacate the property. Dr. Patterson's pride could not face the humiliation of public departure from North Groton. He went by himself to Rumney Station, six miles away, to arrange lodgings, and Abigail Tilton came up in her carriage from Sanbornton Bridge to move her invalid sister. They drove out of town to the mocking accompaniment of churchbells rung by the jubilant Wheets, who were now at last to enter into possession of the property they had purchased six months before. Biographers friendly to Mrs. Patterson said that the Wheets attacked because Dr. Patterson had seduced the elder Wheet's wife. Her enemies said of the move that Mrs. Patterson wouldn't make room for her poor blind servant in the carriage, so that the girl had to follow behind on foot. The Pattersons soon moved into a little house in Rumney Station and settled down once again.

The country was moving toward civil war and Mrs. Patterson's martial spirit was aroused. That muse had awakened earlier when she was living in the South and wrote poems in honor of Henry Clay. Later on, she wrote in this inspired vein to celebrate the victors of the Mexican War:

> *Fill high the rich goblet, its nectar is fraught,*
> *With glory and liberty won from thy veins;*
> *Than the feathery spray — is this foaming draught*
> *(That leaps from the Egean Sea to the plains)*
> *Brighter and purer — more dazzling to the*
> *Swift dragons of battle — brave sons of the free . . .* [27]

She had composed heroics in honor of Franklin Pierce in 1852:

> *. . . Is there no bard imbued with hallowed fire,*
> *To wake the chords of Ossian's magic lyre,*
> *Whose numbers, breathing all his flame divine,*
> *This patriot's name to ages would consign?* [28]

Now, in celebration of worsening relations with the South she spoke for the other side of the political divide:

> *. . . O! weak Buchanan, join thy county's cause,*
> *And aid her champions to defend her laws;*
> *Our Eagle's eye-beams dart unwonted fires —*
> *His kindling glance the warrior's heart inspires.* [29]

This martial attitude was in sharp contrast to the enervated, helpless mournfulness of the poety she wrote at other times and the poems she collected in her scrapbook. Her patriotic passion seemed always to justify itself by expressing the dominant mood of the people she associated with, the southerners in power when she lived in the South, the Democrats when she was surrounded by her Democratic family and their Democratic friends, and the bellicose unionists of the North as the southern states threatened secession.

Her political poetry gave her the opportunity to express

some part of her own passionate personal feelings, usually suffocated under the weight of her inhibitions. The content, the particular political idea, was less important than the pretext it provided for some release of her inner pressures. At these times, when she did not have to stand alone, she could rush to storm the barricades, any barricades, and enjoy a brief moment of exhilarating intensity before she relapsed again into her customary languor. Always searching outside of herself in vain for an organizing theme, she would develop a transient interest in some cause or another, but could not make any of them her own in any sustained way and was unable to focus or to direct her capacities productively.

The outbreak of the Civil War in 1861 did bring two unexpected events, however, one of which was to have a real impact on her life. The first was that her son, George Glover, reacted to the death of his foster mother, Mahala Cheney, by running away from home and joining the Union Army. He thought now of his relatives in New Hampshire and wrote to his mother and to his cousin Albert Tilton, beginning a sporadic correspondence that was to continue fitfully through the years to come.

The second event, this one of more serious consequence, was that Dr. Patterson went off to Washington with a commission from the governor of New Hampshire to smuggle certain funds to northern sympathizers in the South, or so at least it is reported. He went to the encampment at Bull Run to see the sights of war at closer range and stumbled across the lines. He was captured by the Confederate cavalry and thrown into prison whence he wrote his wife, wondering who would care for her now, entrusting her to God. She wrote to her congressman and Franklin Pierce in a vain effort to obtain his release. And so Dr. Patterson was doomed to lie in prison for the moment, striving to keep up his own spirits. His wife revised a poem she had originally written in memory of her first husband and published it now as an amended tribute to her second:

I, too, would join thy sky-bound flight
To orange groves and mellow light,
And soar from earth to loftier doom,
And light on flowers with sweet perfume,
And wake a genial happy lay —
Where hearts are kind and earth so gay.
Oh! to the captive's cell I'd sing
A song of hope — and freedom bring —
An olive leaf I'd quick let fall,
And lift our country's blackened pall:
Then homeward seek my frigid zone,
More chilling to the heart alone. . . .[30]

Chapter Three

Daniel Patterson's decision to seek his fortune in Washington must have marked the decline not only in his material circumstances but also in the relationship between husband and wife; her health had not improved, but he no longer felt the same solicitude that he had earlier in the marriage for her everyday care and comfort. Yet he did attempt to make some minimal provision for her, writing on her behalf to at least one healer, Phineas Parkhurst Quimby of Portland, Maine, saying that his wife had been an invalid for a number of years and was "not able to sit up but a little":

Rumney N.H.   Oct. 14, 1861
Dr. Quimby
    Dear Sir
        I have heard that you intend to come to Concord N.H. this fall to stop a while for the benefit of the suffering portion of our race; do you so intend, and if so, how soon? My wife has been an invalid for a number of years is not able to sit up but a little and we wish to have the benefit of your wonderful power in her case. If you are soon coming to Concord I shall carry her to you, and if you are not coming there we may try to carry her to Portland if you remain there.

Please write me at your earliest convenience and oblige
Yours truly
Dr. D. Patterson
Rumney
N.H.[1]

Quimby did not come to Concord, nor did the Pattersons go to Portland to see him. Mrs. Patterson had other healers in mind as well. For example, she wrote a letter to Dr. William T. Vail, who operated what was called a water cure in Hill, New Hampshire, asking about the possibilities for room and board in his vicinity.

In the late winter, Patterson went off to his adventure, even though no solution had been found for the problem of his wife's care; she, more desperate now, wrote to Quimby herself, presenting her situation in all of its pathos. Apparently uncertain that Quimby would answer her letter and offer to treat her for her own sake, she tried to use a bit of leverage from the recommendations of her more prestigious relatives in Sanbornton Bridge. Her letter offers a clear description of her physical condition and mental attitude:

Rumney, May 29/62
Dr. Quimby
    Dear Sir
        I address you briefly stating my case. I have been sick 6 years with spinal inflammation, and its train of sufferings — gastric and bilious. Last Autumn my husband addressed you a letter respecting my case and has always been anxious for me to see you. I am now unable to go to you. I was getting well this spring but my dear husband was taken prisoner of war by the Southrens and the shock overcame me and brought on a relapse. I want to see you above all others. I have entire confidence in your philosophy as read in the circular sent my husband, Dr. Patterson. *Can* you, *Will* you visit me at once? I must die unless you can save me. My disease is "chronic" and I have been unable to turn myself or be moved by any but my husband for

61

one year at a time. I am just on the verge of such sufferings again. Do come and save me. Do you remember A N Tilton and Geo. W [S?] Baker of Sanbornton Bridge: I am the youngest sister of the latter. Mrs. Tilton is anxious you should see me. Please pardon all the errors. I write in bed and without ceremony. Yours etc. Mary M. Patterson.[2]

Whether Quimby replied is unknown, but he was apparently unwilling to leave his practice in Portland. Mrs. Patterson went to Dr. Vail's establishment, where the baths, kindly encouragement, plain living, and the admonition not to talk about her physical discomforts were not enough to relieve her of her sufferings. In August she wrote a second letter to Quimby:

Dr. P.P.Quimby   Hill   August 1862
    Dear Sir:
        I am constrained to write you, feeling as I do the great mistake I made in not trying to reach you when I had more strength. I have been at this water cure between 2 and 3 months, and when I came could walk ½ mile, now I can sit up but a few minutes at one time. Suppose I have faith sufficient to start for you do you think I can reach you without sinking from the effects of the journey? I am so excitable I think I could keep alive till I reached you but then would there be foundation sufficient for you to restore me — is *the* question. I should rather die with my friends at S.Bridge, hence I *shall go* to you to *live* or to them to *die* very soon. Please answer this *yourself*.

                                        Truly yours
                                        Mary M. Patterson[3]

It took two months more for her to get there, but finally she arrived in Portland on October 10, 1862. Julius Dresser, one of Quimby's patients, described in his diary Mrs. Patterson's entry into their group:

MARY BAKER G. EDDY

FROM A TINTYPE GIVEN TO MRS. SARAH G. CROSBY
IN THE SUMMER OF 1864

At this time she was being treated by P. P. Quimby, the mental healer
of Portland. She was then Mrs. Daniel Patterson

The most peculiar person I have seen of late is Mrs. Patterson, the authoress, who came last Friday, a week ago today, from Vail's Water Cure in Hill, N.H., where Melville, Fanny Bass, and I were; and is now under Dr. Quimby, and boarding also, at Mrs. Hunter's. She was only able to get here, and no one else thought she could live to travel so far, but today she, with Mrs. Hunter and sister, Nettie and I went up into the dome of the "New City Building" up seven flights of stairs, or 182 steps. So much for Dr. Quimby's doings.[4]

Dresser's witness of Mrs. Patterson's improvement was soon seconded by her own testimony, for she wrote a eulogy of Quimby that was published in the Portland *Courier* on November 7. Both this article and a sequel to it illustrate her enthusiastic literary style as well as what she understood Quimby's beliefs to entail. Her own words from this part of her life serve as background against which to examine her attitude toward Quimby later on:

When our Shakespeare decided that "there were more things in this world than was dreampt of in your philosophy," I cannot say of a verity that he had a foreknowledge of P. P. Quimby. And when the school Platonic anatomized the soul and divided it into halves to be reunited by elementary attraction — and heathen philosophers averred that old Chaos in sullen silence brooded o'er the Earth until her inimitable form was hatched from the egg of Night; I would not at present decide whether the fallacy was found in their premises or conclusions, never having dated my existence before the flood . . . when by a falling apple an immutable law was discovered, we gave it the crown of science, which is incontrovertible and capable of demonstration, hence that was wisdom and truth. When from the evidence of the senses my reason takes cognizance of truth, although it may appear in quite a miraculous view, I must acknowledge that as *science* which is truth uninvestigated. Hence the following demonstration:

Three weeks since, and I quitted my sick room en route

64

P. P. Quimby

for Portland. The belief in my recovery had died out of the hearts of those who were most anxious for it. With this mental and physical depression I first visited P. P. Quimby, and in less than one week from that time I ascended by a stairway of one hundred and eighty-two steps to the dome of the City Hall, and am improving ad infinitum. To the most subtle reasoning, such a proof, coupled too as it is with numberless similar ones, demonstrate his *power* to heal. Now for a brief analysis of this power: —

Is it Spiritualism: Listen to the words of wisdom. "Believe in God believe also in me; or believe in me for the very work's sake."

Now then his works are but the result of superior wisdom which can demonstrate a science not understood; hence it were a doubtful proceeding not to believe *him* for the work's sake. Well then, he denies that his power to heal the sick is borrowed from the spirits of this or another world; . . .

Again is it by animal magnetism that he heals the sick? Let us examine. I have employed electro magnetism and animal magnetism, and for a brief interval have felt relief from the equilibrium which I fancied was restored to an exhausted system, or by a diffusion of concentrated action; but in no instance did I get rid of a return of all my ailments, and because I had not been helped out of the error in which opinions involve us, my operator believed in disease independent of the mind, hence I could not be wiser than my teacher. But now I can see dimly at first and only as trees walking, the great principle which underlies Dr. Quimby's faith and works; and just in proportion to my right perception of truth, is my recovery. . . .

After all, this is a very *spiritual* doctrine — but the eternal years of God are with it and it must stand firm as the rock of ages. And to many a poor sufferer may it be found as by me, "the shadow of a great Rock in a weary land."[5]

Another newspaper, the *Advertiser*, pretended to be dismayed by the prodigality of Mrs. Patterson's testimonial to

Quimby. After quoting from her letter to the *Courier*, the *Advertiser* went on:

> The above we clip from a communication in the *Courier*, setting forth the marvellous healing (?) powers of Dr. P. P. Quimby. The expression — "*superior wisdom* which can demonstrate a science not understood" sounds wise enough to be very foolish, and deep enough to be exceedingly shallow. The "not understood" is doubtless true, as all will say who know the Doctor. P. P. Quimby compared to Jesus Christ!! What next![6]

The *Courier* gave Mrs. Patterson space to reply, which she did at length. One paragraph and a postscript are worth quoting here in view of what was to follow:

> . . . P. P. Quimby stands upon the plane of wisdom with his truth. Christ healed the sick, but not by jugglery or with drugs; as the former speaks as never man before spake, and heals as never man healed since Christ, is he not identified with truth, and is not this the Christ which is in him? We know that in wisdom is life, "and the life was the light of man." P. P. Quimby rolls away the stone from the Sepulchre of error and health is the resurrection. But we also know that light shineth in darkness, and the darkness comprehended it not. . . .
> . . . In explanation I would furnish your readers with some quotations from P. P. Quimby's theory of Christ (not Jesus) if he is willing, and you will publish it.[7]

If we were to assume that such florid sentiments testified to genuine appreciation, we would be misreading their author. She could be moved to enthusiasm by a raft of causes and characters of varying importance, and the intensity of her rhetoric more often reflected an outpouring of suppressed inner feeling than what might be a genuinely fervid regard for the immediate subject of her composition. Mrs. Patterson's sudden enthusiasm could not have been based on depth and intimacy of acquaintance with Quimby. Rather, when she came to Portland, she was already primed to find someone who she thought would care for her — and with whom she could involve herself. Quimby's efforts, whatever they were, were sufficient to trigger her exultation. However, the pieces she wrote for the newspaper were to be only a preamble. Her feelings for Quimby and his ideas about healing were to become the dominating influence of her life from this point on.

That he would not think so much of *her* was unimportant. She needed a cause to identify herself with and a person who would not discourage the hopes she would place in him, someone she could idealize whose ideas would resonate with and give shape to her unformed thoughts, who was close enough to be reassuring but distant enough that the wear and tear of real friendship wouldn't get in the way of her illusions. It was by accident that she met him at all and that he became so important to her and that his congenial teachings became the framework of her own philosophy. If she had never met him, she might never have accomplished what she did; on the other hand, what other of his patients ever did half so much? Mrs. Patterson's capacity to use what she found and to cause it to develop and magnify should justify our astonishment. To attribute total and absolute originality to her would be to underestimate her remarkable ability to take what she found and transform it into something uniquely her own.

Quimby gains his place in our story because he filled that place of formative influence in Mary Patterson's development. Yet even if Christian Science and Mary Baker Eddy had never been, Quimby would deserve a vivid paragraph in the history of American medicine for his originality and influence on others and as a prototype of the ingenious, practical, and eccentric Yankee craftsman. However, because there was later to be such intense controversy between Quimby's other disciples and Mrs. Eddy and her followers about these early facts of her relationship with her healer, we are fortunate to have available to us a collection of letters that she wrote to him in the years 1862 to 1865. These letters, along with newspaper clippings about Quimby and manuscripts of his writings, both in his own hand and in the hands of some of his patients who served as his scribes, were deposited in the Library of Congress after the death of Quimby's son George, who had been his secretary and had written the short biography that provides what few facts we have about his life.[8]

One of seven children, Phineas Parkhurst Quimby was born in Lebanon, New Hampshire, on February 16, 1802. His father was a blacksmith. When he was two, the family moved to Belfast, Maine, where he lived for most of the rest of his life. He had little formal schooling. The manuscripts in his own laborious hand, a small portion of those writings that are in the Library of Congress material, show a sketchy command of spelling and punctuation, worse even than Mrs. Eddy's own. His son said of him: "He was very argumentative and always wanted proof of anything, rather than an accepted opinion. Anything which could be demonstrated he was willing to accept; but he would combat what could not be proven with all his energy, rather than admit it as a truth." One imagines a determined young man in hardheaded revolt against his father's authority, making his own way in the world and inspiring in his children a similar grudging admiration, a willingness to acknowledge, but not to emulate. However much he was to inspire certain of his patients, Quimby never could persuade his *children* to carry on his work.

His first trade was that of making clocks with wooden movements. He invented a number of improvements in the manufacturing process, including, for example, a functioning bandsaw, used for cutting small parts, establishing the principle in use today. His openness to new technological discoveries and new ideas led him to an interest in daguerreotypy, and for a time he made a business of taking daguerreotype portraits.

In 1836 and 1837, a Frenchman named Charles Poyen began to demonstrate mesmerism in towns along the New England coast. By 1837, when he published his book *Progress of Animal Magnetism in New England*, Poyen claimed to have introduced the practice to at least forty amateurs, among whom one finds some well-known academicians, including, for example, Professor J. W. Webster and Drs. J. Ware, Francis Dana, and Charles T. Jackson of Boston and Cambridge.[9] Like many who were to follow him, Poyen had first become interested in mesmerism as a way to relieve his own ailments and emphasized that aspect in his demonstrations. In 1838, Quimby was witness to one of Poyen's sessions and began to try the method himself on anyone he could persuade to volunteer. In short order he discovered an enormously suggestible young man named Lucius Burkmar. When Quimby would put him into mesmeric sleep, Burkmar would diagnose the pains of ailing people brought before him and make prescription for their relief.

Quimby himself described an occasion on which Burkmar treated *him* in this manner:

On one occasion, when I had my subject [Lucius] asleep, he described the pains I felt in my back (I had never dared to ask him to examine me, for I felt sure that my Kidneys were nearly gone) and he placed his hand on the spot where I felt the pain. He then told me that my kidneys were in a very bad state, — that one was half-consumed, and a piece three inches long had separated from it, and was only connected by a slender thread. This was what I believed to be true, for it agreed with what the doctors told me, and with what I had suffered; for I had not been free from pain for years. My common sense told me that no medicine would ever cure this trouble, and therefore I must suffer till death relieved me. But I asked him if there was any remedy. He replied, "Yes, I can put the piece on so it will grow, and you will get well." At this I was completely astonished, and knew not what to think. He immediately placed his hands upon me, and said he united the

70

pieces so they would grow. The next day he said they had grown together, and from that day I never have experienced the least pain from them.[10]

We are all very much influenced by the attitudes prevailing in our own times. In Quimby's day, the fashionable notions of what influenced human behavior and therapeutics included phrenology, animal magnetism, and spiritualism. There was less of a spread than there is now between the level of sophistication of the interested intelligent layman and that of the specialist, just as there was less of a difference than there is now between the cultural and intellectual life of a middling small town in Maine and that Hub of its Universe, Boston. The presence today of very good private colleges in odd corners of rural areas testifies to the vitality of intellectual life of those areas a century ago.

Thus Quimby had greater access to the leading edge of investigation in these popular beliefs than we today are likely to expect of a man of his background and education, however talented he might be. Similarly, he expressed his ideas in the style of his age; his distinction lay not in the readiness with which he incorporated the conventional "scientific" attitudes of his time into his practice of mesmerism but, rather, in his capacity to question the conventions and to make new and original observations that would modify his practices and his beliefs.

He was at first very much influenced by prevailing notions of phrenology and of animal magnetism. Here, for example, are excerpts from an account of him published in a Belfast, Maine, newspaper on April 27, 1843:

. . . Mr. Quimby is a gentleman in size rather smaller than the medium of man, with a well proportioned and well balanced Phrenological head, and with the power of concentration surpassing any thing we have ever witnessed. His eyes are black and very piercing, with rather a pleasant expression, and he possesses the power of looking at one object without even winking for a great length of time. Thus when he commences to magnetize, he fixes his eyes upon the subject's, and neither moves nor winks until he entirely accomplishes his object.

We were present a few days since when a subject [Lucius Burkmar] was under the magnetic influence, and saw some few experiments upon local magnetism, clairvoyance, &c. When the subject was thoroughly magnetized, and the bandages placed over the eyes, Quimby placed his finger upon the organ of Self Esteem, and inquired whether it was not very wrong to allow slavery in this country, and was answered, no, *no*! — that slavery was one of the best institutions in the world, and that one half of the world were just fit to be the slaves of the other! He then asked the magnetized, what he thought of himself, and was answered that he possessed all power, that he should one day be a great man, that he should be Governor, and even more, that he should one day be PRESIDENT OF THE UNITED STATES! Just as he had spoken the above, Quimby passed his hand to the organ of Reverence, and the subject instantly changed his tone and thoughts, and said, oh! he should never be anything but a poor miserable mechanic, that he could not do anything, &c[11]

The reporter then went on to describe clairvoyant diagnosis in the presence of only a lock of a patient's hair, and other manifestations of clairvoyance under trance, such as taking the subject in spirit to a place where he had never been, and asking him to describe what he saw in his mind's eye. For instance, Burkmar was taken in spirit to the laboratories of Bowdoin College, where he described all kinds of interesting things and, at the end, thanked the reporter for having suggested such a delightful excursion. Clearly, Burkmar was a performer with great style, thoroughly convincing to his interrogator, who concluded with a formulation of the conventional beliefs of what constituted mesmerism:

. . . Human Magnetism, or Mesmerism, is an indescribable, unseen something, exercised by the magnetizer upon the magnetized, and that it entirely overcomes with sleep the body, through which the mind ordinarily receives its ideas from external objects, and that it gives another and clearer medium of communication of thought to the soul, which acts entirely separate from and independent of the body, — that this communicated power enables the soul to be more like its original self, and that in its existence in this state, there is no such thing as distance and space, — that it can behold all things, however distant or near, and look through all material bodies.

We are not prepared to say to what degree these investigations, if continued, may not progress and improve society and the world.

Quimby was not then primarily interested in using mesmerism to heal but was eager to participate in all kinds of investigations and demonstrations. A report is available of Quimby's being enlisted to induce surgical anesthesia. A letter dated Belfast, Maine, April 19, 1845, from A. T. Wheelock, M.D., to the editor of the *Boston Medical and Surgical Journal* describes an event of the preceding year. A young woman who was to have a nasal polyp removed requested that she be mesmerized so that the procedure might not hurt. Quimby was called in and assisted successfully, much to the surprise of Dr. Wheelock, who had thought that he was simply humoring his patient. He wrote:

. . . she evinced not the slightest symptom of pain, either by any groaning, sighing, or motion whatever, but was in all respects precisely like the dead body. I felt convinced that I might as well have amputated her arm. . . .[12]

Among those interested in "magnetism" with whom Quimby was acquainted was a minister, John Bovee Dods. If Quimby was not then particularly interested in healing, Dods was and borrowed Burkmar for some time, using him to diagnose and prescribe medicines that Dods would then prepare and sell to the patient.

Dods elaborated a physiological theory based on his enthusiasm for electricity as a life principle. He believed that the soul was composed of electricity, which was a weightless "substance," so that the soul could exist and yet be thought immaterial. He set forth his elaborate ideas in a book, *The Philosophy of Electrical Psychology*, first published in 1850 and enlarged two years later.[13]

Burkmar was full of Dods's theories when he returned to Quimby. He was, in the trance state, a confident healer now. Diagnoses and prescriptions composed in Latin rolled off his tongue with professional self-assurance. Quimby was puzzled by the Latin, which Burkmar would recite, but with no more understanding of it than Quimby had. He must have gotten it from somewhere.[14] When Burkmar would come out with one of these expensive prescriptions in Latin, Quimby said, he would mesmerize him again and Burkmar would then prescribe the simple, homely herb remedies that Quimby was more familiar with and that cost less; Quimby observed that the patients seemed to do just as well with these folk remedies as they did with the more sophisticated ones prescribed by Burkmar-Dods. He concluded that the patient's belief in the encounter was the most effective healing force. He had been surprised that Burkmar had been able to make *his* pains disappear and felt that Burkmar's explanation of reconnecting the parts of his kidney hadn't made sense. Could he, too, have gotten better by his own belief in Burkmar? It seemed so to him.

One doubt leads to another. Quimby began to question the other "facts" of animal magnetism, that the trance relationship between people operates by an electrical force from one to the other, a force subject to the same influences as static electricity, such as meteorological conditions and the like. He satisfied himself that he could mesmerize just as effectively in a moist as in a dry atmosphere, if only he were confident in his capacity to do so. He could mesmerize in the midst of a lightning storm if he wanted. And he began to experiment with the healing technique, eliminating the middleman, Burkmar, and treating the patient directly, either by putting him in a trance and suggesting health or by convincing the patient directly, without recourse to mesmerism at all.

The notion had been that it was Burkmar who healed, not Quimby. Burkmar's capacity to heal was supposed to reside in some innate talent for clairvoyance, which could be released from the bondage of everyday conventionality when Burkmar was put into a mesmeric trance. In this state, it was thought, Burkmar could see into the patient's body, divine thereby what was amiss, and prescribe accurately. It was thought, then, that the prescription was the curative agent but that this technique of diagnosis and prescription was more accurate than that of ordinary doctors simply because *they* didn't have access to the same insight into the patient's body as Burkmar, clairvoyant in his trance.

What Quimby did now, though, was to reject the notion that the patient was healed by medicine. Belief, he said, was the powerful agent in the encounter, the patient's belief that he was sick and the patient's belief that he would be cured. The healer's practice served only to verify the patient's beliefs — in the illness and in the cure.

Quimby thought it possible to attack the notion of illness more directly. In his evolving view, people visited illness upon themselves by their own notions of illness. It wasn't that the illness was imaginary. It was real enough, but it was caused by the patient's beliefs, by his mental state. If only the patient's attitude toward illness could be changed, if only he could be convinced that illness was a matter of belief, then the harmony between his mental state and his body could be reestablished and the body would heal itself.

The process of healing practice, according to Quimby, ought to be the healer's helping the patient redress his mental attitude toward illness; once that was done, the aim of healing — absence of illness — would be accomplished by the patient's own body, in conjunction with his purified mental state. That was the goal that Quimby sought in his practice. His technique was described by his son George:

> Instead of putting the patient into a mesmeric sleep, Mr. Quimby would sit by him; and, after giving him a detailed account of what his troubles were, he would simply converse with him, and explain the causes of the troubles, and thus change the mind of the patient, and disabuse it of its errors and establish the truth in its place; which, if done, was the cure. He sometimes, in cases of lameness and sprains, manipulated the limbs of the patient, and often rubbed the head with his hands, wetting them with water. He said it was so hard for the patient to believe that his mere talk with him produced the cure, that he did this rubbing simply that the patient would have more confidence in him; but he always insisted that he possessed no "power" nor healing properties different from any one else, and that his manipulations conferred no beneficial effect upon the patient, although it was often the case that the patient himself thought they did. On the contrary, Mr. Quimby always denied emphatically that he used any mesmeric or mediumistic power.[15]

Quimby believed that he discerned the patient's pain without requiring that the patient show or describe it. When he would sit beside the patient, pains would arise in his own body, which would serve then as a reflection of the patient's body. By attending to his own inner feelings, he would have a sure guide to a sense of the *patient's* inner feelings. Then he could describe accurately what the patient felt. This accuracy would presumably convince the patient of Quimby's authority, and the patient would be ready to receive Quimby's theory of illness.

It was believed that the healer took upon himself, in some part, the burden of the patient's suffering and that once a connection to the patient had been made, one could exert an influence in spirit from some distance, without the requirement of one's corporeal presence. Such ideas were in common currency at the time. When Mary Baker had married her first husband and left with him for the South, for example, she had made the quite matter-of-fact arrangement with her mother that they would hold meetings in spirit at a particular hour each day. This was thought to be a perfectly reasonable way to bridge the loneliness of separation.

Such was the form, then, that Quimby's practice had taken by 1859, when he established his office in the International House Hotel in Portland, Maine. He would occasionally make healing tours to other areas and had prepared an advance circular, which was used for promoting the tours and could be sent to those, like Dr. Patterson, who expressed some interest in consulting with him. In the circular, in addition to warning prospective patients not to put their trust in quacks, traditional healers, and employers of trance states and spiritualist messages from the dead, Quimby described in some detail his own philosophy and practice of healing:

TO THE SICK

Dr. P. P. Quimby would respectfully announce to the citizens of ———— and vicinity that he will be at the ———— where he will attend to those wishing to consult him in regard to their health, and, as his practice is unlike all other medical practise, it is necessary to say that *he gives no medicines and makes no outward applications*, but simply sits down by the patients, tells them their feelings, and what they think is their disease. If the patients admit that he tells them their feelings, &c., then his explanation is the cure; and, if he succeeds in correcting their error, he changes the fluids of the system and establishes the truth, or health. *The Truth is the Cure.* This mode of practise applies to all cases. If no explanation is given, no charge is made, for no effect is produced. . . . If patients feel pain they know it, and if he describes their pain he feels it, and in his explanation lies the cure. Patients, of course, have some opinion as to what causes pain — he has none, therefore the disagreement lies not in the pain but in the cause of the pain. He has the advantage of patients, for it is very easy to convince them that he had no pain before he sat down by them. After this it becomes his duty to prove to them the cause of their trouble. This can only be explained to patients, for which explanation his charge is _____ dollars. . . .[16]

The dogmatic, exhortatory style of this broadside, with its warnings against quackery and fraud, must have had some influence in determining who would consult with Quimby. "Put yourself in my hands," he seems to say, "and if only you can believe what I tell you, you'll feel better." Quimby was a man who did not hesitate to contend that he was right where others were wrong. He was not the dispassionate investigator that some of his disciples were to describe later. Yet those patients who wrote of him agreed that he was kindly with those who submitted themselves to him, even though he would dismiss brusquely those who came as doubters.

During this period of his life when he was practicing in Portland, he began to think of publishing his theories of healing, but found it hard to express himself on paper. He wrote slowly and with great labor. His son George and some of his patients served as scribes, taking down his words or copying out his notes, submitting the result for correction and then making revised copies. Some of these were open to his patients for perusal, others not. Mrs. Patterson referred to these writings in her second letter to the Portland *Courier*.[17]

When she first came to Quimby in 1862 to be restored to amazing health, she already had some idea of his practice, attitudes, and personal style. She had read his broadside and had heard testimony of him from other patients. All that remained was to see him herself, to feel his presence, to discover whether his ideas would retain their attractive force. As we now know, she was convinced immediately and gave good testimony both by her well-being and by her published tributes.

Her husband, meanwhile, was one of a group who escaped from the Confederate prison and made their way northward, scrounging along the way. Patterson himself, we are told, was too scrupulous to steal, but he did allow himself to eat the food that his fellow escapees obtained whichever way they could, and they in turn tolerated his scruples for his good company.[18] When he got home after an absence of nine months, he discovered his wife transformed. She was wholly devoted to Quimby and his healing ideas. She no longer needed him. The bond of their mutual dependence, already tenuous, was weakened still further. Mrs. Patterson had turned herself to Quimby, she the sunflower and he the sun. In the first letter she wrote to Quimby after her husband's return, she said that he was already thinking seriously of leaving her again to return to Washington. But now she was not helpless, as she had been before. She even felt enough in command of Quimby's principles to consider engaging in a little healing herself. She had not wholly given up her various physical complaints and thanked Quimby for coming in spirit to care for her, but she was conducting herself as a substantially healthy person. This is the first serious testimony in Mrs. Patterson's own words of her ambition to become a healer:

Sanbornton Bridge
Jan 12/63

Dr. P. P. Quimby
Dear Sir,
Yours of recent date was received with pleasure. My felon finger must account for bad penmanship in answering it. Yesterday I took care of a woman in fits, and in the Spasm she grasped my finger, which has made it somewhat troublesome today. Your angel visit [i.e., in spirit rather than in person] here removed all my stomach pain, the particulars of which were very remarkable and some time I will narrate them to you.
I am to all who once knew me a living wonder and a living monument of your power; five or six of my friends

79

are going to visit you. My sister, Mrs. Tilton, will not find it convenient to leave at present. I am at this time with her, and company from Boston will detain her at present. She wishes me to accompany her son to Portland to see you and probably he will visit you soon.

Capt. Colby's disease [decease] was somewhat unlooked for! but I know the theory too well to ever for a moment doubt. I am sorry to see the levity with which his death is named here. I heard one *remark* "the Dr. knew better than to save such a rascal" but I always wish to tread softly on the ashes of the dead.*

I eat, drink and am merry; have no laws to fetter my spirit now, though I am quite as much of an escaped prisoner as my dear husband was. Many thanks for your kind wishes for my future. I mean not again to look mournfully into the past, but wisely to improve the present, and go forth to meet the future with a woman's courage. I somewhat expect my husband will take up arms to defend our nation's rights, he yearns to do it and I shall try to acquiesce.

My explanations of your curative principle surprises people; especially those whose minds are all matter are convinced by the external appearance of errors in their exit; as for instance the sores that have visited me, and yet I never lost my faith, or cursed *wisdom*, but have lived to receive all with usury again.

The Dr. wishes to be kindly remembered —

Yours ever
Mary M. Patterson[19]

By the end of the month, though, she was sick again, and wrote for Quimby's help. She was taking meals with her sister Abigail's family, and their food, or what one had to swallow along with it, didn't agree with her. She permitted herself a bit of convenient deceit in her letter; she and Quimby shared the belief that people are subject to illness

* That is, one of Dr. Quimby's patients has died. How does one explain failures of a method of cure that promises so much? This was to be a continuing problem.

for their first thirty-nine years, but that life begins at forty. She wrote:

> . . . You know I am less than one year from the 39 of supposed disease, and the habit is yet so strong upon me that I need your *occasional* aid.[20]

At the top of the page, by the date, she had written: "1863

$$\frac{1863 \quad 39}{1824}"$$

She was, in fact, born in 1821, not 1824, and was two or three years older at the time of writing than she admitted to. Well, it was a small thing, the readiness to bend the facts a little to decorate a fancy. Reality would not have served so well.

Her sister Abigail took her son Albert to Quimby in Portland to make him give up smoking, but he started again as soon as he returned home. Mrs. Patterson herself was trying to cure him. She found, though, that her attempts to make Albert give up the urge succeeded only in causing the urge to arise in her.[21] *She* wanted to smoke now, too. This was to be her invariable experience with attempts at healing; she would take on the symptoms of the sufferer and her own stability would be shaken.

Albert's smoking and drinking were considered grievous sins. Abigail and Mary did everything they could to reform him. They distrusted his friends, and when Mary misplaced a piece of jewelry while they were all rooming together in Portland, she was wholly convinced that one of Albert's companions in evil, who lodged in the same house, was guilty of theft. She hired a detective and opened Albert's mail.[22] Lack of evidence did nothing to lessen her suspicion. She was as sure of her intuition in this matter as she had been when she put her faith in Quimby's powers of healing.

Dr. Patterson finally decided to resume his dental practice, working with a colleague in Lynn, Massachusetts. In the summer of 1863 the Pattersons traveled to Saco, Maine, to vacation with his family. Mrs. Patterson did not prosper there. She wrote Quimby from Saco, asking him to come in his "omnipresence," that is, in spirit, to heal her.[23] He may, she says, come when he likes, just so he comes, and at least once a day, please, until she is better.

She visited with Quimby again in the winter, staying for two months, not only for the relief of her ever-changing aches and pains but even more for a kind of spiritual communion, a discussion of the theory of healing with Quimby and his other patients, and for the enjoyment of the fellowship of the disciples. As we have seen, Quimby was in the habit of wetting his hands and rubbing the heads of his patients while he tried to change their minds about their symptoms. After each treatment, the ladies would retire to their rooming house and spend hours talking together while they let down their long hair to dry.

The wetting was a vestige of mesmerism. It was supposed to foster the transfer of electricity between patient and healer. Quimby himself would have preferred to do without it and felt it shouldn't have been necessary. But he found that for many patients, talking alone, sitting down together without the laying on of hands, was too austere and ungratifying to produce the healing result he desired.

The group discussions that took place as the ladies let down their hair must themselves have contributed to the healing result, too. The activity had metaphorical meanings. Talking things over together fostered exchanges of confidence, which helped ease the minds of the sufferers and relieved those tensions that had brought them into Dr. Quimby's hands.

In the course of this mutual enterprise, Mrs. Patterson became particularly friendly with two of Quimby's other patients, Miss Mary Ann Jarvis and Mrs. Sarah Crosby. Miss Jarvis had severe asthma and, while she felt she benefited from Quimby's healing, she did not seize upon the idea of it and doubted her capacity to remain well after returning home. Mrs. Crosby was more attuned to Mrs. Patterson; their friendship had more of mutual affinity in it and less of dependence and reassurance. When she returned home, it was with the expectation that Mrs. Patterson would visit her there when she was ready to leave Portland.

As soon as Miss Jarvis returned home, though, she collapsed and begged Mrs. Patterson to come and help her. It is worth noting that Mrs. Patterson was able to convince both of these women that she was a very special person. She went to Miss Jarvis as friend and companion but also as Quimby's handmaiden, as the delegate of his healing powers. She wrote him almost immediately, telling him of her troubles with Miss Jarvis in a letter that carries the flavor of the situation there:

Warren, Maine, March 31, 1864

Dr. P. P. Quimby —
My dear Doctor,
 I am here after a ride of two days, first day to Wiscassit where I stopped over night, next morning at 10 o'clock got into a vilanous old vehicle and felt a sensation of being in a hencoop on the top of a churn-dash for about 6 hours! When the symptoms began to subside and so did the old cart.

Found my friend glad at *last* that I had got here. She was not a little disappointed on Thursday and Friday at not seeing me; said her brother kept watch for me until the stage came in at ½ 2 o'clock Friday morning; every night she had a cry, 'till Sunday when she gave me up for lost or never to come. She is in a peculiar condition, last Saturday she had a paroxism of what she called "difficulty of breathing on account of the easterly wind." I sat down by her, took her hands and explained in my poor way what it was, instead of what it *was not*, as she had understood it. In a little, her breath became natural, and to my surprise even, she raised phlegm easily and has scarcely coughed any since, till today. So I have laughed at her about the wind veering according to P P Quimby. I say to her, "Why even the winds and waves obey him."[24]

The friendly, conversational, observant qualities revealed in this letter show a different side of Mrs. Patterson's capacities. Her writing up to this time had seemed more designed for effect than for communication. But note how carefully she describes Miss Jarvis's neediness and the shifting balance between Miss Jarvis's symptoms and her fear of losing Mrs. Patterson:

> But last evening we made a mistake. I had a letter from Mrs. Crosby which I read aloud (unwisely) and in which she anticipated the time when I should again be with her. I stopped as by intuition, looked at Mary and she was the picture of despair. This morning she told me her night was sleepless, that she felt I should leave her and all she had tried to live for was to see me. What could I say? I must of course leave her, but I told her not until she was more self-reliant and willing I should go. Still she is weeping and I can't yet get her out of it. When I sit by her she seems frightened and nervous, I cannot feel any physical suffering of hers as I did of Hannah.
>
> Her nervousness has got into my errors in a lump. I wish you would come to my aid — help me to sleep and relieve the confined state of the bowels.

That is, being in the presence of Miss Jarvis's symptoms had caused Mrs. Patterson's physical discomforts to become more insistent. She continues:

> Dear Doctor, what could I do without *you?* I feel less physical strength this spring than I did last, my nervous excitement at one time weakened me. I then had a jaw of trouble and still have so I can't eat enough, all this and *more* of *this* is what's the matter, is it not? I do not want to return to Portland to stop if I can avoid it. If I could have my husband with me and be at home, I would like it there; but! but! but!

Here the tone of Mrs. Patterson's letter shifts, becoming less explicit, more self-justifying and angry. One possible

84

explanation is that Dr. Patterson was displeased with his wife's intense interest in Quimby and his healing and with her plans to visit others rather than returning to him directly, once her own treatments were concluded:

> I like people of common sense, and common justice, or else I like to laugh where the joke comes in. I cannot be deceived in character — I have seen not a little of life in most conditions, and I cannot stoop to conditions. I will not bow to wealth for I cannot honor it as I do wisdom, I despise an individual who does. I respect my "household God" and give it an identity, call it by no name, but always know it when I see it. It never appears in envey, or jealousy, but loves all good attainments in every one, pleased to acknowledge them better than riches and exalting above all else their possessor. Love to George.
>
> Ever with Esteem
Mary M Patterson

> Will Geo please forward all letters or papers
> Dr, won't you continue to help me by thinking of myself.

There follows a flood of letters in very short order. Miss Jarvis would improve with the attention of her guest but would relapse with every sign of the guest's impending departure. Furthermore, Mrs. Patterson was so suggestible that she fancied herself afflicted with all of the ailments from which she was trying to free her hostess. Her system was not strong enough to withstand such buffets. She wrote Quimby again and again to come to her in spirit, and to heal her and heal Miss Jarvis. She even says that she saw his apparition:

> Last Wed. at 12 M. I saw you in this parlor where I am now writing. You wore a hat and dress coat. I said to your Doctorship How dyedo? Whereupon you answered not again, but left, which I called dodging the question. Well, I sighed! "am sorry I spoke" — but really he need not have gone so suddenly. I was not intending to ask him to have

staid to my lecture! But I did see you and was not thinking of you at the time.[25]

Mrs. Patterson then went on to tell Quimby of a lecture she had given about his mental science. It was thinly attended, but she was enough encouraged that she would give another one later in the month. She was attempting, she said, to counteract the notion that Quimby was a spiritualist and that she was one, too. She was pleased with her attempts at public speaking and testified to her continuing devotion to her teacher.

Despite his best efforts at distant healing, however, she continued to suffer from Miss Jarvis's pains. Finally she wrote, almost in exasperation:

> I thank Wisdom that you were not a hopeless invalid ever; hence your power to resist the Devil. When Miss Jarvis would come to my bed it invariably would set me to coughing. . . . I did feel once Why hast thou foresaken me? i.e., your wisdom; am all right now — Please come occasionally [in spirit] and if you make my nights sleepy and bowels act again I can go on without fear.
>
> Ever with Gratitude
MMP[26]

She escaped Miss Jarvis, finally, to return to Quimby briefly and then to go on to Dr. Patterson in Lynn. He was now in practice for himself. Despite a modest success, he and his wife did not prosper together. His enterprise was not wholly expended in the practice of dentistry; Mrs. Patterson received a letter from a friend giving a detailed account of an attempt by Dr. Patterson on that lady's virtue. Mrs. Patterson left home and went to spend a season with Mrs. Crosby in Albion, Maine. The two women talked together in a rush, Mrs. Patterson in the lead. She became attached to the notion that her dead brother Albert was Mrs. Crosby's spiritual guide. When Georgine Milmine was collecting data for her long, careful series in *McClure's Maga*-

zine, Mrs. Crosby was still alive and wrote a detailed memorandum of the events of this time. She still felt the power of Mrs. Patterson's presence, of her attractive, imaginative intensity. As Milmine described the situation:

> One day Mrs. Patterson and Mrs. Crosby sat together at opposite sides of the same table. Suddenly Mrs. Patterson leaned backward, shivered, closed her eyes, and began to talk in a sepulchral, mannish voice. The voice said that "he" was Albert Baker, Mrs. Patterson's brother. "He" had been trying, the voice continued, to get control of Mrs. Patterson for many days. "He" wished to warn Mrs. Crosby against putting such entire confidence in Mrs. Patterson. "He informed me," Mrs. Crosby continues, "through her own lips, that while his sister loved me as much as she was capable of loving any one, life had been a severe experiment with her and she might use my sacred confidence to further any ambitious purposes of her own." . . . Several times, in the course of this visit, Mrs. Patterson went into trances. In one of these, Albert Baker's spirit told Mrs. Crosby that if, from time to time, she would look under the cushion of a particular chair, she would find important communications from him.[27]

Milmine went on to quote two of these notes, both of which were in Mrs. Patterson's handwriting. The first, which appeared while Mrs. Patterson was a visitor in the house, exhorted Mrs. Crosby to put her trust in Quimby. A second, presumably received from Albert by Mrs. Patterson after she had returned home and sent on by her to Mrs. Crosby, deserves quotation in full:

> Child of earth! heir to immortality! love hath made intercession with wisdom for you — your request is answered.
>   Let not the letter leave your hand — nor destroy it.
>   Love each other, your spirits are affined. My dear Sarah is innocent, and will rejoice for every tear.
>   The gates of paradise are opening at the tread of time; glory and the crown shall be the diadem of your earthly

pilgrimage if you patiently persevere in virtue, justice, and love. You twain are my care. I speak through no other earthly medium but you.[28]

Could one but imagine the impact of such extravagance on the workaday world of a Maine farmhouse! Mrs. Crosby did not know what to make of the spirit of Albert warning about his sister and concluded that Mrs. Patterson was sincere. Others have wondered whether she was perpetrating a conscious hoax. Conscious or not, deliberate or not, the words Albert was reported to have spoken certainly reflected an accurate perception of one part of Mrs. Patterson's character, and it is clear that Mrs. Patterson was one of those rare people who are in touch with a part of their own motivations that most people prefer to ignore in themselves.

Mrs. Patterson was changing as a result of her contact with Quimby. Capacities that had been latent were now having a chance to develop for the first time. She had never before been able to talk at length with someone with whom she could share an intense, deep involvement in a common interest. She was becoming more communicative, trying new kinds of activities, finding ambitions and objectives of her own. Her brother Albert had been the most ambitious and accomplished member of her family, and it is oddly appropriate that it was his voice speaking through her own, in this peculiar situation, as if she in her burgeoning ambition had identified with and drawn strength from her memories of him.

In later years, of course, these revelations were to bring pain to Mrs. Eddy and her followers. How were they to explain such antics? It was all a kindly, well-meant hoax, they would say, designed by Mrs. Patterson to cure her friend of her credulity, of her belief in spiritualism. Mrs. Crosby herself was outraged by such an assertion. She knew nothing of spiritualism, she said, and Mrs. Patterson would not then consciously have acted the part of a charlatan:

. . . I shall defend her from such aspersions at the time when her ambition for money and power had not yet been kindled; when she was a devoted and humble follower of Dr. P. P. Quimby . . . aspiring only to follow in the footsteps of her teacher in humility of spirit. I am sure she was too honest then, too much of a lady to use the identity of an honored brother whose memory I think she revered, to attempt to practice a wicked fraud upon one who trusted her, for no purpose except to deceive. . . .[29]

Mrs. Patterson returned from Mrs. Crosby to her husband apparently with the mutual compromise that he would cease his attention to other women if she would dampen her ardor for Quimby. Her letters to Quimby were interrupted now for several months. The Pattersons devoted themselves to social matters in Lynn. They became involved together in a temperance lodge and she began again to write accounts of local affairs for the newspapers, resuming also her practice of refurbishing bits of prose and poetry taken from other authors or other times and suited, now, to new occasions.

But Quimby was not to be forgotten. Early in 1865 he became so weakened from an abdominal tumor that he was forced to give up his practice in Portland and stay with his family in Belfast. Mrs. Patterson visited him there, for the last time, in April of 1865. In July she sent him a strange letter:

Lynn, July 29th 1865

Dear Doctor,

     I have just received a letter that has well nigh separated soul and body and the first thing I thought of doing was to go to you like the mother of old.

A letter informs me from the house where George my son is stopping that he is but just alive not able to sit up with what they call consumption of the bowels. He reached Enterprise, Minnesota on his way home to me and there had to stop too feeble to get farther. If I am with this body next Mond. I shall start for him with it although I am sick today and know nothing of the route to him. O Doctor, tis only in you I have any hope, and can't you save him? He is too good too noble and self sacrificing to be lost to this world even in example.

All I ask all I hope for is that he may be spared to me Save him Save him if you can He shall be brought to you if he can possibly bear the journey

Since the above something tells me not to start. That it is now too late.

Oh Doctor I know not what I have written.

M. M. Patterson[30]

This letter could not have been provoked by news of her son. He was in the South at the time and never had any illness like the one she described. Quimby was ill, certainly, and so was her father, and her marriage was sick enough. Her distress appears genuine. Perhaps she wanted to reassure herself that Quimby, despite his own infirmity, still could heal on her behalf, if only the need were great enough. That is really what she asked in her letter.

But on October 13, 1865, her father died, leaving the bulk of his estate to his son George Sullivan Baker and one dollar to each of his three daughters.* Two months later, on January 16, 1866, Quimby died too. These men had been each a strong arm, a "shadow of a great Rock in a weary land," and Mary was bereft.

---

* Mark Baker was not necessarily being mean to his daughters. His son Sullivan had provided him with the only male heir to carry on the family name. Daughters, however much they were loved, became the responsibility of their new families once they married.

Chapter Four

Mrs. Patterson's first *public* reaction to Quimby's death was what past performance would have led one to expect — a poetic eulogy — dated six days later, January 22, 1866, and published in the Lynn *Reporter* on February 14:

Lines on the Death of Dr. P. P. Quimby,
Who Healed with the Truth that Christ Taught
in Contradistinction of all Isms.

Did sackcloth clothe the sun and day grow night,
All matter mourn the hour with dewy eyes,
When Truth, receding from our mortal sight,
Had paid to error her last sacrifice?

Can we forget the power that gave us life?
Shall we forget the wisdom of its way?
Then ask me not amid this mortal strife —
This keenest pang of animated clay —

To mourn him less; to mourn him more were just
If to his memory 'twere a tribute given
For every solemn, sacred, earnest trust
Delivered to us ere he rose to heaven.

Heaven but the happiness of that calm soul,
Growing in stature to the throne of God;
Rest should reward him who hath made us whole,
Seeking, though tremblers, where his footsteps trod.[1]

This stirring of the poetic impulse did not necessarily indicate any real depth of feeling, because Mrs. Patterson saw it as her duty to celebrate any newsworthy occasion with suitable verse. But an accident befell her two weeks after Quimby's death that symbolized how much support she had gotten from him and what his loss would mean to her. She fell on the ice on February 1, 1866, and the aftermath of that fall, celebrated in Christian Science as its founding moment, was to show very clearly that this was to be a turning point in her life.

Several quite disparate descriptions exist of this "Fall on the Ice." Putting them side by side permits a view of Mrs. Patterson and the history of Christian Science that conveys much more of metaphorical truth than could be obtained from any one single version.

The first and simplest was the account, perhaps slightly overblown, found in the Lynn *Reporter* on February 3:

> Mrs. Mary Patterson of Swampscott fell upon the ice near the corner of Market and Oxford Streets on Thursday evening and was severely injured. She was taken up in an insensible condition and carried into the residence of S. M. Bubier, Esq., near by, where she was kindly cared for during the night. Dr. Cushing, who was called, found her injuries to be internal and of a severe nature, inducing spasms and internal suffering. She was removed to her home in Swampscott yesterday afternoon, though in a very critical condition.[2]

Dr. Alvin Cushing remembered it somewhat differently, that there was less of critical internal injury and more of intense emotion. Forty years later, when Georgine Milmine and her associates were preparing the series for *McClure's Magazine*, they found Dr. Cushing still alive and with his office records intact. In his description of the event, he said that when he saw Mrs. Patterson shortly after her fall she was ". . . nervous, partially unconscious, semi-hysterical, complaining by word and action of severe pain in the back of her head and neck. . . ." He gave her medicine every fifteen minutes till she was quieter, visited her later that night and again next morning, when he found that she had slept some and that she was ". . . quite rational but complaining of severe pain, almost spasmodic on moving. . . ." Dr. Cushing found that she had a remarkably profound reaction to the very small amounts of morphine he gave her for her pain. ". . . She told me she could feel each dose to the tips of her fingers and toes, and gave me much credit for my ability to select a remedy. . . ."[3]

The intense effect of the almost vanishingly small amounts of narcotic (one eighth of a grain, progressively diluted, according to Dr. Cushing) suggests that Mrs. Patterson was drawing greater relief from the doctor's presence than from his medicine. She spoke to him of ". . . a Dr. Quimby of Portland, Maine, who had treated her for some severe illness with remarkable success. She did not tell what his method was. . . ." Dr. Cushing made his final visit on February 13, when ". . . she seemed to have recovered from the disturbance caused by the accident and to be, practically, in her normal condition."

On the very next day, February 14, she wrote a letter to Julius Dresser, another patient of Quimby's, announcing for his benefit that she had fallen on the ice and that her symptoms had returned again, as bad as they were before she knew Quimby. She did not volunteer that she had been discharged from medical care by the time she was writing this letter but asked Dresser to take Quimby's place and heal her:

93

Lynn, February 14, 1866

Mr. Dresser:

Sir: I enclose some lines of mine in memory of our much-loved Friend, which perhaps *you* will not think over-wrought in meaning, *others* must of course.*

I am constantly wishing that *you* would step forward into the place he has vacated. I believe you would do a vast amount of good, and are more capable of occupying his place than any other I know of.

Two weeks ago I fell on the sidewalk and struck my back on the ice and was taken up for dead, came to consciousness amid a storm of vapors from cologne, chloroform, ether, camphor, etc., but to find myself the helpless cripple I was before I saw Dr. Quimby.

The physician attending said I had taken the last step I ever should, but in two days I got out of my bed *alone* and *will* walk, but yet I confess I am frightened, and out of that nervous heat my friends are forming, spite of me, the terrible spinal affection from which I have suffered so long and hopelessly. . . . Now can't *you* help me. I believe you can. I write this with this feeling: I think I could help another in *my* condition if they had not placed their intelligence in matter. This I have not done and yet I am slowly failing. Won't you write me if you will undertake for me if I can get to you? . . .

Respectfully,
Mary M. Patterson[4]

Dresser had been married only a short while; his wife too had been a patient of Dr. Quimby's. They had just had their first child. Their family life was full. They had little need to find replacement for Quimby. Dresser's reply, dated March 2, was a model of detachment and included reflections on Quimby's career that, even as they expressed a way of thinking that was very close to her own, must have convinced Mrs. Patterson that Dresser was not available to her:

* A reference to her husband, who felt abandoned by her total absorption in Quimby.

94

As to turning doctor myself, and undertaking to fill Dr. Quimby's place and carry on his work, it is not to be thought of for a minute. Can an infant do a strong man's work? Nor would I if I could. Dr. Quimby gave himself away to his patients. To be sure he did a great work, but what will it avail in fifty years from now, if his theory does not come out, and if he and his ideas pass amoung the things that were, to be forgotten? He did work some change in the minds of the people, which will grow with the development and progress in the world. He helped to make them progress. They will progress faster for his having lived and done his work. So with Jesus. He had an effect that was lasting and still exists. He did not succeed nor has Dr. Quimby succeeded in establishing the science he aimed to do. The true way to establish it is, as I look at it, to lecture and by a paper and make that the means, rather more than the curing, to introduce the truth. To be sure faith without works is dead, but Dr. Quimby's work killed him, whereas, if he had spared himself from his curing, and given himself partly and as considerately, to getting out his theory, he would then have, at least, come nearer success in this great aim than he did.[5]

Mrs. Patterson shared Dresser's belief that the healing practice weakened the healer, whether by distracting his attention from his own self or by causing him to take onto himself the symptoms of the sufferer. The healer felt pain and the patient felt relieved and well. When she was with Miss Jarvis, Mrs. Patterson had written to Quimby that as Miss Jarvis would give up her symptoms, Mrs. Patterson would take them on, and when she tried to cure her nephew of smoking, she had succeeded only in giving herself the urge to smoke. It would require only a very subtle shift in position for the healer to see himself as a scapegoat, that is, a victim of other people's intentions, however motivated, which Mrs. Patterson-Eddy was so often to do. Dresser was reluctant for obvious reasons to take on the healing mantle and recommended that it would be safer to practice theory oneself and let someone else bear the burden of the healing.

That Mrs. Patterson was to pursue this very program is not proof that she was inspired to it by Dresser's recommendation. She and he thought alike in these respects. Whatever their other dissimilarities, they were both responsive to Quimby's view of life and of the nature of illness and the Divine mission, and they both drew the same conclusion — that it was Quimby's work that had killed him.

The capacity to dramatize oneself, to transmute ordinary experience into that mythic event that creates an aura of special significance, had been one of Mrs. Patterson's special qualities, not yet perfected in practice, perhaps, but constantly nurtured and exercised. This "Fall on the Ice" was such an experience, dramatized from the start, conveying her dismay at the loss of Quimby, and used as an expression of her pitiful need in an attempt to convince Dresser to take Quimby's place. It had an emotional meaning that transcended the physical significance of whatever trivial injuries she might have sustained. In later years, when she was to disavow Quimby, it was to become transformed into that critical moment of Divine revelation that would legitimize Mrs. Patterson as the one true prophet of the Divine Healer and would justify the very existence of the Church of Christ, Scientist. The 1907 version, composed by Sibyl Wilbur with Mrs. Eddy's acquiescence and encouragement, was heavily influenced by the Gospel accounts of the death and resurrection of Jesus:

> Mrs. Eddy's account of this accident differed from the physician's and she knew what healed her and how she was healed and when it occurred. She was not responsible for the calling of the physician and only took his medicine when she was roused into semi-consciousness to have it administered, of which she had no recollection. After the doctor's departure on Friday, however, she refused to take the medicine he had left, and as she has expressed it, lifted her heart to God. On the third day, which was Sunday, she sent those who were in her room away, and taking her

Bible, opened it. Her eyes fell upon the account of the healing of the palsied man by Jesus. . . .

A spiritual experience so deep was granted her that she realized eternity in a moment, infinitude in limitation, life in the presence of death. . . . In that moment all pain evanesced into bliss, all discord in her physical body melted into harmony, all sorrow was translated into rapture. She recognized this state as her rightful condition as a child of God. Love invaded her, life lifted her, truth irradiated her. God said to her, "Daughter, arise!"

Mrs. Patterson arose from her bed, dressed and walked into the parlor where a clergyman and a few friends had gathered, thinking it might be for the last words on earth with the sufferer who, they believed, was dying. They arose in consternation at her appearance, almost believing they beheld an apparition. . . . She stood before them fully restored to health. . . .

Mary Baker did more than experience a cure. She in that hour received a revelation for which she had been preparing her heart in every event of her life. . . .[6]

Dr. Cushing did not sympathize with this kind of mythification. He contradicted Sibyl Wilbur's account. He had treated Mrs. Patterson later that same year of 1866 for another relatively minor illness, he said, and she had made no claim to him of having been touched by Divine Healing:

> . . . I did not at any time declare, or believe, that there was no hope of Mrs. Patterson's recovery, or that she was in a critical condition, and did not at any time say, or believe, that she had but three or any other limited number of days to live. Mrs. Patterson did not suggest, or say, or pretend, or in any way whatever intimate, that on the third, or any other day, of her said illness, she had miraculously recovered or been healed, or that, discovering or perceiving the truth of the power employed by Christ to heal the sick, she had, by it, been restored to health. As I have stated, on the third and subsequent days of her said illness, resulting from her said fall on the ice, I attended Mrs. Patterson and gave her

medicine; and on the 10th day of the following August, I was again called to see her, this time, at the home of a Mrs. Clark, on Summer Street, in said City of Lynn. I found Mrs. Patterson suffering from a bad cough and prescribed for her. I made three more professional calls upon Mrs. Patterson and treated her for this cough in the said month of August, and with that ended my professional relations with her.[7]

Good Christian Scientists have tended to see the time before "the Fall" as one of preparation for revelation and the period after as one demonstrating the progressive transmission of that great light to an enlarging body of believers. Others, like Dr. Cushing more critical of Christian Science, have supposed that these events were of no great significance but that they were elaborated in retrospect to suit Mrs. Eddy's purposes in claiming a source of divine inspiration for her teachings and in wishing specifically to deny any continuity between Quimby's beliefs and her own.

My own view differs from both of these. The later events of her life suggest that Mrs. Eddy's "Fall" was an important event, although not necessarily a *cause* in itself. It marked in dramatic fashion her reaction to Quimby's death and perhaps to that of her father, just before. She now had no one on whom to rely. She was hurt, in the most literal sense. But who, now, could gather her into his arms and comfort her? Her husband had drawn away from her, alienated by her attachment to Quimby. Her father was dead, her family largely uninvolved, and she was forty-five years old, no longer young, fresh, appealing. And it had all happened before, more than once. Her attempts to cope in her usual way, by finding an immediate replacement, were unavailing. It was, then, as if she decided that this time would be different — that she would never again put such hope in any human being; instead, she would become the person who brought hope and help to others. She would not depend on them, but they on her. She had, after all, a method, the one she had gotten from Quimby, for whom there could be no easy replacement.

This attitude did not spring forth openly, at once fully developed, but the guiding principle was there, working its way toward being realized, and she had models for such an attitude of exaggerated independence in her memories of her father, in the example of her sister Abigail, and in the personality of Quimby himself.

Moderation and compromise were not native to Mary Patterson's temperament. Drama and self-concern had always taken precedence over humdrum ordinary reality, and so they would now. She would become not *more* independent, but wholly so. She would make *entirely* her own way in the world. Her acknowledgment of needing other people was now to be stringently denied, the exact opposite maintained. All of her latent talents were to be drawn into the struggle to maintain that fiction. That was to be her remarkable accomplishment — that a helpless woman of forty-five, without formal training or serious preparation, would struggle with her feelings of helplessness so persistently and with such resourcefulness and opportunism that she would succeed both in creating a kind of security for herself and in disguising the emotional cost of the struggle from herself and from others. And in her struggle she would win the enthusiasm and veneration of a large group of people who needed, as she did, to wrestle with their own conflicting needs for warmth from others and for independence; they would see in what she appeared to accomplish a worthy example, a model for their own life conduct.

Our mental life — our thoughts, feelings, attitudes — has been likened to one of those magical cities planned by Leonardo da Vinci in which the wealthy citizens live their lives on one level while the servants, who do the work of maintaining the establishment, use underground rooms and roadways, out of sight and largely ignored. If Mary Patterson was going to live her later life in denial of a very important emotional reality — her need to depend on others —

then we can be sure that that reality, like da Vinci's servants, would have a very active subterranean part in her life, showing itself in recurrent eruptions that would contrast with the superficial consistency of her attitude. It was the drama of that conflict, between the calm, confident public presence and the impulsive, pain-ridden, nightmare-obsessed, vengeful, suspicious private person, that was so to embarrass her friends and followers — and to provide material matter for the rueful amusement and outrage of her opponents.

Our premise in examining the second half of her life is that it was like a mirror image of the first half. Her helplessness and need for others, the dominating qualities of her earlier life, were now to become subterranean passions — and her capacities for independence, determination, organization, and initiative, suppressed before, were now to come out into the light. Where before she had sought someone constantly to lean upon, now she was to try to be wholly independent; and where before she had sought anyone's purpose for her momentary use to assure herself of an instant of fitful attention, now she was to have a consistent program and purpose of her own. To accomplish these ends, she was to mobilize capacities and resources that had heretofore been hidden, largely neglected, or misused but that now, shaped by a serious need, she would become adept in managing.

Her need for others to lean on was to persist, as strong as before, but hidden even from herself, invading her thoughts and dreams and providing the secret motive to those aspects of her behavior which would seem least consistent. The drama of her accomplishment would be that she would reassemble old materials in new ways. The second half of her life was to be startlingly different from what went before, but by an odd principle of economy nothing wholly new was to be introduced as life force for this transformation. Old traits would find new expression, old talents, heretofore denied free development, would now come into their own, and old tendencies to cripple one's gifts would now be pushed away from the center of attention. All of this marvelous metamorphosis was set into being by Quimby's death and Mrs. Patterson's realization of a loss for which there could be no replacement.

We have already seen that she and her husband had never regained for each other the regard that had been so marked early in their marriage. His departure for Washington and her infatuation with Quimby's ideas and with Quimby himself had solidified a disaffection from which they never recovered. Patterson seems to have been one of those men who feel most masculine and best about themselves when they have a beautiful, helpless, admiring woman to care for. His wife's defection to Quimby surely troubled his self-esteem. And when she still did not return to nestle in his heart, even after Quimby had died, then he could no longer bear to live with her. They separated, not on wholly unfriendly terms, for he agreed to provide her with an allowance of two hundred dollars a year, enough in those days for decent room and board, but with little left over, and they joined together for a short time in an abortive lawsuit against the town of Lynn, saying that the town's negligent maintenance of the public way was what had caused her to fall on the ice. There was no indignant outcry then about Patterson's infidelities, and he apparently went to Sanbornton Bridge in good standing to explain to the family his reasons for leaving his wife. It was not until years later, when Mrs. Eddy felt that she needed to justify herself for the separation and the subsequent divorce, that she told the conventionalized story of the good woman who was so outraged by her husband's immoral conduct that she could not permit him to remain by her side. The Pattersons still lived together, part of the time at least, as late as the early fall of 1866, although in progressively poorer circumstances. After they separated, Patterson continued with diminishing success his luckless profession of wandering dentist. His remittances continued for a few years before petering out, and in 1873 Mrs. Patterson was divorced from him, charging desertion.

He died in 1896, to be buried, it was said, in a pauper's grave.

This time, after Patterson's departure, Mrs. Patterson didn't try to return to her sister's house. She lived instead with a succession of acquaintances, saving up her little bit of money, outstaying her welcome over and over again, and then moving on to stay with someone else. She alienated her hosts by refusing to pay for her room and board or by justifying herself with the claim that she had cured some member of the household of this or that illness. Most of these beneficiaries denied that she had either practiced on them or healed them.

When Georgine Milmine was collecting affidavits for the *McClure's* series, forty years later, many of the witnesses from that time were happy to deny Mrs. Patterson and to testify still how unpleasant they had found her to be, how pretentious or how unbending. We could be led to suppose that her claims were meaningless. Perhaps they were, in a strictly realistic sense, but she needed both to hoard her small bit of money and to avoid the appearance of needing someone else's help. Her only expendable capital lay in Quimby's healing method, but she had some fear of practicing the method herself, believing that it would weaken her body when she was already most alone and vulnerable. After all, as Julius Dresser had written, "Dr. Quimby's work killed him." But to accept charity is humiliating to a proud spirit. We cannot wonder, then, that Mrs. Patterson would always insist that she gave more than she received and that her healing more than justified the bread and shelter that she did her hosts the favor of accepting.

She had to move at least eight times during that year of 1866, driven by dwindling finances and the exhaustion of her hosts' patience. The seventh of these sojourns was at the boardinghouse in Lynn of a Mr. and Mrs. George Clark, who attracted to their table the kind of person who might be interested in mystical and spiritualistic phenomena. Séances were often held there. Mrs. Patterson apparently was careful to make it clear that she was not really of *this* group, being interested in Quimby's healing, which denied alliance with spiritualism or hypnotism. She attracted the interest of a young man named Hiram Crafts, a shoemaker from East Stoughton, Massachusetts, who was boarding there while he worked for a time in a shoe factory in Lynn. After returning home and discussing the matter with his wife, Crafts decided to try the healing practice and invited Mrs. Patterson to come and stay with them while she taught him. He was to share the proceeds of his practice with her, in return for which she was not to teach anyone else Quimby's method. She is quoted as having said, over and over again, "I learned this science from Dr. Quimby and can impart it to but one person."[8]

Five months later, in April 1867, Crafts moved the trio to Taunton, Massachusetts, where he opened an office, and on May 13 his advertisement appeared in the newspaper:

TO THE SICK

DR. H. S. CRAFTS
Would say unhesitatingly, *I can cure you*, and have never failed to cure Consumption, Catarrh, Scrofula, Dyspepsia and Rheumatism, with many other forms of disease and weakness, in which I am especially successful. If you will give me a fair trial and are not helped, I will refund your money.[9]

The venture might have gone well if Mrs. Patterson had not felt that Mrs. Crafts was an unnecessary impediment to its success and tried to get Crafts to divorce her. At least, that is the story that Mrs. Crafts's brother told many years later. Others claimed it was a dispute over money. Perhaps both were true. Mrs. Patterson left precipitously and Crafts gave up the practice and went back to shoes. After looking about for a place to stay, Mrs. Patterson was directed to a Mrs. Nathaniel Webster in Amesbury, a lady who had the reputation of taking in stray souls with whom she might share her interest in spiritualism.

While she was staying with the Crafts, though, Mrs. Patterson had paid a brief visit to her brother and sisters in Sanbornton Bridge. Her brother was gravely ill and died soon after her visit. It was claimed that she went to cure her niece, Ellen Pillsbury, who was said to be dying from gastroenteritis and who had been given up by three doctors as a hopeless case. But Ellen repudiated her, and Ellen's mother did not seem, either then or ever, impressed by the therapeutic intervention. Her mission seems more likely to have been in search of some kind of help, but the high-handed, independent line that she was taking in those days was not one that would have endeared her to her family. Her sister Abigail was the absolute first lady of her community and had little tolerance for others who, like herself, insisted on their pride. When Mary was meek and helpless and agreeable, she was Abigail's favorite; but when she was her own woman, Abigail could not abide her.

The Webster household in Amesbury was a most unusual establishment. Nathaniel Webster, a wealthy retired sea captain, was manager of a mill in Manchester, New Hampshire, too far away in those days for him to live at home. He visited only every other weekend. His wife was a spiritualist, that is, a medium, and a charitable soul who filled her fifteen-room house with a variety of waifs, ailing people anticipating mediumistic cures, and assorted spiritualistic colleagues, who participated in séances and intense discussions of mutual interest. Mrs. Glover, as Mary Patterson now called herself again, fit right in with the other inhabitants of this menage. She had a room of her own, was not expected to contribute to the expenses of the household, and set herself up to use Mrs. Webster's séance room as a study. Hard at work on an ambitious project to which she devoted several hours each day, she was writing a commentary on the Bible from the perspective of Quimby's concept of the Divine Healing Mission, as she understood it from Quimby and interpreted it herself. This project was to continue for several years, although never advancing beyond Genesis. Later, she would shift her focus to suit other purposes.

There is some controversy, naturally, about how actively she entered into the spirit of the household. Mrs. Webster's granddaughter said much later that Mrs. Glover was a wholehearted and even a leading participant in the séances; surely, when she had been Mrs. Crosby's guest only three years before, she had entered with gusto into communication with spirits from the other world. Many years later, after she had become famous, such matters were considered less respectable and certainly unsuitable for the leader of a church that had to struggle for legitimacy and acceptance. In more recent times, Mrs. Glover thus came to be portrayed as a saintly person, without any self-interest at all, her mind wholly devoted to serious pursuits, and only a passive and unwillingly acquiescent spectator to the spooky goings-on. But she so loved to be the center of interest in any gathering that one cannot imagine how she could have resisted taking center stage in Mrs. Webster's productions, whether she believed in them or not (perhaps even upstaging her hostess). That good lady was reported by her granddaughter to have become less enchanted by her guest as time went on, but without being able to make her move from the house, in which she lived from the early fall of 1867 until the early summer of 1868, when she was finally expelled.

That is the only word for it — expelled. Mrs. Webster had had a daughter who had died, leaving her husband with three young children to raise. He would bring them up from New York City each summer to spend the school vacation with their grandmother in the country, but since he disapproved of her houseguests and felt that the spiritualistic atmosphere was bad for the children, he would insist that the house be cleared before they arrived. But Mrs. Webster was unable to get Mrs. Glover to go. Where, indeed, might she have gone, given her penury? So Mr. Ellis came up to add the weight of his commanding presence and, that being still not sufficient, had her trunk put out of doors, herself then with it, and the door then locked with her outside — all of this at night and in the rain. It became a vivid family anecdote and he always marveled, his daughter said, that he had been compelled to do something that was so alien to his own notion of a gentleman's proper conduct.

Although the story concerns Mrs. Glover in particular, two other inmates were evicted at the same time, one of whom, Richard Kennedy, was only eighteen years old then. He was destined to reappear in her life shortly.

Mrs. Glover went to the house of Sarah Bagley, a maiden lady with spiritualist interests, who took her in for a small sum and learned from her something of the Quimby method, enough at least to enable her to make a modest living as a healer. Mrs. Glover was looking for pupils and advertised that summer in the *Banner of Light*, a spiritualist weekly:

> Any person desiring to learn how to heal the sick can receive of the undersigned instruction that will enable them to commence healing on a *principle of Science* with success far beyond any of the present modes. No medicine electricity, physiology or hygiene required for unparalleled success in the most difficult cases. No pay is required unless this skill is obtained. Address Mrs. Mary B. Glover, Amesbury, Mass., Box 61.[10]

There is no sign of a vigorous response to this advertisement, but Mrs. Glover did enter into negotiation with yet another spiritualist, Mrs. Sally Wentworth of Stoughton, whom she had met the year before when she was a member of the Crafts household. In addition to having spiritualist interests, Mrs. Wentworth was what we might today call a practical nurse. One of her children, a daughter, was thought to be "consumptive," which in those days might have meant anything from having a tendency to cough, at one end of the spectrum, to having severe pulmonary tuberculosis, at the other. This girl was taken to a variety of healers, among them Hiram Crafts, at whose home Mrs. Wentworth met

Mrs. Glover and was very favorably impressed by her. Mrs. Wentworth agreed to pay Mrs. Glover three hundred dollars in room and board if she would come and instruct Mrs. Wentworth in the healing art. Mrs. Glover left Miss Bagley abruptly and set herself up at the Wentworths', where she was to stay from the fall of 1868 until the early spring of 1870.

The Wentworths found Mrs. Glover to be a charming guest, especially at first, and it is clear that she set herself the task of being a wise and loving oracle. The statement that she had been in the habit of repeating to the Craftses, "I learned this science from Dr. Quimby and can impart it to but one person," was now amended to "I *learned* this from *Dr. Quimby*, and he made me *promise* to teach it to at least *two* persons before I *die*," delivered in a sweet, sententious, rhythmic, emphatic voice.[11] Although family visitors to the household were critical of Mrs. Glover's self-importance and bossiness, Mrs. Wentworth and her daughter Lucy, at least, were staunch in defense of her good qualities. Mr. Wentworth accepted her presence, too, although with less enchantment.

During this time Mrs. Glover was working on her commentary on Genesis. When it was finished she took it to Boston to be published but found that the publisher would accept it only if she paid for it herself, the required sum being six hundred dollars. She didn't begin to have that kind of money and asked Mr. Wentworth for it. When he wasn't about to give it to her, the battle lines were drawn. It is chiefly from Mrs. Wentworth's niece, Catherine Isabel Clapp, and from her elder son, Horace Wentworth, that we have the stories about the disintegrating relationship. Apparently Mrs. Glover tried to retaliate first by trying to get Mrs. Wentworth to leave her husband and then, that failing, by trying to make his life at home unpleasant by, for example, pounding on the floor above when he was sick in bed. It was clear that she would have to leave yet another refuge, but again she refused as long as she could and then chose for her departure a day when the family was away, and without letting them know she had gone. Horace Wentworth wrote about the event:

A few days after Mrs. Glover left, I and my mother went into the room which she had occupied. We were the first persons to enter the room after Mrs. Glover's departure. We found every breadth of matting slashed up through the middle, apparently with some sharp instrument. We also found the featherbed all cut to pieces. We opened the door of a closet. On the floor was a pile of newspapers almost entirely consumed. On top of these papers was a shoveful of dead coals. These had evidently been left upon the paper by the last occupant. The only reasons that they had not set the house on fire evidently were because the closet door had been shut, and the air of the closet so dead, and because the newspapers were piled flat and did not readily ignite — were folded so tight, in other words, that they would not blaze.[12]

Other family members later repudiated Horace Wentworth's extreme version, and Sibyl Wilbur told yet another, in which Mr. Wentworth escorted his guest to the train and carried her bags for her. Whatever version one credits, Mrs. Glover had again, at least, outstayed her welcome.

She returned to Amesbury and to Sarah Bagley, with whom she had maintained correspondence during her stay with the Wentworths, as she had with Richard Kennedy, the lad who had left the Webster house with her that rainy summer night, two and a half years before. Kennedy had visited her in Stoughton and had studied with her and instructed Miss Bagley. She and Kennedy decided to go into partnership, he to heal and she to teach and continue her writing.[13] In February of 1870 they entered into a first agreement, that he would pay her one thousand dollars in quarterly installments of fifty dollars each, in recognition of her having taught him during the preceding two years. Then, in preparation for a regular working relationship, they entered into a second agreement: that Mrs. Glover was to have half of Kennedy's earnings but could keep all to herself whatever money she would make, presumably from her teaching activities.

They moved together in May 1870 to Lynn, there to begin their partnership, she forty-nine and he twenty-one. It is a wonderful demonstration of the ambiguities and contradictions that are so much a part of life that Mrs. Glover had found in Richard Kennedy a pair of strong arms to comfort her, at the same time that their formal relationship established him as her pupil, protégé, and dependent: it was to her that he owed his training, half of what he earned, and all the respect that youth traditionally accords to wisdom and maturity.

Chapter Five

At the beginning, the partnership worked out very well indeed, young Dr. Kennedy* as healer and Mrs. Glover as teacher and theoretician. Kennedy rented the upper half of a building that housed a private school. He charmed the proprietress, a Miss Susie Magoun, who thought, when he first came to inquire, that he was seeking the doctor's office and quarters for his father. But it was for himself, the young man said, for himself and an elderly lady, his teacher, who appeared shortly and treated Miss Magoun to an impromptu lecture on Quimby's method of healing. The couple were accepted as tenants, the disparity in their ages putting to rest whatever doubts there might have been about the propriety of their joint occupancy.

Mrs. Glover kept very much to herself and worked away at her writing. Kennedy, when he wasn't occupied with his practice, helped out with the schoolchildren downstairs. He was pleasant and his method of healing, which combined friendly interest, the conviction that he could be useful, and the laying on of hands, made many people feel better, so that he quickly developed a modestly thriving clientele. Those patients who were interested in the theory of heal-

---

* It should be apparent that at this time in American history the title "Doctor" was bestowed more to express the function a person was intended to perform than to signify the education and training he was supposed to have received.

ing, he referred to his partner. She also advertised independently:

MRS. GLOVER, the well-known Scientist, will receive applications for one week from ladies and gentlemen who wish to learn how to HEAL THE SICK without medicine, and with a success unequalled by any known method of the present day, at DR. KENNEDY'S OFFICE, No. 71 South Common Street, Lynn, Mass.[1]

By the autumn of 1870, then, Mrs. Glover had assembled one or two groups of potential students, perhaps a dozen in all. She entered into a formal tuition agreement with each of them, much as she had with Kennedy. At first she required a pupil to pay one hundred dollars in advance for a course of twelve lectures and either ten percent of subsequent earnings from practice or, if a student didn't practice, a sum in default of one thousand dollars. She very shortly raised her initial fee to three hundred dollars, a substantial sum that, in later years, she felt the need to justify by attributing it to Divine Guidance.

The content of her lectures derived heavily from what she had gotten from Quimby. She used his "Questions and Answers" manuscript, somewhat modified by her own interpolations, as her major text.[2] A large proportion of the students she attracted were women; one was proprietress of a small shoe factory, another a person primarily interested in odd religious ideas, a third a shoe-shop worker, and there were at least a couple who came mostly because they thought that this easily learned technique would make it possible for them to earn a good living. Among the men, one was foreman in his uncle's shoe factory, one worked in his father's box factory, yet another was an accountant who was later to have a successful business career, and still another was a sailor, just ashore from a stint at sea.

One of the students, Samuel Putnam Bancroft (known as Putney), who was to be very close to Mrs. Glover for the next several years, later published his reminiscences of that time under the title *Mrs. Eddy as I Knew Her in 1870.*[3] He described the procedure of those first teaching sessions. The group would gather in Mrs. Glover's apartment. Before beginning, each student would be treated by Kennedy, who would manipulate the pupil's solar plexus and head. As Bancroft understood it, these were supposed to be the most sensitive areas of the body, whose arousal by manipulation would put the students in the best possible frame of mind to receive Mrs. Glover's teaching. Bancroft said that he and apparently others of the students felt, however, that such rubbing and the rationale for it were inconsistent with the message that Mrs. Glover was trying to inculcate, namely, that there was no sensation in matter and that whatever feeling there was came from belief.

Some of the students must have felt not only a philosophical but also a physical uneasiness. The "expectant readiness" that manipulation of those "most sensitive areas of the body" could arouse, rather than preparing pupils for a learning experience, might very well have distracted them from such intellectual endeavors entirely, for touch can be either a most potent instrument for healing or a persuasive ancillary to seduction, depending on the intent of the healer and the experience of the patient. It is this ambiguous, various quality of touch, with its evocation of layers of experience, in infancy, in childhood, and in later years, that makes it such a problem for the inexperienced or poorly trained or falsely motivated physician.

The earliest experiences of a child with a good mother, the soothing touch, comforting, reassuring, inviting feelings of contentment and well-being, all of these memories of tactile impressions contribute to the power of touch's healing and to the submissive respect that so many patients accord to their physicians. However, as children grow, the generally comforting quality of being touched is superseded at times and in particular parts of the body by the special quality of becoming sexually aroused. Part of the process of growing up is to develop the capacity to separate one's responses, to make a distinction between being touched to be comforted or healed and being touched to be aroused. Similarly, one hopes to separate out the capacity for using touch to comfort from that of using it to invite erotic exchange. But these separations are rarely wholly complete; caressing is a part of sexual stimulation and sexual intercourse is often a form of comforting and of being comforted. In ordinary experience, the distinctions are usually recognized and the differences in intent observed, but many patients with their physicians are particularly vulnerable to confusion because of the complexity of their needs and desires and because of the way physicians can so easily become the focus for reawakened confused longings from their patients' past lives.

Mrs. Glover and Richard Kennedy and those first pupils of Mrs. Glover's classes in mental healing were as vulnerable to these susceptibilities as any such group might ever be. We know how important being held and rocked and comforted had been for Mrs. Glover and have surmised that she had decided not ever again to succumb to such dependence on anyone. Such a decision, if taken, cannot, however, quiet the yearning. Rather, a struggle is set up between contradictory wishes. For some people, such a struggle will be conscious; for others, it will be perceived only as uneasiness in certain poorly defined situations, or as an anger or a dislike or a sudden impulse to do something or change something or go somewhere.

We have no way of knowing how much *conscious* conflict Mrs. Glover experienced when Kennedy laid his hands upon her. She was, Bancroft tells us, so often in need of healing care herself, at that time. Perhaps, too, Kennedy's manipulations, or those of other students, evoked protests from patients, even accusations of seduction. Perhaps one of the students was an opportunist, or got so carried away by his own feelings that what started out as an attempt to heal became, in the passion of the moment, a much more intimate interchange.

We can be sure at least of *Mrs. Glover*'s susceptibility to touch, of her need to struggle against succumbing to such care from any man. She tried to convince Kennedy to give up the touching part of his practice. He was reluctant, feeling as Quimby had that it was a powerful vehicle into the patients' sensibilities, a powerful support to his therapeutic efforts, and that without it, his practice — his livelihood — would suffer. The difference between them was irreconcilable, and in April of 1872 Mrs. Glover and Richard Kennedy broke up their partnership and divided their assets. Her share was close to $6,000, a substantial sum for those days!

It was also said that Kennedy had become interested in a woman of his own age, that he found Mrs. Glover becoming increasingly controlling as she felt more and more neglected. How could one know for sure?

But Mrs. Glover was once more alone. No one was prepared to step forward as healer in Kennedy's place to generate a sustained income. Her teaching did not offer a very dependable living since her success in teaching had been uneven from the very beginning. Some of her students had fallen away almost at once, even forcing her to return their tuition money, although they had to take her to court to get it, claiming that she had promised much more than she could ever deliver.

She was a dogmatic teacher. She would not tolerate questioning and closed off discussion to avoid confrontation. She liked to feel that she could dispose of her pupils' lives, that she could command their most lively obedience. Some of her students could tolerate such control, even welcomed it. Others felt that the promise of an easily acquired source of livelihood justified submitting to such demanding and capricious tutelage. Still others — and perhaps this was true of all of the people who stayed close to her for any length of time — were captivated by several deeply affecting qualities: her intense, single-minded interest in her healing method; the very natural sense of self-importance that she conveyed; and her capacity to admit another person into her enterprise, to convey to him or her that they two together were embarked on a journey of the utmost seriousness for mankind's future, that theirs was a quest that transcended the petty day-to-day activities of ordinary people.

Since there was no money from healing coming in, and little from teaching, and since she felt the need to guard her modest financial capital, she began to live with one and then another of her remaining students, urging them to practice healing and needing them to treat her own symptoms, which now, in the absence of Kennedy's strong arms, were particularly troublesome. Bancroft described in his book an example of her need, which he heard about from George Barry, one of the younger students most devoted to her. One day Barry went to call upon Mrs. Glover. After bidding him enter in a faint voice, she fell into a deep swoon and appeared as if in a coma. Barry thought she was traveling to the Great Beyond and tried to call her back mentally, but without effect. He went for Miranda Rice, another student, who often cared for her. Mrs. Rice called, not mentally, but with a loud, clear, firm voice. Mrs. Glover answered faintly, as if from far away, but soon she came to herself again. Her students had felt that she was surely dying and that Mrs. Rice had saved her life.[4]

Mrs. Glover's attacks were caused in some part by her struggle to cast Kennedy out of her life. It had become particularly hard for her to acknowledge even to herself that she yearned for someone, anyone, and that she regretted the loss of this man to whom she had been so close. As she explained it to herself, people defected from her because they had become tainted with error or malicious belief, and her pains and spells were caused by the bad thoughts of those who had formerly been her allies. It was necessary for her, in her own mind, to disassociate herself from these former disciples and to characterize the evolution in her own theory of healing that would show how she had advanced and they had remained behind.

Fortunately, she had available to her a model, Quimby himself, who could show her how to define the progression in her own beliefs. Quimby's evolution had followed the path of moving from the practice of mesmeric healing to one of attempting to cure by convincing people to give up their belief in the reality of their own illness. He had taken great pains to repudiate the mesmeric cure and to clarify the evolution of his own theory because the change represented such a dramatically different conception of the origins of illness and the functions of patient and healer. The theory of the mesmeric cure, as he knew it, presupposed that the healer in a trance simply saw more clearly into the patient's body and could, therefore, make a better diagnosis. Quimby knew that this was not true and that in some way it was the patient's belief in the encounter that led to his improvement. Illness was cured, therefore, not by specific diagnosis and treatment, he thought, but by an attack on the very root of illness — false belief. When Mrs. Glover had been Quimby's patient and disciple, she too had gone to particular lengths, as we know, to repudiate mesmerism and to prove that Quimby was free of any taint of mesmeric influence. She had adopted Quimby's repudiation of mesmerism and it was only natural now that she disassociate herself from Kennedy by the very same logic she had learned from Quimby. She had progressed to a higher plane of wisdom, she said, and in doing so, she had progressed beyond mesmerism, which was discredited. All that was required was a simple redefinition of mesmerism to equate it now with Kennedy's practice, with the use of manipulation in the service of mental healing.

This being done, Kennedy could be cast out *in principle* as morally tainted, as using an evil and discredited technique. Struggles over principle are as old as the struggle between God and the Devil, and as vigorous, and this instance was to be no exception. The struggle over principle was paralleled now by the struggle between helplessness and independence, personified in Mrs. Glover's own largely unacknowledged attachment to Kennedy. Her very great yearning for fatherly comforting, with all of its implications of holding and rocking, soothing and lulling, struggled with her need to repudiate dependence on any man and served to intensify her horror of Kennedy and to sharpen her resentment of him.

Another product of this conflict, however, was a redefinition of her relationship to Quimby, for he too had practiced the laying on of hands. If she had dispensed with this procedure, if she now found grounds *in principle* to turn away from it, then she could claim that she had made significant advance over Quimby and had become not merely the disciple of a great man, but a prophetess who discovered new truth where before there had been error. This certainly, she felt, represented such a fundamental change in attitude and one that was to have cosmic implications.

It took a whole decade after his death for Quimby to be substantially supplanted. When Mrs. Glover had used his text of "Questions and Answers" as a basis for her teachings to Hiram Crafts and Mrs. Wentworth, for example, she had prefaced it with an introduction of her own, making clear the distinction between her contribution and his and acknowledging him as the prophet, herself as the disciple. Later on, when she taught her students in Lynn, she continued to use "Questions and Answers," but now the preface was merged into the body of the text and the distinctions in authorship blurred, although major acknowledgment was still given to Quimby. By 1875, however, with the publication of the first edition of *Science and Health*, Quimby's ideas and phraseology would be incorporated with only minimal acknowledgment into a text that was mostly her own, and later yet, Quimby would be repudiated disdainfully as no more than a well-meaning mesmerist whose disciples were claiming as his own thoughts ideas that he had really taken from Mrs. Patterson when she was his patient and his *mentor*. Struggles for priority are not uncommon, and the process of repudiation was one that was necessary for Mrs. Glover's peace of mind, even if what she experienced was not really peace but only an unquiet truce.

In the years after she and Kennedy had parted, and before the publication of *Science and Health*, Mrs. Glover felt she was without anyone she could really count on. Her small group of pupils were occupied more than she would have liked with their own personal concerns and family interests. Bancroft, for example, decided to marry, which Mrs. Glover felt to be a sign of disloyalty, and she chided him for it even as she acknowledged the inevitability of such worldly behavior. She sent him a bitter letter one Thanksgiving Day, when no one had invited her to share the holiday, saying that her students were selfish hypocrites and threatening to break up all of her class meetings with them. She lived in Bancroft's house for several months but found that his wife's activities interfered with her own, and she moved elsewhere when she was able to find some new pupils.

In 1874 she devised a plan whereby Bancroft would move to Cambridge and open a practice there, near Harvard College, where there would surely be a continuing source of good patients. She would come to lecture and, ultimately, to live, she said, and would by her most intense spiritual efforts encourage Bancroft's venture. He did go to Cambridge, dutifully leaving his family behind in Lynn and putting out his shingle, but without very much success. He arranged some meetings for Mrs. Glover to address, but she never would appear. A real estate man had been commissioned to find her a house in Cambridge, but according to Bancroft the realtor really wanted to keep her in Lynn and marry her himself, so *that* plan fell through. Bancroft, alone, dispirited, and running out of money, had to confess defeat to his teacher, who accused him of faintheartedness and insufficient loyalty and said that he couldn't expect to succeed if he gave himself only three months for the attempt. Furthermore, she said, his efforts were being sabotaged by Dick Kennedy, who, she knew, was following after Bancroft and exerting his evil mental influence to harm him. She had very much the feeling that this influence, which she called Malicious Animal Magnetism, was being turned against her. She had to gather all of her forces to repel Kennedy's influence. The claims for attention that her pupils made on her, she said, distracted her from repelling the evil that came from Kennedy, and this left her vulnerable to great pain.

We would have to say, I think, that she herself had Kennedy very much in her thoughts and that her anger with him and her yearning for him persisted, despite all her efforts not to think of him, and that this caused her pain. But it was not Mrs. Glover's style to look to her own feelings; she put all the responsibility onto Kennedy; he was the villain and she the victim.

The antipode to these concerns was her writing, her own work, in which she persisted despite all of her personal distractions and sufferings. She was not one to write in a tower, insulated from the life around her and with a mind and heart at peace. Rather, she was most often in a state of emotional turmoil, and her writing was the refuge to which she attached enormous value.

As the year 1875 began, four separate strands of her life came together in a most particular way. She finished the first edition of *Science and Health*[5] and saw it through to publication, albeit at her pupils' expense. She used the money she had saved from her partnership with Kennedy to buy her first piece of real estate. She found a name, Christian Science, under which her enterprise was ultimately to flourish. And she found yet another man who would serve, for a time, again, as the repository of her most enthusiastic hopes.

The book was what she had been working on, especially since her separation from Kennedy, but really it was the agglomeration of all of her preoccupations from the time of her enthusiastic conversion to Quimby, thirteen years earlier. As such it embodied everything that she acknowledged to be of value, and if it rambled and digressed, at least it contained within its covers all of her thoughts about life and healing and religion. Naturally, then, a Christian Scientist would search its pages for the sources of all that is good in his religion and might find in its ambiguities and prophetic utterances the fountain of true wisdom.

To one not so inclined, it is hard to see how her thoughts and sometimes even her phraseology differed very much from Quimby's, particularly as they related to God and to healing, although she included a broader range of thoughts about the sum of life than Quimby had and, with her need to parcel out feelings in extremes, was considerably more preoccupied with Evil than Quimby ever had been. Quimby's own essays, however, had never been published; publication of Mrs. Glover's essays bestowed upon them a priority of great significance, regardless of the origin of some of her conceptions.

She believed with Quimby that the essence of God was Goodness, that everything that flowed from God was Good, and that God could be identified with Truth, Wisdom, Harmony, and Principle. This was the only reality. Health was Good and illness evil. Health must proceed from a state of the proper relationship with God, with Principle, Harmony, Wisdom, and Truth, and it was Christ's mission on Earth to bring to Mankind the keys to this proper relationship, the healing mission, now rediscovered after so many centuries of misunderstanding. Illness was evil and could not have been created by God. How then could such things exist, since all of God's Creation was Good? Such things *didn't* exist, according to this sophisticated reasoning. These bad things had no reality. They flowed from mistaken ideas, from the aberrations of men's minds, from false beliefs, the divagations of minds that turned away from Principle and Harmony, Wisdom and Truth, that preoccupied themselves with such false notions as material being, physiology, concern about the body or about the things of this world, Man's imperfect perception of Truth, but not the real Truth.

Thus Truth, Principle, Wisdom, and Harmony, regaining the center of Man's belief and understanding, would restore him to Goodness and to Health. This was the only cure. Illness came from false belief. Health would come from true belief. Illness came only from aberrations of mind, and only a mental process would restore health again, a process that could be discovered by reading *Science and Health* and by being taught by the author of *Science and Health*.

Of course, Mrs. Glover's whole range of ideas, expressed in a somewhat rambling way, was not restricted to these principles. The first edition of *Science and Health* is 456 pages long and is divided into eight chapters, beginning with Natural Science, that is, with The Basis of All Things, and ending with her chapter on Healing the Sick, with discursions along the way into her ideas about what constitutes proof, what constitutes reality, how she attempts to reconcile the notion of God as all-powerful and all-creating with the idea of God as all-good. There are also chapters on prayer, which she tended to see as an unworthy substitute for the Good Life; on Marriage; and on Physiology, which she felt was essentially a false distraction, reflecting as it did a preoccupation with things, with matter, with the body, rather than a concern about Principle and Harmony. "Physiology is anti-Christian; it teaches us to have other gods before 'Me,' the only Life of man."[6]

The last chapter, "Healing the Sick," begins with a long warning against mesmerism, the "one possible way of doing wrong with a mental method of healing . . . whereby the minds of the sick may be controlled with error instead of Truth."

Filled with revenge and evil passions, the malpractitioner can only depend on manipulation, and rubs the heads of patients years together, fairly incorporating their minds through this process, . . . Through the control this gives the practitioner over patients, he readily reaches the mind of the community to injure another or promote himself, but none can track his foul course. . . . Controlled by his will, patients haste to do his bidding, and become involuntary agents of his schemes, while honestly attesting their faith in him and his moral character. . . . Try it, whoever will, manipulate the head of an individual until you have established a mesmeric connection between you both, then direct her action, or influence her to some conclusion, . . . you will find the more honest and confiding the individual, the more she is governed by the mind of the operator. . . . We thank Wisdom, that revealed this great error to us before these pages went to press, that the years we have labored to bless our fellow-beings be not wholly lost through this trepass upon the blessing of mental healing.[7]

Here it becomes clear that Mrs. Glover is describing her understanding of her own experience with Kennedy. She gives in this section some acknowledgment to Quimby, relegating him to the place of precursor and claiming him to have been a mesmerist still, because he used the laying on of hands in his healing practice:

In defence of mesmerism is urged, that Dr. Quimby manipulated the sick. He never studied this science [that is, Mrs. Glover's science], but reached his own high standpoint and grew to it through his own, and not another's progress. He was a good man, a law to himself; when we knew him he was growing out of mesmerism; contrasted with a student that falls into it by forsaking the good rules of science for a mal-practice that has the power and opportunity to do evil. Dr. Quimby had passed away years before ever there was a student of this science, and never, to our knowledge, informed any one of his method of healing.[8]

Such sketchy comments and quotations cannot encompass a large work that attempts, beginning from very simple premises about the nature of God, to construct a whole world view. That is, of itself, a very ambitious scheme, and the enormous importance that Mrs. Glover gave to her book can be readily understood. It was a source of comfort and the object of her continuing preoccupations; it was her own product, one which she wished to free from any debt of acknowledgment to anyone else, and her attempt to produce something that would be more dependable than parents or children or family life or the company of dear friends.

As a final touch to her work and, Bancroft tells us,[9] as a specific decision made that same year, "Christian Science" was introduced as the formal name for Mrs. Glover's belief. The term of Christian Science had been used by Quimby at various points in his writing, but he did not make any attempt to frame it as the title to a school of thought. Bates and Dittemore identify at least two other contemporaneous uses of the title: one in a book, *The Elements of Christian Science; a Treatise Upon Moral Philosophy and Practice*, by the Reverend William Adams, published in 1854, of which Mrs. Eddy possessed a copy; and the other in a poem, "The Vigil of Love," by the popular poetess Sarah Josepha Hale, in which the line occurs, " 'Tis Christian Science makes our day."[10] That doesn't mean that Mrs. Glover took the meaning itself or even the title from either of these latter sources. She may not even have known about them, then. She had certainly heard it used by Quimby, but most important of all, it was the kind of title that fit with the spirit of the times and one that would not be burdened with the taint of secularism that made "Moral Science" objectionable as a title for a movement. This did not mean, either, that the Christian Scientists considered themselves a religious sect. Mrs. Glover said unkind things in *Science and Health* about creeds, rituals, and prayer, and professed to share Quimby's distaste for formal religious organizations. For example, on page 165 of *Science and Health*, first edition, she says, "Christianity is not a creed, doctrine or belief; but the demonstration of Life, Love, and Truth; . . ." and goes on to state those attitudes about organized religion that have been quoted so often:

We have no need of creeds and church organizations to sustain or explain a demonstrable platform, that defines itself in healing the sick, and casting out error . . . the mistake the disciples of Jesus made was to found religious organizations and church rites. . . . No time was lost by our Master in organizations, rites, and ceremonies, or in proselyting for certain forms of belief: . . . a magnificent edifice was not the sign of Christ's Church.[11]

Science and Health being ready for publication, and the name of the movement, Christian Science, having been chosen, Mrs. Glover now invested $5,600 of her nest egg in a house at 8 Broad Street, Lynn, which was suitably adorned with a large sign that read:[12]

MARY B. GLOVER'S
CHRISTIAN SCIENTISTS' HOME.

Since she had also taken over a mortgage for $2,800, which she did not have the means to pay, she rented out most of the house into apartments and set about to teach once again, to use the energies liberated from the task of writing.

Among her half-dozen students in that late spring of 1875 was Harry Spofford. He had been a fellow foreman with Putney Bancroft in the shoe factory five years earlier, when his wife, who had gone to young Dr. Kennedy for treatment, had introduced both him and Bancroft to Mrs. Glover's circle. Mrs. Spofford had been one of Mrs. Glover's first students. Although Spofford had studied his wife's copy of Quimby's "Questions and Answers," the text that Mrs. Glover had been using at the time, he himself had not studied with her. In 1875 he was practicing some kind of mental healing in the Lynn area, and, according to Bancroft, Mrs. Glover heard of him and invited him to become her student. He was a handsome and quietly impressive man, self-reliant and more effective in setting up and operating a practice than Bancroft had been when he had made his unsuccessful attempt in Cambridge the year before. Mrs. Glover began to rely on him more and more and soon gave him responsibility for the management of the sale of *Science and Health*, which came from the printer in the fall of 1875 in an edition of 1,000 copies. George Barry and Elizabeth Newhall, students of Mrs. Glover, had advanced a total of $2,200 for the venture, in compensation for which they became the Christian Science Publishing Company. The price of the book was set at $2.50 a copy. It sold poorly. Obviously, Barry and Miss Newhall couldn't hope to make a profit and were acting out of devotion to their teacher. Spofford sent a great many copies out for review, with the request that only favorable reviews be published. As a result, the book was largely ignored. The Boston *Globe* did carry a critical review, which was answered by an indignant letter in the *Traveller*, apparently written by Mrs. Glover herself, that said in part:

> . . . because she understands the hidden working of mind, . . . [the author] would say it is the *sensualism* of the critic that prevented his clearer perception of its supersensual truths![13]

Spofford threw himself with great zeal into his labors for Christian Science and for Mrs. Glover, so much zeal, in fact, that he set about to divorce his wife so that he might be free to marry Mrs. Glover, although he was perhaps twenty years her junior. She may explicitly have encouraged this plan; certainly she never had much use for the spouses of her students, particularly her male students. The court, however, would not grant the divorce, a mishap that was attributed to Richard Kennedy's malicious mental influence, but Mrs. Glover continued to lean heavily upon Spofford and actually turned over to him much of her teaching responsibility so that she could preserve her own efforts for the task of warding off Kennedy's evil powers.

Late in 1875 Spofford introduced one of his patients into

the Christian Scientists' circle. This man, Asa Gilbert Eddy, was a sewing-machine salesman who had become interested in the method after finding that it helped him. He undertook the usual course of training to become a healer himself, which at that time required only three weeks of study.

A man more in contrast with Kennedy and Spofford could hardly have been imagined. Although Eddy was devoid of fire and originality, retiring in manner and unprepossessing in appearance, he nevertheless had in good measure traits of dutifulness and self-restraint, both important to Mrs. Glover. He was one of the youngest of seven children, born into an unusual farm family in Londonderry, Vermont. His mother was the more remarkable parent. She never did care much for her children beyond the having of them but, it was said, would spend her days on the move, driving her horse and buggy about the countryside in all weathers, shielding herself from the cold and damp with an invention of her own, a kind of protective hood into which she had inserted a nine-by-ten-inch pane of glass to see through. When the children were sick, she called in to look after them a woman who would go into trance states during which, like Lucius Burkmar, she would diagnose and prescribe for the sufferer.

Gilbert, growing up in this bizarre and disorganized household, became a specialist in self-possession and orderliness, making, washing, and ironing his own clothing and doing his own cooking. His most notable scholastic accomplishment was the cultivation of a fine, regular, careful, elegant style of writing. He was said to enjoy drawing pictures for children and playing the violin a little. And he loved to shoot birds.

He was short and slight, and combed his hair neatly, high upon his head. His early jobs were as a laborer in spinning mills, but in his middle thirties he returned to care for his parents on the family farm, which was deeded to him as part of the arrangement. His parents died soon after and he subsequently rented out the farm and moved into other jobs, mostly selling, until that winter of 1875–76 when he encountered Spofford and entered for his brief part in this story.

He and Mrs. Glover began very soon to call each other Gilbert and Mary, a familiarity denied to her other students. Now she had two devoted men among her disciples, Eddy and Spofford, the one more tractable, the other more enterprising, and it seemed for a time as if she didn't know quite what to do with them. Spofford was an attractive teacher, successful healer, and energetic manager of the distribution and sale of *Science and Health*, but Mrs. Glover, like all totalitarian rulers, feared the possibility that he might develop his own following in the group and diminish her authority. She couldn't tie him to her by marriage because he couldn't get a divorce from his wife.

Eddy was tractable and not at all threatening, but not nearly so engaging. Mrs. Glover required of Spofford that he turn over to Eddy all of his practice so that he would be freer to devote himself to the book. He complied, perhaps forewarned. Mrs. Glover seems now to have had the same problem that she had had with Kennedy, that is, that she was attracted to Spofford and had to fight against it. She seems to have tried to use her attachment to Gilbert Eddy as a shield. Spofford apparently complained of her disaffection, and on December 30, 1876, she sent him a letter of renunciation, of which the following portion is available to us:

Now, Dr. Spofford, won't you exercise *reason* and let me live or will you *kill* me? Your mind is just what has brought on my relapse and I shall never *recover* if you do not govern yourself and TURN YOUR THOUGHTS wholly away from me. Do for God's sake and the work I have before me let me get out of this suffering I never was worse than last night and you say you wish to do me good and I do not doubt it. Then won't you *quit thinking* of me. I shall write no more to a male student and never more

trust one to live with. It is a hidden foe that is at work read
Science and Health page 193 1st paragraph[14]

The paragraph to which she referred Spofford is as follows:

. . . Sin is thought before it is deed, and you must master
it in the first, or it conquers you in the second instance.
Jesus said, to look with foul desire on forbidden objects,
breaks a moral precept; hence, the stress he laid on the
character of a man that is hidden from our perception.
Evil thoughts reach farther, and do more harm than individual crimes, for they impregnate other minds and fashion
your body. The atmosphere of impure desires, like the
atmosphere of earth, is restless, ever in motion, and calling
on some object; this atmosphere is laden with mental
poison, and contaminates all it touches. When malicious
purposes, evil thoughts, or lusts, go forth from one mind,
they seek others, and will lodge in them unless repelled
by virtue and a higher motive for being. All mental emana-
tions take root and bear fruit after their own kind. Consider, then, the guilt of nurturing evil and impure thoughts,
that send broadcast discord and moral death. Sooner suffer
a doctor infected with small-pox to be about you, than
come under the treatment of one that manipulates his patients' heads, and is a traitor to science.[15]

She goes on with her letter to Spofford:

No STUDENT nor mortal has tried to have you leave
me that I know of. Dr. Eddy has tried to have you stay
You are in a *mistake*, it is *God* and not man that has separated us and for the reason I *begin* to learn. Do not think
of returning to me again I shall never again trust a *man*
They know not what manner of temptations assail God
produces the separation and I submit to it so must you.
There is no cloud between us but the way you set me up
for a Dagon* is wrong and now I implore you to return

* Dagon: a Babylonian deity.

forever from this error of *personality* and go alone *to God* as I have taught you.

It is Mesmerism that I feel and is killing me it is *mortal* mind that only can make me suffer. Now stop thinking of me or you will cut me off *soon* from the face of the earth.

The very next night, Mrs. Glover had Eddy bring to Spofford the news that she and Eddy were to wed, and charged Spofford to notify the clergyman who had been selected to perform the ceremony. As he remembered the event for Miss Milmine thirty years later, Spofford said to Eddy:

"You've been very quiet about all this, Gilbert."

"Indeed, Dr. Spofford, I didn't know a thing about it myself until last night."[16]

That night Mrs. Glover

. . . had a dream in which she wanted to cross a wheat-field but was prevented by "dark swinish forms" moving about in it, until Gilbert appeared on the other side calling, "Come on, Mary, I will help you."[17]

Mrs. Eddy told this dream many years later and, like many of her dreams, cherished it as a sign of the direction she should take for the good of her movement. One cannot confidently interpret a dream without hearing the dreamer's thoughts in association to the dream's contents, but we can at least suppose that this dream represents the feeling that her marriage to Eddy was designed to protect her against her own intense yearnings for Spofford.

Mary Glover and Gilbert Eddy were married next day, January 1, 1877, to the dismay of many of her students, even though she assured them that the marriage was only a spiritual one. She was fifty-six years old, he forty-six. Their ages were listed on the marriage certificate as forty each, and the explanation was given that such things as dates of birth were mere technicalities.

Eddy retired from his healing almost immediately to devote himself to his wife, who suffered now renewed spasms of pain. The struggle between her attraction to strong men and her fear of losing her independence was as intense as ever. For the sake of her movement, the course she chose was undoubtedly the wiser one, but it was taken only at the cost of great personal suffering.

She was preparing a second edition of *Science and Health* for the press and wanted Spofford to see it through and to finance it himself, giving her a twenty-five-percent royalty. Some of his devotion to Mrs. Glover had understandably evaporated. He was winding up final disposition of the first edition now and was in a position to know just how much money one could lose by sponsoring one of Mrs. Eddy's publications. He temporized and made a final accounting, turning over $600 in receipts for the book to George Barry and Elizabeth Newhall, who had paid for the edition and lost over two thousand dollars on it. Mrs. Eddy was furious, claiming that the book was hers, that Barry and Miss Newhall had merely advanced her the money for it, and that the $600 ought by rights to have gone toward publication of the second edition. It is theirs, Spofford said, and if they want to advance it for the second edition, well, let them do it. Barry, meanwhile, had brought suit against Mrs. Eddy for a total of $2,700, saying that this represented an accurate, careful accounting of the worth of his services to her over the preceding five years. During all that time he had been her amanuensis until he had been displaced by Eddy, of whom he was bitterly jealous. He no longer felt toward her as he had when he had called her "mother" and had written the following poem in her honor:

> O, *mother mine, God grant I ne'er forget,*
> *Whatever be my grief or what my joy,*
> *The unmeasurable, unextinguishable debt*

I owe to thee, but find my sweet employ
Ever through thy remaining days to be
To thee as faithful as thou wast to me.[18]

The jury trial required three days of detailed testimony, including a spirited appearance by Mrs. Eddy, who loved the limelight. Barry's services had obviously been accorded in a voluntary spirit, but the court finally found for him to the modest extent of $350. Spofford had testified for Barry and was now officially expelled from the association with the following notice:

> Dr. D. H. Spofford of Newburyport has been expelled from the Association of Christian Scientists for immorality and as unworthy to be a member.
> > Mrs. H.M. Kingsbury
> > Secretary of the Christian Scientists' Association
> > Lynn, Jan. 19, 1878[19]

This notice, along with more generous elaboration, was published in the newspapers. Barry and Miss Newhall came to Spofford's defense, which made their anathematization even more complete.

Mrs. Eddy rushed into publication an abbreviation of her new edition of *Science and Health* in order to make an attack on Spofford, whom she had now discovered to be a mesmerist just as Kennedy was, even though Spofford didn't manipulate his patients.[20] Mrs. Eddy still felt an attachment to Spofford but preferred to believe that that feeling came from Spofford's evil machinations rather than from her own susceptible heart:

> Mesmerism is practiced through manipulation — and without it. . . . Since *Science and Health* first went to press, we have observed the crimes of another mesmeric outlaw, in a variety of ways, who does not as a common thing manipulate, in cases where he sullenly attempted to

avenge himself of certain individuals, etc. But we had not before witnessed the malpractitioner's fable without manipulation, and supposed it was not done without it; but have learned it is the addenda to that we have described in a previous edition, but without manipulating the head. . . . unless the efforts he makes through mind to injure the body are found out, and exposed by the metaphysical experts that can find him out, it is dangerous to employ him under any circumstances. . . . he can gain what he esteems an advantage, or gratify a revenge, etc., . . .[21]

Mrs. Eddy was now officially estranged from Spofford, even though, as her dreams would show, she was never to give him up in her secret thoughts. She came, however, under the sway of a passion for yet another enterprising man, Edward J. Arens, an unsavory person who had been seriously implicated in a swindling operation but who spoke with a convincing tongue. He apparently urged her to revenge herself on her enemies by taking them to court. She was not immune from litigious impulses herself and enjoyed the publicity of the courtroom even when the decision went against her, an outcome that she would always attribute to the designs of her growing list of personal enemies. So she brought suit against Kennedy, against Spofford, and against at least two of her other students for various sums that she claimed they owed her from their original contracts. All of these cases were either decided against her ultimately, or dismissed before coming to trial.

On May 14, 1878, Mrs. Eddy appeared in the Salem court with Arens to present a bill of complaint against Spofford, then practicing mental healing in Boston, accusing him of having practiced malicious mesmerism against one of her students, Lucretia Brown, on whose behalf the complaint was submitted:

> . . . that Daniel H. Spofford . . . is a mesmerist and practices the art of mesmerism and by his said art and the power of his mind influences and controls the mind and bodies of

other persons and uses his said power and art for the purpose of injuring the persons and property and social relations of others and does by said means so injure them.

. . . [He] caused the plaintiff by means of his said power and art great suffering of body and mind and severe spinal pains and neuralgia and a temporary suspension of mind . . .[22]

The Newburyport *Herald* had this to say about it:

In the Supreme Judicial Court, at Salem, on Tuesday, a bill in equity was brought more befitting the new institution at Danvers [the State Hospital for the Insane] than the highest tribunal of the Commonwealth. . . . we suspect the real complainant is Mrs. Mary B. G. Eddy, of Lynn, who has a power of attorney to appear for the plaintiff in the case. Mrs. Eddy professes to cure disease miraculously, and to be able to impart her power, and Spofford was one of her pupils, with whom she has since quarreled. She tried some time since, to induce us to publish an attack upon Spofford which we declined to do, and we understand that similar requests were made to other newspapers of the country. At last the matter has come into court, and the bill in equity is a curiosity such as might have been looked for in the court records of two hundred years ago. The witchcraft delusion is not yet dead, even officially. . . .

Edward J. Arnes [Arens?] has power of attorney with Mrs. Eddy to appear for the plaintiff, and he says that Spofford wields an awful influence, according to a *Boston Globe* reporter. He can, by his will, destroy and blight our homes, and this influence he can make felt all over the Universe. What good the Court can do does not appear, inasmuch as prison walls could not restrain such power, and since death would not be likely to terminate it. Nevertheless the Court has granted a hearing and granted an order of notice on Spofford. So the old madness is revived, and a witchcraft case is to be heard in the highest Court of Massachusetts.[23]

On the date set by the judge for Spofford to appear in court, his attorney came and filed a demurrer, which the judge sustained, saying that the suit against Spofford was based presumably not upon what he had *done*, but what he had *thought*. To control Spofford's mind was not within the power of the court. An appeal was filed but ultimately waived, and the matter appeared to drop. A newspaper reporter interviewed Miss Brown's sister, who said that

> . . . she and her family believed that there was no limit to the awful power of mesmerism, but she still had some faith in the power of the law, and thought that Dr. Spofford might be awed into abstaining from injuring her sister further.[24]

Some of Mrs. Eddy's disciples were very much troubled by her preoccupation with these evil influences. She had selected twelve students to concentrate their thoughts against Spofford in relays of two hours each, and Bancroft wrote that she had requested him to turn his thoughts against Spofford at 4:00 A.M. and at 4:00 and 9:00 P.M., the hours Spofford was most likely to work against her.[25]

The unsuccessful outcome of the suit only made Mrs. Eddy the more uneasy about Spofford. She could not get him out of her thoughts — or, as she would have felt it, he kept directing his evil influence against her so that she couldn't sleep. Finally, it appears, Eddy and Arens decided to take more definitive action.

In October of that year, 1878, they were arrested and charged with conspiring to have Spofford killed. A Boston saloon-keeper named Sargent said that they had promised him $500, $75 of it in advance, if he would do the job. Sargent was in some difficulty with the police and thought to improve his relations with them and at the same time to milk Arens and Eddy for as much as he could. With the assistance of Spofford and the police, a trap was laid for Arens and Eddy, who were arrested and brought before the judge. Bail was set and the case scheduled for the Superior Court, where it was, however, discharged with-

134

out trial at the behest of the district attorney in January of 1879. The district attorney had decided not to prosecute after some of the witnesses recanted their testimony. It was thought that they had been bribed to do so. Arens and Eddy were still required to pay court costs, which they did without protest, happy to be out of the matter. The motive and intent one can most charitably ascribe to this adventure was that they wanted to frighten Spofford, to make him go away and stop thinking of Mrs. Eddy. Sargent might have been directed, as part of such a plan, to approach Spofford and warn him that his life was in danger, with the hope that he might flee the area. Whether or not Eddy did have it in mind to murder Spofford, he and his wife really believed that Spofford was trying to murder *them*.

Naturally, all of this litigation cost a lot of money in legal fees, even excluding the Brown-Spofford witchcraft case, which Mrs. Eddy's own lawyer felt was so bizarre that he wouldn't handle it. Mrs. Eddy didn't have the money to pay those fees and tried to deny ownership of her one asset, the house at 8 Broad Street, by conveying it to a succession of straw owners. Her attorney did succeed in attaching the house, though, and held on to it for six months, until her debt to him was paid. During that time, the Eddys lived in Boston, going from one boardinghouse to another, largely because Mrs. Eddy would quickly become suspicious of the people at each successive new house and precipitate a scene, requiring her departure. She thought of migrating to Cincinnati, so low were her circumstances, so strong her desire to put distance between herself and the potential influence of Kennedy and Spofford. On impulse, she sent a telegram to her son, George Glover, whom she had not seen for so many years, asking him to come east to Cincinnati and meet her there. He complied, but when he got to Cincinnati, his mother was not to be found. After searching for several days, he telegraphed the chief of police in Lynn, asking his help in finding his mother. Alerted, she sent him a telegram saying that she had changed her mind but inviting him to come to Boston. He came and got caught up in the malevolent atmosphere of her circle, becoming more angry and more suspicious, until finally he went one day to Kennedy's office and threatened to blow Kennedy's brains out if he didn't stop using his black arts to ruin his mother. That did the trick, Glover later said, for after that threat the boardinghouse problems ceased and the family did not have to move for the rest of the winter.[26]

One might expect an ordinary person to have been wholly undone by all of these fears, yearnings, suspicions, and rages, and by the need to move over and over again from one unappetizing boardinghouse to another. But Mrs. Eddy experienced her painful feelings and thoughts not as generated by wishes from within, but as attacks from her enemies outside, or as claims made upon her by students who wanted her to cure them of their own travails. She was remarkable for the steadfastness of her attachment to her purpose, to her desire to become wholly independent by capitalizing on her one resource — what she had made of Quimby's method. In the midst of all of this chaos, and even though she was considering flight to Cincinnati or New York in order to escape from the malicious influence of Kennedy and Spofford, she was able, every Sunday, to put her fears and yearnings aside and pull herself together to preach to a modest but faithful group of followers, half audience and half congregation — the makings of a movement if not yet of a sect.

In the summer of 1875 a small group of her followers had pledged themselves to pay her a modest weekly sum and to hire a hall so that she could preach every Sunday. There was no breath of church attached to this arrangement, for, as we know, formal religion was officially despised by those admirers of the first edition of *Science and Health*. The Sunday lessons of 1875 did not prosper because Mrs. Glover disliked the questions that were asked by some of the people who were attracted to her talks, and she did not yet have the facility to disarm or ignore her critics.

Later on, there were other, more private prayer services, with Putney Bancroft and his wife coming to Lynn from Swampscott to provide the music. Bancroft wrote that those early prayer meetings consisted of a reading from the Scriptures by Mrs. Eddy, following which she would give an extemporaneous commentary on the portion she had read, usually recasting it into the context of her own beliefs.[27]

When she and Eddy were living in Boston during the period when their house was encumbered in Lynn, she continued to preach each Sunday, many of her students from Lynn making the trip regularly and constituting a large part of her small audience. Weekly reports of the meetings, written by her or by her husband, appeared in the newspapers and gave the impression of a grander assemblage than there really was. Eddy acted as usher and directed to his wife those new visitors who appeared interested in what she was saying. Some of these people became important to Mrs. Eddy, following her back to Lynn when her house became available once again, and became dependable students, converts and, in the fullness of time, important members of the Church and props to her old age. They often came to Christian Science from other schools of healing. One, Arthur Buswell, had been a hydrotherapist, employed in an establishment similar to the one Mrs. Patterson had attended almost two decades earlier, before she had gone to Quimby for the first time. Another of these men was a phrenologist, and a third, although making his living in business, was particularly interested in astrology.

When she returned to Lynn during that summer of 1879 with her husband and some new students from Boston, she set about organizing a definitive church. In August the application was made and granted for a charter of the Church of Christ (Scientist), of which she was president. Again, she considered moving out of New England to escape her enemies and sent one student to New York and another to Cincinnati, each to open a practice and test the receptiveness of the local atmosphere. Both experiments failed, and Mrs. Eddy decided, as usual, that her enemies' influence operated even at long distance and that her students were never as consistently devoted and enterprising as the importance of her discoveries justified. She was, however, determined to pursue the larger audience that a big city offered and the relative anonymity that would protect her and her followers from the scrutiny of the more conformist, small-town community of Lynn.

She continued her Sunday services in Boston, moved there again for a time in late 1879–80, and did everything she could to dress up the new sect with all of the trappings of a formal, established church organization. She even founded for her Church a Sunday school, although there was only one candidate for its services, a frightened five-year-old boy who appeared on the platform at a regular Sunday meeting. He was presented as a representative of the religious school of which he was in fact the entire student body and said a brief piece to testify to the excellence of his instruction, which he had not yet really begun to receive.

As a further instrument of the Church, the Massachusetts Metaphysical College was chartered, Mrs. Eddy again president. The state law at the time chartered institutions of higher education without investigating their facilities and faculties of instruction and without making any attempt to verify that they could in fact deliver what they promised. The seat of this college was Mrs. Eddy's house in Lynn. She was, for practical purposes, the sole instructor, as she had been before, and the classes were no different from what *they* had been earlier, except that now she had the formal recognition to which her charter entitled her.

All of this progress in her Church's affairs was temporarily impeded by two unexpected developments. The first was the disaffection of Arens, who in 1881 published a pamphlet of his own in which he minimized Mrs. Eddy's contributions to mental healing, although he quoted twenty pages of *Science and Health* verbatim without acknowledging her as their author. A preface to the third edition of Mrs. Eddy's book was composed by Gilbert Eddy with the express purpose of demolishing Arens and making him one of that growing company of important enemies, of which Kennedy and Spofford were already the most prominent members.

The second event was the revolt and public resignation of eight of Mrs. Eddy's most devoted followers, who issued the following statement:

> We, the undersigned, while we acknowledge and appreciate the understanding of Truth imparted to us by our Teacher, Mrs. Mary B.G. Eddy, led by Divine Intelligence to perceive with sorrow that departure from the straight and narrow road (which alone leads to growth of Christlike virtues) made manifest by frequent ebullitions of temper, love of money, and the appearance of hypocrisy, *cannot* longer submit to such Leadership; therefore, without aught of hatred, revenge or petty spite in our hearts, from a sense of duty alone, to her, the Cause, and ourselves, do most respectfully withdraw our names from the Christian Science Association and Church of Christ (Scientist).
>
> > S. Louise Durant,
> > Margaret J. Dunshee,
> > Dorcas B. Rawson,
> > Elizabeth G. Stuart,
> > Jane L. Straw,
> > Anna B. Newman,
> > James C. Howard,
> > Miranda R. Rice.
>
> 21st October, 1881[28]

Dorcas Rawson and Miranda Rice had been two of Mrs. Eddy's first and most devoted pupils. The only man in the group, James Howard, had just been through the experience of shepherding the third edition of *Science and Health* through the press and had been serving as Mrs. Eddy's amanuensis and paying tenant at the house in Lynn, a mixture of responsibilities that few could tolerate for very long. Two other women were to resign shortly — Mrs. F. A. Damon, in whose home the regular Church meetings were being held, and Miss A. A. Draper, secretary of the Church. Another of the original Church directors had left just shortly before. This group of defectors constituted half the membership, leaving Mrs. Eddy with barely a dozen regular followers. She did not respond immediately.

The meeting at which the October 21 declaration was made was held in her house. She didn't comment when the manifesto was presented but went silently to her room. Two of her still loyal followers remained to comfort her after the others left. They spent the whole night talking with her about the situation. In the morning, another student came, who had not been at the meeting the night before. She found her teacher emerging from a trance in which she spoke ecstatic words, biblical phrases, taken down by Calvin Frye, one of those who had stayed with her that night:

> Is this humiliation, the humility the oppressor
>   would heap upon me! O, the exaltation of Spirit!
> I have made thee ruler over many things.
> Height upon height! Holiness! Unquenchable light!
>   Divine Being! The Womanhood of God!
> Well done, good and faithful, enter thou into the
>   joy of thy Lord.
> One woe is passed, and behold, another cometh
>   quickly; and no sign shall be given thee.
>   Sufficient unto the day is the evil thereof.
> Woe, woe unto my people! The furnace is heated,
>   the dross will be destroyed.
> And the false prophet that is among you shall
>   deceive if possible the very elect, and he
>   shall lead them into forbidden paths. And
>   their feet shall bleed upon the jagged rocks.
>   And the briars shall tear the rags from them.

For they are not clothed with a garment of
righteousness.
And I will give to thee, daughter of Zion, a new
heritage and a new people.
Her ways shall be ways of pleasantness and ways of
peace.[29]

The reader who notices the transformations of gender
in some of the passages quoted from the Bible may conclude
that Mrs. Eddy, under the spur of her disappointment, had
identified herself with the Man of Sorrows, who was despised, rejected, and acquainted with grief. But she recovered her sense of herself, arose the more erect from her
humiliation, and arranged her own ordination, three weeks
later, as the first official pastor of the Church. Early in the
winter, she left Lynn forever, preaching one last lesson at
her departure, her text taken from the seventeenth chapter
of the Gospel of John, in which Jesus prays for the church
before he is to be captured and taken before Pilate.

The Eddys went first to Washington, where Gilbert
Eddy made a study of the copyright laws and Mrs. Eddy
recruited students, distributing a notice that said:

CIRCULAR

Mrs. Eddy, President of the Mass. Metaphysical College,
Will interest all who may favor her with a call at her rooms.
13 FIRST STREET, N.E.
With her Parlor Lectures on Practical Metaphysics and
the influence that mind holds over disease and longevity.

How to improve the moral and physical condition of
man to eradicate in children hereditary taints, to enlarge
the intellect a hundred per cent., to restore and strengthen
memory, to cure consumption, rheumatism, deafness, blindness and every ill the race is heir to.

We have a certificate from the most celebrated and skill-
ful Obstetrician and Surgeon in Massachusetts, stating our
qualification to teach Obstetrics. And what is better, our

system prevents the suffering that has attended accouchment, and with the great auxillary of Mind, obviates the use of medicine.

CONSULTATIONS FREE.

First Lecture Free, and the First Course, which includes twelve lectures, commences Feb. 10th, at 8 p.m.[30]

Mrs. Eddy was becoming an impressive speaker, convincing to many people, and she wrote to her followers back home that she had been very busy and successful. But she was still much troubled by her physical complaints and concluded that the evil influence of her enemies could be exerted all the way from Boston to Washington.

Upon their return to Boston in April of 1882, the Eddys established their residence at 569 Columbus Avenue, the new home of the Massachusetts Metaphysical College, where four of her followers, three women and a man, came to live. She started a new class the very next month with seven pupils, six of them women and five either older married women or widows. Even more now than before, her movement was particularly attractive to women who had not been trained in their youth to support themselves, but whom the circumstances of later life had forced into that need.

Her undertakings were just beginning to prosper that spring, when her husband suddenly became ill. He was examined by a physician, Dr. Rufus K. Noyes, who made a diagnosis of organic heart disease and warned that Eddy could die at any moment. Mrs. Eddy was certain, however, that her enemies were the cause of Gilbert's illness; particularly was she afraid of Arens, and she called in to confirm *her* diagnosis one "Dr." Charles J. Eastman, a founding director of the Massachusetts Metaphysical College, the obstetrician and surgeon to whom her circular in Washington had referred but whose practice consisted primarily in performing abortions. She deputized various others of her followers to offer mental surveillance to protect Eddy from

Arens's malicious influence, but all without benefit, for Eddy became progressively weaker and died in his sleep on June 3, 1882, just two months after their return from Washington.

Whatever the warmth of their mutual regard, the Eddys' marriage had not really been a success, no matter how it was to be idealized later on. Mrs. Eddy had not been able to free herself from her preoccupation with Kennedy and Spofford and had even, for a time, come under the influence of such a man as Arens. Her attachment to Gilbert Eddy did not provide the stability that she needed to free herself even in part from her suspicions and her ever-recurring physical complaints. And now that marriage had confronted her with the greatest embarrassment possible. How was one to reconcile Eddy's death with the pretensions of his wife's healing method? Mrs. Eddy chose the characteristic course of insisting on her own point of view, whatever the consequences and as publicly as possible. She called in Dr. Noyes to perform an autopsy, certain that he would find evidence of foul play. He found the death to have been caused by serious disease of the aortic valve of the heart, even showing that organ to Mrs. Eddy to demonstrate his conclusion. She transformed his findings in a unique way. Since he had not found evidence of arsenical poisoning, she said, it proved that Dr. Eddy had been killed by metaphysical arsenical poisoning, which leaves no trace. "Dr." Eastman was happy again to concur with her diagnosis and she issued a statement to the Boston newspapers, saying:

My husband's death was caused by malicious mesmerism. Dr. C. J. Eastman, who attended the case after it had taken an alarming turn, declares the symptoms to be the same as those of arsenical poisoning. On the other hand, Dr. Rufus K. Noyes, late of the City Hospital, who held an autopsy over the body to-day, affirms that the corpse is free from all material poison, although Dr. Eastman still holds to his original belief. I know it was poison that killed him, not material poison, but mesmeric poison. My husband was in uniform health, and but seldom complained of any kind of ailment. . . . Circumstances debarred me from taking hold of my husband's case. He declared himself perfectly capable of carrying himself through, and I was so entirely absorbed in business that I permitted him to try, and when I awakened to the danger it was too late. I have cured worse cases before, but I took hold of them in time. . . . One of my students, a malpractitioner, has been heard to say that he would follow us to the grave. He has already reached my husband. While my husband and I were in Washington and Philadelphia last winter, we were obliged to guard against poison, the same symptoms apparent at my husband's death constantly attending us. And yet the one who was planning the evil against us was in Boston the whole time. . . .[31]

The funeral services were held in the Eddy home, the Massachusetts Metaphysical College. The body was taken then to Tilton to be buried in the Baker family plot, but the grieving widow did not accompany it to its final resting place.

Chapter Six

Although Gilbert Eddy's death was a great misfortune, both because of Mrs. Eddy's need of him and because of the embarrassment it might bring to a woman who claimed to be able to cure anyone of anything, she was not now a person who would allow herself to be undone by such tribulations. In her earlier days she had collapsed into the arms of sympathetic strangers. Even as late as 1866, when Quimby died, her first response had been to appeal to others out of a sense of her own neediness. Her experience at that time had shown her that she could rely on her own initiative and on the raw materials of what she had gotten from Quimby, material which she had transformed by now into the foundations of Christian Science. The future of that new Church constituted for her a moral imperative with which her own fate was fused. She no longer appealed for help; she commanded assistance.

Her first orders went out to her own son, George Glover, and to her student, Arthur Buswell. George had been willing to come to his mother's aid three years before, at the time of the Cincinnati fiasco; now, however, he was unwilling to respond to such peremptory summons, and deferred his visit until a time of his own choosing.

Buswell showed himself to be a more willing disciple. Mrs. Eddy had sent him to Cincinnati two years earlier to found a practice and a congregation. He had not achieved either task but had remained faithful during the defections of her followers the preceding year, and he answered her summons now, eager to be useful in any way he could. He offered her the use of his house in Barton, Vermont, as a retreat. She went there with him and one of her other students, Miss Alice Sibley, and stayed for the month of July, nursing as much grief for Eddy as she could muster, struggling through her nightmare reminiscences of Kennedy, Spofford, and Arens, and enduring and attempting to suggest away the cloud of physical symptoms that was always waiting to envelop her in troubled times. And while these furies assailed, in the moments of her greatest misery as well as at more lucid times, she was constantly at work considering ways to rescue herself from her misfortunes and put her practical affairs in order.

The situation was not wholly bleak. While the death of Gilbert Eddy had shaken the faith of many of Mrs. Eddy's disciples and had provided strong ammunition for those who disliked her teachings and her presumptions, the will to believe is strong enough in many people to withstand very powerful countervailing arguments. Thus, while some responded to Eddy's death by becoming disillusioned, others, in their need to defend themselves against their own doubts, became even more insistent in their faith. Mrs. Eddy had already discovered that the serious defection of her followers in Lynn the year before had not destroyed her movement. She was able to keep the remnant of her congregation together and, in Boston, to attract new adherents from a much larger population. Life in the town is more constrained by the push toward conformity than is life in the city. In the relative impersonality of the city she was less vulnerable to the power of public opinion than she had been in Lynn.

The more immediate difficulty imposed upon her by Eddy's death was that she was deprived of the reliable presence of a comforting man. While Eddy was not distinguished by force of personality, a quality that would have brought him into serious conflict with his wife, he did symbolize for her that repository of parental concern which had always been so important to her, and he had served at least as a counterweight to her attraction to Spofford and her unquiet memories of Kennedy.

It is hard to know whether she had much personal regard for Eddy. It had always been her way to replace one person with another, and now, when she set about to compose a poetic eulogy for Eddy, she simply took up a poem that she had first published thirty-odd years earlier for another man, her suitor John Bartlett, and revised it to make it do for Gilbert. In that earlier poem, "The Meeting of Two Spirits," she had used the convention of her grief for Bartlett as an opportunity to write some lines about herself.[1] Now she had recourse to the same device, producing "Meeting of My Departed Mother and Husband," in which Abigail Baker offers Gilbert Eddy, newly arrived in Heaven, the opportunity to speak some compassionate lines about the widow he has left behind but, naturally, very little about himself.[2]

To rectify the emptiness of her household, Mrs. Eddy now summoned Calvin Frye to serve her. He had demonstrated his loyalty the year before when, on the night of October 21, the group of Mrs. Eddy's eight followers had presented her with their statement of resignation. He had kept vigil with her all that night and had written down the prophetic phrases which she had uttered as she awoke the next morning from her state of shock. Faithfulness was to be one of his most valued characteristics in the years to come. He, like Gilbert Eddy, came from a family in the last stages of disintegration.[3] His forebears had given their name to a village that was to be incorporated into Andover, Massachusetts, and his grandfather, a modestly prosperous lumber and grain miller, had sent his son, Frye's father, first to Phillips Academy at Andover and then to Harvard College. This son, who suffered from some kind of lameness or paralysis, earned a meager living as a grocer. His wife, who bore him five children, became psychotic shortly after

Calvin was born and remained so thereafter, with but brief periods of intermittent lucidity. An elder sister who had been widowed cared for the parents. Frye was an indifferent student, slow to learn to read and write, and became a machinist. He married when he was in his mid-twenties, but his wife died within the year and he rejoined the somber family household. He struggled to maintain the standards of gentility set by his grandfather's generation and showed as his most marked characteristic a guarded, steady demeanor and an exemplary faithfulness of attendance at church services.

In 1881 Clara Choate, a student of Mrs. Eddy's, came to undertake the treatment of Mrs. Frye, Calvin's mother, who appeared to blossom, even if it was only to be for a short while, in the warmth of Mrs. Choate's enthusiasm. Frye and his sister were so impressed that they sought out Mrs. Eddy's teaching and after three weeks of instruction, returned to Lowell to found a halting healing practice and to await the summons that was to come in the following summer.

Frye joined Mrs. Eddy, then, in early August of 1882; he was thirty-seven years old. His sister followed to work as a domestic in Mrs. Eddy's house. However, she became ill after only a short while and returned for surgery to Lowell, where she stayed for the few remaining years of her life.

Not so Frye. He was to remain Mrs. Eddy's servant until the end of her life, twenty-eight years later. Perhaps unwittingly, she had evolved just that woman-man relationship which would offer her the greatest stability, one that would provide the best opportunity for deriving comfort and support while demanding the least abdication of control over her own initiative. This is not to say that Mrs. Eddy would not require the assistance and daily attendance of other men as well. That would certainly continue, but her relationship to Frye was to be for these remaining productive years the axis of her everyday life. He was never to leave her side for as much as a whole day. On one occasion, when his father died, he started off for the funeral but changed his mind midway and returned home. He didn't attend his mother's burial or his sister's, either.

Mrs. Eddy found him to be an excellent object for the exercise of her temper. Only once did he respond to one of her attacks by quitting and leaving. Another member of the household came quickly to find him and begged him to return, threatening that if he didn't return that very evening, Mrs. Eddy was resolved to discharge him forever. He returned immediately, of course. Like Gilbert Eddy, who also had an eccentric mother, the cord that bound him to this imperious and often irrational woman was too strong to be broken by momentary resentments.

He confided his private feelings only to his diary, which he wrote out every day on a calendar pad. He recorded sensitive matters in shorthand.[4] This diary shows that in addition to doing household errands, keeping budget records, representing Mrs. Eddy in financial transactions, and serving as general guardian of the household and even as Mrs. Eddy's coachman, Frye performed his most important functions by taking care of her when she was beset by "beliefs" and "visions," that is, by her physical torments and her nightmares. As an example of his treatment of her "beliefs," the following is quoted from his diary entry of November 15, 1883:

> Mrs. Eddy has had a belief of difficulty of breathing for the last two days and got only temporary relief from it, this morning at about four o'clock she called me to help her. I attempted (to) do so for about ten minutes when she told me I made her worse afterwards told me she could not rise from the bed to speak to me because of the suffocating sense it produced; worked for (her) faithfully last evening with little result. When we were together this morning at about 9:30 she discovered that the mesmerists were arguing to her inflammation and paralysis of spinal

nerve to produce paralysis of muscles of lungs and heart so as to prevent breathing & heart disease with soreness (?) between the shoulderblades.

She experienced the greatest relief when she and I took up Kennedy & Arens to break their attempt to make her suffer from aforementioned beliefs, and she said "I have not breathed so easy for two days."[5]

That is, it was Frye's responsibility to exert his own mental force as protection for Mrs. Eddy from the malicious mesmeric influences exerted upon her, she thought, by her enemies.

The technique for this kind of antimesmerism occupied a great deal of Mrs. Eddy's attention during the first years after Gilbert Eddy's death and constituted a most important part of her teaching at the Massachusetts Metaphysical College. The formulas of defense often took the form of repelling the evil wishes of the enemy and causing the harmful effects of his bad thoughts to turn around and be visited upon *him*. Later on, as the Church became more successful and more insistently peaceable, this aggressively retaliatory part of the mental treatment would be denied and positive and conciliatory aspects of the treatment stressed instead.[6] But, as a participant from that time later described to Georgine Milmine, Mrs. Eddy organized a Private Meeting Society, which met daily after breakfast and at night after supper to "take up the enemy" in thought:

. . . Mrs. Eddy was not always present at these sittings, but she usually gave out the line of treatment. She would say, for example: "Treat Kennedy. Say to him: 'Your sins have found you out. You are affected as you wish to affect me. Your evil thought reacts upon you. You are bilious, you are consumptive, you have liver trouble, you have been poisoned by arsenic,' " etc. Mrs. Eddy further instructed her practitioners that, when they were treating their patients, they should first take up and combat the common enemy, mesmerism, before they took up the patient's error. . . .[7]

The belief in malicious mesmerism was so extreme that people felt they were being shadowed when they left the house, that mailboxes were mesmerized so that letters deposited in them would get mislaid, and that to send a telegram to Chicago one had to go in secret to the telegraph office in West Newton, presumably outside the area of surveillance and evil force. Frye's diary contained many examples of this attitude of siege that he apparently never questioned.

The examples from Frye's diary that are available to us come because of certain dissensions that occurred within the Church after Mrs. Eddy's death. Shortly before Frye died in 1917, many parts of his diary that he thought it would be important to preserve were removed and given to John V. Dittemore, who was a Director of the Church and Frye's friend. It was felt that the diary might be destroyed if it were to be given intact to the Archives of the Mother Church along with his other papers relating to Mrs. Eddy. Dittemore had photostats made of these materials and later, after he had broken with the Mother Church, allowed some specimens to be quoted in the second edition of Edwin Franden Dakin's book,[8] an edition that was published after attempts by members of the Church to suppress the first edition had failed.

In the book that Dittemore himself then wrote with E. S. Bates, he took from Frye's records some data about Mrs. Eddy's dreams, although he did not quote the records directly. Mrs. Eddy would dictate these dreams to Frye, who called them visions. She would then interpret them as revelations of the truths of Christian Science, as Bates and Dittemore illustrate in their summary:

. . . The first dreams were usually of water; then came an interval of serpents; then water again; then all manner of beasts. Calvin Frye could only recall these "visions" in pious wonder, interpreting them, according to the instructions of the dreamer herself, as further revelations of the truths of Christian Science.

Thus, when Mrs. Eddy dreamed that she was driving over a bridge with runaway horses, but escaped from danger by leaping from the carriage, Calvin was careful to add the gloss that it was a bridge over unconscious mind. Similarly when she dreamed that she was about to be swept over a cataract but climbed up to safety by catching hold of the water, he explained that she was out in the stream of mortal mind. When a black fish swam up from the water and lay in her lap, this was taken to be a sign of good luck. When Mrs. Eddy told him that while she was lying down, a gorilla seemed to seize her, put a large paw over her mouth, and hold her motionless, for all her desire to arise, Calvin after the word "gorilla" added in shorthand: "Arens."

Kennedy and Arens appeared constantly in these dreams. She saw Kennedy prosperous, surrounded by many friends, laughing at her because she was wasted away with consumption. Or Kennedy and Arens told her to look in the mirror and see how old she looked, and they "made a law" that if she told Frye about it, she would suffer. Or she saw Kennedy with a huge elephant and a watch-dog, and the elephant followed her into the house and chased her from room to room, while the watch-dog waited for her outside. Or Kennedy met her and was very agreeable, but then led her into a house of assignation, where all the doors were locked so that she could not get out.

The last theme was repeated in the most elaborate vision of the series. Mrs. Eddy dreamed that she was facing a congregation who were all talking against Christian Science; then someone came behind her, saying that he loved her, and threw his arms around her. Her son George appeared and cried: "Hands off!" The nameless lover then slowly opened a case which contained a pistol, and George retired. She was again seized, and George reappeared, but this time dead drunk. She then broke away from the person holding her and fled into a house; he followed, locked the door, and laughed; it was a house of assignation. When she realized this, the vision vanished.[9]

One other characteristic of Mrs. Eddy's personal and domestic arrangements deserves attention before we look outward into the progress of her movement. From the time she and Patterson separated, shortly after Quimby's death and her own decision to push forward the healing work herself, Mrs. Eddy had turned away from anything that might be considered a purely *private* life, in the conventional sense. Her life was that of teacher and leader, and her whole existence woven into the texture of her career. Whenever she had a home, it was a home for Christian Science, and her students were expected to demonstrate the same wholehearted involvement, both to Christian Science and to her. They were to live in her house, share her table and her expenses, be prepared to arise at any hour and turn their thoughts onto this enemy or that one who might be exerting a malign influence on Mrs. Eddy. They might expect to be summoned to duty at any time, sent off to distant cities as messengers of the new faith, forswearing other ambitions in their service to her cause. Those who were unwilling, insufficiently devoted, dropped away. Those whose personal needs brought them into conflict with hers were made to feel her disapproval or, at best, her toleration. From this time on, Mrs. Eddy was to occupy the most cherished place in an increasingly complex and populous household; her presence there would make this household the absolute heart and mind of the Christian Science establishment.

Now, at the same time that these dark terrors were visited upon Mrs. Eddy and her household — the productions of her own thoughts and feelings but perceived as if from outside — Christian Science itself was experiencing a modest but burgeoning success, gathering adherents, students, healers, and missionaries. Some measure of this growing success can be taken from the enrollment in Mrs. Eddy's classes in the Massachusetts Metaphysical College. From

1883 onward until 1888, the year before it closed, she conducted sometimes four or five but usually six classes a year. The number of students rose from forty-three in 1883 to one hundred thirty in 1887 and in 1888, and her income from these classes over the six-year period was more than a hundred thousand dollars.[10]

The Christian Scientists were only a small corps in a whole army of diverse practitioners known generally in the 1880s as "mental healers." Just as Quimby's work developed in the context of a wide interest in psychic phenomena, so too did Mrs. Eddy's sect occupy only one part of a very broad field. Many of these healers were frank opportunists of the sort described by Henry James, for example, in *The Bostonians*, a novel set in the post-Civil War period, in which social reformers, feminists, and confidence men all come together at an intersecting point of common interest. As James characterizes Selah Tarrant, a mental healer and the father of the novel's heroine, he was

> . . . false, cunning, vulgar, ignoble; the cheapest kind of human product . . . a young man who had begun life as an itinerant vendor of lead pencils, . . . had afterwards been for a while a member of the celebrated Cayuga community,[11] where there were no wives, or no husbands, or something of that sort, . . . and had still later (though before the development of the healing faculty) achieved distinction in the spiritualistic world. . . . He had "considerable many" patients, he got about two dollars a sitting, and he had effected some most gratifying cures. A lady in Cambridge had been so much indebted to him that she had recently persuaded them to take a house near her, in order that Doctor Tarrant might drop in at any time. He availed himself of that convenience — they had taken so many houses that another, more or less, didn't matter — and Mrs. Tarrant began to feel as if they had really "struck" something.[12]

Many of these mental healers were eager to try new techniques, without much interest in or respect for whatever might have been of real substance in the method, and some of these people drifted in and out of Christian Science, adapting one or another of its elements to lend impressiveness to their own style. Others saw in Christian Science a competitor, still others a salvation. The regular medical establishment had entered the field, too, for it was now beginning to give attention to those painful feelings which seemed not to be associated with the known organic diseases and which, while they were accompanied by weakness and other kinds of debilitation, never were fatal and seemed never to progress to some change in the body that could be identified by the investigators in the new and growing field of microscopic pathology.

These symptoms, which, in a general way we recognize today as psychosomatic, were then grouped together under the term "neurasthenia," a term that had been invented in 1869 by an American physician, George M. Beard, who included within this rubric a whole host of symptoms that were called "functional"; that is, without being accompanied by detectable changes in the physical structure of the patient's body.[13]

At an earlier time, these symptoms might have been seen as evidences of sloth, of slackness of character, or of malingering, or they might have been confused with diseases of a more frankly physical cause and with a more dire prognosis. Now they were recognized often to respond to some element in the personality of the healer, his optimism, perhaps, or his kindness, or, perhaps, to the treatment regimen he prescribed — one that often emphasized rest, distraction, and removal from everyday cares. The medical people were men then, almost invariably, the field largely being closed to women, but, as we'll see, mental healing, which operated under a looser apprenticeship and which welcomed new practitioners, did not impose the same restrictions and offered great opportunity to women.

It is often difficult, even today, to distinguish between pain caused by anguish and pain that warns of a physical disease process. But it was infinitely more difficult a hundred years ago, before the discoveries of pathological anatomy and bacteriology, before the discovery of the X rays and their application to medicine, before the invention of the techniques of nerve-cell staining that made possible the mapping out of the central nervous system. Furthermore, the discoveries of the great psychologists at the end of the nineteenth century and into the twentieth were yet to come, so that physicians and their lay counterparts, while they could rely somewhat on their experience of living and of observing others, had even more fragmentary understanding than we do today of what it might be in a person's life that could give rise to such apparently incomprehensible sufferings.[14]

Another set of factors that contributed to the general interest both in healers and in unorthodox religious teachers was a pronounced shift in American religious and moral attitudes, starting particularly in the Northeast. The Civil War, industrialization, and the growth of the cities were accompanied by a shift of the center of agriculture in the North from New England farms to the wider and more fertile fields of the Midwest. The concomitant widening in the structure of society, away from the agrarian democracy of the early nineteenth century and toward greater extremes of wealth and poverty, contributed to a loosening of religious ties. In particular, fundamental deterministic Protestantism seemed less relevant in an urban social order that confronted men and women every day with the inequity of life and that offered to each person the hope that his own efforts might propel him on the way to his own material salvation. A God who required acceptance of the way things were was more acceptable to a largely agricultural community, bound to the land and the seasons and the accidents of nature. But a God who offered hope for the amelioration of one's lot came to be more in keeping with the values of those members of the new society who were predisposed to struggle toward affluence.

With urbanization during this period, the actual experience of life in the American family was changing. Husbands and wives were sharing less of the family activities as joint enterprise. Husbands were becoming more the absent breadwinners and wives more the keepers of the home and children. These changes affected the psychological climate of the household and the patterns of child rearing as well. In addition, family size was decreasing, education was becoming more specialized and prolonged, and the usual age of young men and women at marriage was being pushed back later and later. Thus, added to the problems and conflicts engendered by these social and psychological transformations, pressure was building for prolonged chastity and against sexuality. As is the American way, early sexual experience became not simply expedient but downright immoral. It might have been not so much the *prohibition* of sexual expression as the moral *conflict* about it that made so many young people increasingly susceptible to various forms of psychological symptoms as an outward expression of inner tensions.[15]

In short, the phenomenon of mental healing was experiencing striking growth at a time when the concept of what constituted illness was being revised and broadened to include disorders having a psychological basis and amenable to psychological modalities of treatment. At the same time, society was changing in the direction of urbanization, accentuation of differences in income and opportunity, and a great postponement in the age for marriage and for legitimized sexual activity for certain large groups of young people. These changes in the social order were accompanied, naturally enough, by widespread disaffection with the traditionally accepted village Protestantism, which strongly emphasized the divine order, predestination, and adherence to a rigid morality that was appropriate for a relatively static and egalitarian rural community.

Some of the problems and opportunities that Mrs. Eddy experienced in shepherding the development of her new

Mary Baker Eddy in 1886

healing religion may be seen against this social backdrop. She would have to do two things at once. First, she would have to separate Christian Science from other forms of mental healing, to distinguish it as having a special position and message, an attractive form of unique authenticity. At the same time, she would have to make it respectable enough to appeal to the wider group of prosperous middle-class people with whom she identified herself in terms of both her origins and her idealization of the value of struggling against adversity.

Christian Science is the only reasonably thriving survivor from this period of a hundred years ago. That is one mark of her success. And yet, she was to enlist in her struggle those very same traits, capacities, and interests which in her earlier years had seemed merely trivial. Earlier, they were not yet integrated by an intense purpose. But now, Mrs. Eddy had become *Christian Science*, and in ensuring its survival she was fighting for her own. A love of publicity, the pursuit of a career as an authoress and in journalism, a tendency to see things only from the point of view of her own immediate advantage, a need constantly to rewrite her own history in order both to dramatize herself and to make herself more middle-class-ordinary than she was — all of these old characteristics of Mary Baker were now enlisted in her fight for Christian Science.

Central to the undertaking was the new *Journal of Christian Science*, which she organized almost immediately, and the first issue was published on April 14, 1883. She was listed as editor. Buswell, although unlisted, was assistant editor and in charge of legwork. We are familiar with Mrs. Eddy's love of drawing grand historical parallels, as she had, for example, when writing for the newspaper in praise of Quimby. This is how she opened the first issue of her journal:

The ancient Greek looked longingly for the Olympiad; the Chaldee watched for the appearing of a Star, to him no higher revelation than the horoscope hung out upon empyrean . . .[16]

and went on to say, by contrast, that Man ought to look closer to hand for his salvation. A general discourse upon Christian Science followed, with the immodest disclaimer:

> While we entertain decided views as to the best method for elevating the race physically, morally and spiritually, and shall express these views as duty demands, we shall claim no especial gift from our divine origin, or any supernatural power . . .

but concluded decently enough with a succinct declaration of purpose, with whose intentions, certainly, no one could find fault, whatever one's reservations about the method:

> Dear reader, the purpose of our paper is the desire of our heart, namely, to bring to many a household hearth health, happiness and increased power to be good, and to do good. To brighten so pure a hope will be to aid our prospect of fulfilling it, through your kindly patronage of the *Journal of Christian Science*, of which this is our first issue, and for which we are needing funds to establish its more permanent publication.

A more specific objective was acknowledged elsewhere in the same issue:

> An organ from the Christian Scientists has become a necessity. Many questions come to the college and to the practising students, yet but a little time has been devoted to their answer. Further enlightenment is necessary for the age, and a paper devoted to this work seems alone adequate to meet the requirement. Much interest is expressed everywhere on this subject of metaphysical healing, but in many minds it is confounded with mesmerism and so-called spiritualism, so that the vastness of its power is lost where it is not correctly understood.

That is, it was to be a main purpose of the *Journal* to disseminate an awareness of Christian Science and to distinguish it from all other forms of mental healing as a movement, a religion having distinctiveness and a genuineness of its very own.

The *Journal* became a monthly the next year. Its name was simplified to *The Christian Science Journal* the year after that. In the first six years of its publication it was to have at least five managing editors, for although responsibility was delegated to the editor of the moment, authority always remained with Mrs. Eddy herself, and she, continually preoccupied with the presentation of herself as the embodiment of Christian Science, expressed a steady stream of homemade contributions, orders, and counterorders; her editors despaired and would leave after a year or two in harness, in some instances to join or to found rival and opposing mental-healing publications.

This pattern of delegating responsibility but keeping the authority to herself made it possible for Mrs. Eddy, by speaking through someone else's mouth, to publicize herself as much as she wanted without appearing immodest or self-seeking. It was the convention that she had used in her poetic eulogy of Gilbert Eddy. For years she had been writing letters to the newspapers signed with someone else's initials, letters in which she defended Mrs. Eddy against attack or brought to the attention of an eager public some impending manifestation of Christian Science. Now she could do that in her own journal and, further, could test out new proposals by making them appear to be someone else's suggestions and then assessing the response they elicited.

The *Journal* served other purposes as well. From the very first issue, an important part was devoted to the cards of Christian Science healers. These announcements were, at first, voluntary, but soon became obligatory and provided a certain source of revenue. Since this listing was official, it also became the record of who had become disaffected with

Mrs. Eddy or had been expelled from authorized participation. It also provides data about the growth and other characteristics of Christian Science in those years. In April of 1883, for example, there were fourteen cards. Two years later there were forty-three, and two years after that, one hundred ten. Of those fourteen first healers, twelve were women. In Volume 1, Number 6, the first announcement appears for a healer from outside New England, from Milwaukee, and in Volume 2, Number 8, cards appear for healers in New York and Chicago. One can chart the further geographical expansion, volume by volume.

The *Journal* also included a question-and-answer feature, both questions and answers often being contributed by Mrs. Eddy, and a regular feature of later volumes was the list of presents given to Mrs. Eddy for Christmas each year. Any donor could be assured of notice in print by sending Mrs. Eddy a box decorated with inlaid butterfly wings or a needlepoint vista of Pike's Peak. Then there were the special articles, the testimonials to healing, and the important columns devoted to malicious mesmerism.

The special articles covered a wide range of topics, anything Mrs. Eddy wanted to contribute herself or to accept from her disciples. In fact, she seems often, especially at first, to have suffered from a dearth of contributions. Sometimes she would delve into the scrapbooks that she had filled with items that caught her fancy in her lonely days as Mrs. Patterson, when her husband was on the road. These assorted inspirational articles were now often rescued and printed in the *Journal* as if she had written them herself; sometimes they were even reprinted later and then, later still, collected and included in volumes of her own works. It's not known what she ever thought of this plagiarism, or whether she ever wondered if the provenance of these pieces might ever be traced. More often than not, they weren't any better than what she might have produced herself. The space was there and the piece to fill it came ready to hand.

The testimonials covered a wide range, some frankly

ludicrous, as, for example, one, widely quoted, in which a dog was cured of rattlesnake bite by the Christian Science devotion of its mistress;[17] and many of the early testimonials were written not by the patient but by the healer and served as a kind of self-advertisement. For example:

I do not like to speak of my cases, but so much is said that I will submit one or two for the encouragement of doubters. A case of chronic dysentery I healed in three treatments. Another, who had not stepped her right heel on the floor for seven years, walked three miles after the fourth treatment, and went home entirely cured. I saw a poor insane woman four times, and treated her against her own wishes. She thanks God for reason restored by the application of His word through my humble instrumentality. A severe case of constipation of many years' standing was cured in three treatments. A child in great pain from eating unripe fruit I relieved almost instantly. Another child in convulsions of agony from some unknown cause, I was able to put into peaceful sleep within ten minutes after I entered her presence. . . .[18]

Other letters, written by the sufferers, reveal the kinds of illnesses that responded to Christian Science healing, illnesses with all kinds of vague and wandering symptoms. These letters in particular must have offered great hope to others in similar circumstances. Here is just one example:

Dear Journal: I read with interest your columns; and as I have been heretofore a great sufferer, I wish to show to the public what Christian Science has done for me. I had been sick for about five years, being confined to my bed about four years, and was a very great sufferer all the time, hardly one moment without the most intense pain. I had what the doctors termed spinal, kidney, and stomach trouble, and a number of other ailments. My spine was so sore that I could not turn myself in bed. My feet and limbs were numb. My stomach would not retain anything, not even a teaspoonful of gruel. The physician said there was an obstruction in my stomach, and I could not get well. . . .[19]

The writer then went on to describe the salutary effects of the intervention of a Mrs. Robinson, a healer from a nearby town, and on the next page there appeared a letter from Mrs. Robinson herself, describing other people she had cured. The testimonials provided good advertisement not only for Christian Science in general but for specific Christian Science practitioners in particular and must have been powerful incentives to aid in the distribution of the magazine.

Every healing method has its failures and must develop a method of dealing with them. Either the healing method has been applied too broadly, or something hasn't been understood by the healer, or there is some unexpected complication. Failures indicate something unanticipated, that is, the possibility for learning something new. The whole possibility for growth lies in the study of such accidents.

Christian Science dealt with its defeats in another way. It elevated malicious mesmerism to great importance as the major source of disappointment to Christian Science practitioners' efforts for cure.

A particularly poignant example of this demon's invocation to explain away disaster involved a woman from a small town in Dakota who had become a Christian Scientist and practitioner and had withdrawn from her local Methodist Episcopal church. When her eleven-month-old boy became ill, she called upon another healer and friend to help her cure him. As this friend wrote to the *Journal*, the mother was sure that the child was ill because members of the church with which she had formerly been affiliated resented her defection. She thought that they prayed in the hope that "God would remove the . . . child so that they [the parents] might come back into the church." The child lingered for days, the Christian Scientists exerting their best efforts on his behalf, reading the Bible and *Science and Health*, attempting to repel by their concentrated efforts of thought the evil influence of the hostile community, and telegraphing respected healers from distant places to ask their assistance by absent treatment.

> . . . At least six times little Edward seemed to have passed. We recognized it as another temptation, took up animal magnetism and each time he rallied. Finally about 5:30 A.M. of Friday, Jan. 25th, he passed on. I took him on my lap. Mrs. Nixon [his mother] and I realized it must be the last temptation, hence the greatest. We had no fear and did not admit he had passed on for several hours. We kept reading the promises "according to thy faith," etc., and did not call an undertaker until evening. When Mrs. Nixon's little Philip passed on a few months ago her faith alone should have raised him. But this time her faith was coupled with understanding and did not waver for a moment. Why this termination? I wish we could have some light on the subject.
>
> We recognized no disease, and as first symptoms would appear — beliefs of paralysis, spasms, fever, etc. — we would realize the allness of God, and they would disappear. It was a clear case of ignorant and malicious magnetism. Why was it not mastered? . . .[20]

Naturally, if one is going to give the keys of healing to Everyman, one is handing over not only a grave responsibility but a frightening burden as well, for few people are trained or emotionally disposed to investigate disaster with a wish to learn from it. One will, then, have to provide him with an explanation for failure that can be readily grasped and that absolves the practitioner from responsibility for the defeat. For this, mesmerism served very well, and the section on mesmerism, which became for a time a regular department of the *Journal* beginning in 1887, occupied a particularly prominent position. It was called Malicious Animal Magnetism, often simply M.A.M., and contained general warnings and preachments about the topic as well as specific examples of its operation and specific instances of how it might successfully be combated.

The *Journal* was from the very first an inexpensive way to broadcast Mrs. Eddy's message. She exercised her ingenuity to see that it was very widely distributed, sending it into even very small towns in remote places. Who would know, in advance, where a responsive heart might be found? The very authority of the *Journal*, with its glorification of Mrs. Eddy as founder and, more, as messenger of God's word, served to set her apart from the raggle-taggle band of faith healers who could not afford such an expensive, authoritative organ for their own promotion, or who lacked the ingenuity or foresight to avail themselves of such pretentious and effective publicity. And Mrs. Eddy was careful from the very beginning to make a distinction between official, "legitimate" Christian Scientists and other healers, warning her readers of the unfortunate consequences of employing healers who had not been certified by Mrs. Eddy herself and by the Massachusetts Metaphysical College.

As another effort to protect her own special position, Mrs. Eddy brought suit against Edward J. Arens on April 6, 1883, saying, correctly, that his pamphlet *The Understanding of Christianity, or God* represented plagiarism of her own writings.[21] This suit was the result of Gilbert Eddy's studies of copyright law in Washington in January of 1882. Arens could not deny plagiarism but planned to justify it by maintaining that *Science and Health* itself was not original but contained substantial borrowings from Quimby's writings, for which no copyright had been obtained.

To this end, he entered into correspondence with all of those whom he could track down from the Quimby years, particularly with Quimby's widow and son George; with Julius and Annetta Dresser, the first of whom, as we know, had been Mrs. Patterson's own nominee for successor to Quimby in 1866; and with the Misses Emma and Sarah

Ware, who had copied out Quimby's writings for him. Arens's argument to all of these people was, apparently, that Mrs. Eddy was usurping Quimby's rightful place in history and that he, Arens, had undertaken the worthy mission of setting the matter to rights and vindicating Quimby.

One of the Ware sisters lived in Washington with her father, a justice of the U.S. Admiralty Court. The other lived in Scotland with her husband. They apparently favored Arens's battle with Mrs. Eddy but didn't want to be involved. George Quimby, too, had no wish at all to participate and refused to allow Arens to use his father's manuscripts as part of Arens's defense against Mrs. Eddy's lawsuit. He even led Arens to believe that he had had the manuscripts conveyed to Scotland for safekeeping so that they could not be commandeered as evidence on Arens's behalf for the trial.

The Dressers, who had been living in the West, had now come to Boston and, whatever their motives, were not loathe to participate. They enagaged in an acrid exchange of letters with Mrs. Eddy in the columns of the Boston *Post*.[22] Julius Dresser set forth as he knew them the facts of Quimby's practice, of Quimby's belief that he had discovered a science of healing which could be taught to any man, and of his treatment of Mrs. Eddy, then Mrs. Patterson. Dresser described the letter Mrs. Patterson had written him when Quimby died, the letter in which she asked him to take Quimby's place, and he offered to show this letter and other documents to whoever was interested.

Mrs. Eddy contended that Quimby had always been a mesmerist, asserted that she herself was the author of Quimby's writings, and went on to give some of her own history, underlining her solid place in the middle class. She wrote of Patterson, for example, that he was one of the most prosperous dentists in Lynn and that their marriage broke up when he ran away with the wife of one of the town's leading citizens, leaving a note proclaiming her the best wife a man could have. The emphasis was on prosperous dentist, leading citizen, best wife. She even promoted Glover, her first husband, to colonel, and gave the names of worthy citizens down in South Carolina who were connected with the Masonic order and whom the interested reader might contact for verification of her history. Only let him not, she implied, contact Dresser in Boston.

She made her own attempt to extract from the Quimby years some testimony that would verify her own position. Just before the case was to come to trial she attempted to get from Sarah Crosby in Maine an affidavit supporting the originality of her own teaching materials, that is, a denial of her indebtedness to Quimby. Mrs. Crosby had been the patient of Quimby's whom Mrs. Patterson had herself visited in 1864 and entertained in spirit sessions with her brother Albert. Mrs. Crosby was a court stenographer, and Mrs. Eddy had brought her to Lynn in 1877 to make a record of the lectures she was using to teach her classes, meaning to provide Gilbert Eddy with a text that he could use in sharing in the teaching. But Mrs. Crosby refused to cooperate and later wrote out for Georgine Milmine her memory of the experience, saying that Mrs. Eddy had requested that she "make an oath to what was not true." She could attest, Mrs. Crosby wrote, that "Mrs. Eddy's teachings in 1877 and Dr. Quimby's teachings in 1864 were substantially the same." [23] When she informed the attorney sent by Mrs. Eddy to prepare the statement that she would not give it, he threatened to summon her to the trial, but she said, "I think I made him understand that I would not be a desirable witness on his side of the case." She knew her way around in the courtroom, knew enough not to be intimidated, and so she was not pursued further.

The case at law was found against Arens. Quimby's writings were not produced; he had had no copyright for them, in any event. Mrs. Eddy did have a valid copyright for hers, from which Arens had lifted whole sections for his pamphlets. These pamphlets were ordered destroyed and he was enjoined from publishing and distributing them further.

Mrs. Eddy said the court had vindicated her claim to the originality of her works, which, of course, it hadn't at all. It had merely affirmed her copyright without making a judgment about the origin or merit of the material to which she had the copyright. But such fine points can easily get lost in polemic discussions.

Arens was destroyed by the experience. He struggled on for another few years, attempting to found his own equivalent of the Massachusetts Metaphysical College, calling it the University of the Science of Spirit, which was to offer among its degrees that of "Defender of the Faith." This grandiosity was, for him, the prelude to madness, and he died in a mental hospital.

The Dressers, however, were not to give up their fight. In 1887, Julius Dresser published a pamphlet, *The True History of Mental Science*, in which he quoted at length from the testimonies Mrs. Patterson had written with so much enthusiasm back in 1863.[24] She established her line of defense in the *Christian Science Journal* of June 1887:

. . . Did I write those articles, in Mr. Dresser's pamphlet, purporting to be mine? I might have written them, twenty or thirty years ago, for I was under the mesmeric treatment of Dr. Quimby from 1862 until his death in 1865. He was illiterate, and I knew nothing then of the Science of Mind-healing; and I was as ignorant of mesmerism as Eve, before she was taught by the serpent. Mind Science was unknown to me; and my head was so turned by Animal Magnetism and will-power, under his treatment, that I might have written something as hopelessly incorrect as the articles now published in the Dresser pamphlet. . . . I was not healed until after the death of Mr. Quimby; and then healing came as the result of my discovery, in 1866, of the Science of Mind-healing, since called Christian Science. . . .[25]

So the battle lines were drawn and the war continued, without victory on either side, but also without defeat. From Mrs. Eddy's point of view, the real issue was the survival of Christian Science, not the literal truth of whether or not she owed a substantial debt to Quimby. For her the more important matter was that Christian Science be her own creation, in its message and structure, financial solidity, and future as an institution, as an extension of her own being. In this very special sense, the Quimby controversy was irrelevant to her own purposes, and her answers to Arens and the Dressers have to be understood not as honest or dishonest representations of historical fact, but as examples of her way of defending herself and her own creation. The irrationality of her defensive statements was a measure of her fear of acknowledging dependence an anyone, even someone whom she had loved as best she could. The enemy was the same enemy she attacked in Kennedy and Arens and, for a time, Spofford, that is, that part of her feelings which hungered to put trust in others but which feared, at the same time, that she would weaken herself by giving in to the yearning.

The Quimby controversy attacked Mrs. Eddy's claim to have discovered the principles of Christian Science but did not question those principles themselves. It was inevitable, however, that the practice of Christian Science healing would lead to *some* disasters, at least, and that these would become the source of attacks on Christian Science and on Mrs. Eddy and, furthermore, that they would create very special problems within the movement. After all, even if malicious mesmerism could be invoked to reassure faltering practitioners, it could not be expected to satisfy doubting critics. Although there had been disasters attendant on the practice of Christian Science healing, the first well-publicized example from close to home threatened the very foundation of the Church.

In the spring of 1888, a Christian Science practitioner from West Medford, Massachusetts, Mrs. Abby H. Corner, attended her own daughter in a complicated childbirth in which hemorrhage occurred, and both the daughter and the infant died. Mrs. Corner was indicted for murder but was eventually acquitted on the ground that the *medical* treatment for hemorrhage in those days would not have been able with any certainty to prevent death. Of course, from the Christian Science point of view the hemorrhage simply shouldn't have occurred, so that theologically it was an uncertain defense.

Christian Science practitioners had had some considerable success with their obstetrics practice, one analogous to what we would today call natural childbirth. The dramatic contrast between the experience of those who were taught to see in childbirth a natural process, unattended by beliefs in pain, and that of those for whom travail was an expected accompaniment to delivery must have been an especially striking mark in favor of the whole method. But although most deliveries are unaccompanied by complications, not all of them are, and the Christian Science practitioners were poorly prepared for the inevitable.

As late as 1886, the curriculum of Mrs. Eddy's Massachusetts Metaphysical College was extremely limited, offering only three courses with a total of no more than twenty-four lectures.[26] The Collegiate Course in Christian Science Metaphysical Healing included only twelve lessons for a tuition of three hundred dollars. The Normal Class, open to those who had taken the first course, was composed of six daily lessons for a tuition of two hundred dollars, and the Course in Metaphysical Obstetrics consisted of six daily lectures, announced now for the first time but not given until the following spring, open only to students of the college for a tuition of two hundred dollars. The main conditions for matriculation were that students be healthy themselves, of good character, and able to pay the tuition in advance.

Although Mrs. Eddy had advertised her qualifications to teach obstetrics as early as 1882, this was the first formal offer of instruction on the topic. A set of notes taken by a student in that first class in 1887 indicated that five of the six lectures in metaphysical obstetrics consisted of instructions for dealing with Malicious Animal Magnetism, and the last for dealing with the complications of delivery:

> The practitioner is first to take up in thought the subject of premature birth, and to deny the possibility of such an occurrence in the case he is then treating.
> He is to deny one by one some of the dangerous symptoms which may attend childbirth. Mrs. Eddy takes these symptoms up at random and with no consideration for their relation to each other.[27]

Thus, when the inevitable complication presented itself at childbirth, all the denial in the world simply wouldn't set it right.

When Mrs. Corner was indicted, the group of Christian Science practitioners wanted to defend her, both individually and as a group. Mrs. Eddy, however, wished to disassociate herself and Christian Science from the very painful publicity that attended the matter. She wrote the following notice, which was published in the Boston *Herald* for April 29, 1888, typically not under her own signature but under that of the Committee on Publication, Christian Scientists' Association, which, however, did not know of the letter before it appeared in the newspaper:

> The lamentable case reported from West Medford of the death of a mother and her infant at childbirth should forever put a stop to quackery. There has been but one side of this case presented by the newspapers. We wait to hear from the other side, trusting that attenuating circumstances will be brought to light. Mrs. Abby H. Corner never entered the obstetrics class at the Massachusetts Metaphysical College. She was not fitted at this institute for an accoucheur, had attended but one term, and four terms, including three years of successful practice by the student, are required to complete the college course. No student graduates under four years. Mrs. Eddy, the president of this college,

requires her students to use the utmost precaution in practice, and to be thoroughly qualified for their work. Hence the rapid growth of this system of mind-healing, its safety and success. The West Medford case, so far as is known, is the first instance of death at child-birth in the practice of Christian science. This fact is of vital importance, when compared with the daily statistics of death on such occasions caused by the use of drugs and instruments. Does medical malpractice, and the mortality that ensues, go unnoticed because of their frequency? Christian scientists are called daily to heal chronic cases of disease caused by the malpractice of physicians of the regular school, and they heal these cases in a majority of instances. All professions are subject to impostors, Christian science included. But the history of science is by no means at the mercy of charlatanism. Recreant practitioners in any school of medicine are a disgrace to it. The mind curer, faith curers and mesmerists, who never touched the attitude of scientists, are reckoned among them all the same. The Globe reports the leader of faith cure, Dr. Cullis, saying that he always employs drugs, hygiene and material methods first, and God last, in his practice. The scriptures say: "Seek ye first the kingdom of heaven." When one's faith in matter is foiled, and as a dernier ressort one exercises some faith in God, what thanks has he? Dr. Cullis admits that God has all power — then he questions this power to even "raise a man who has fallen in the street." He reasons that God cannot deliver a mother in travail, for this is the proper province of drugs, the knife and the forceps.

Are the medical scoffers who sit in judgment on mind-healing willing to lift the veil on the charnel house for others to read the records of their blunders and count the number of their victims. (Signed)

Committee on Publication,
Christian Scientists' Association

In effect, the letter started out with a frank disavowal of Mrs. Corner, saying that she had not had the requisite regular training for Christian Science practitioners. In the process, it gave a false picture of those training requirements in terms of number of classes, duration, and provisions for supervision, which simply didn't exist. It then went on to attack medicine and nonmedical healing practices other than Christian Science, saying both that they had their practical limits and that they, like Christian Science, may have had a few quacks among their serious practitioners.

When Mrs. Eddy's followers read this letter, many of them were appalled. They felt that Mrs. Eddy had abandoned Mrs. Corner and, perhaps as bad, had set impossible and nonexistent standards for training that none of them could measure up to, so that if *they* got into trouble, they could not count on Mrs. Eddy's support any more than could Abby Corner. They were in no position to understand Mrs. Eddy's insecurity — or even to recognize it as such — for while they were, at times, insecure themselves, they counted on her to be as she was in public, absolutely confident, a buttress for each of them.

In her own way, Mrs. Eddy tried to maintain that very same appearance of confidence. She contended that this letter was *not* a rejection of Mrs. Corner and should have been read instead as a *defense* of her. Furthermore, after Mrs. Corner was in fact acquitted, Mrs. Eddy said that no defense of her had been necessary, because Mrs. Eddy knew all along that acquittal was inevitable. They had all, she said, been a flock of panicky sheep.

The association of Christian Scientists was planning to meet to argue the matter officially. Mrs. Eddy summoned her most loyal partisans, hoping to pack the meeting, but perhaps fearing the results of an open fight, changed her mind and advised the association that she had now decided to attend, instead, the convention of the National Christian Scientists' Association in Chicago, which was to meet in mid-June. Away from Boston and the troubles of that ungrateful town, she might inspire a show of popular support that would temper her critics at home. This was not her first visit to Chicago. In 1884 she had taught a class there, which had served as a nucleus for the thriving movement in the Midwest. To those in Chicago, Mrs. Corner and the tragedy in West Medford would seem very far away and of slight importance.

The meeting in Chicago was a great personal success for Mrs. Eddy. Although she had not planned to speak, the organizer of the meeting had announced that she would, and so a crowd of four or five hundred delegates and many other spectators were on hand on the morning of June 14 to hear her. The Chicago *Times* carried a detailed story of the convention, reporting part of it in a straight tone and part with some irony. After describing the audience as ". . . a notable body of sweet-faced, middle-aged matrons, whose features wore a pleasing expression of benevolence," it described Mrs. Eddy:

> . . . Mrs. Eddy is fully seventy-five years old [she was only 67], of rather slight build, and affects a peculiar air of magnetism in her actions. . . . When [she] came upon the rostrum she sat down upon a chair, folded her hands, closed her eyes, and seemed to be conjuring the audience. She was very deliberate in her movements and opened the bible with the peculiar rolling of the eyes which mesmerists affect. She spoke distinctly and with effect, though her talk was lacking in unity and coherence. . . . When the speaker concluded the audience arose en masse and made a rush for the platform. There were no steps provided for getting on the rostrum, but that did not deter those who wanted to shake hands with the idolized expounder of their creed. They mounted the reporters' table and vaulted to the rostrum like acrobats. They crowded about the little woman and hugged and kissed her until she was exhausted and a man had to come to her rescue and lead her away.
>
> "I must leave you now, dears. You must let me pass now," and followed with expressions of "what a dear good woman she is" she made her exit.[28]

The report of the morning session concludes with a long summary of Mrs. Eddy's extemporaneous talk, which consisted of a review of Christian Science theory without any reference to the actual problems that Mrs. Eddy was facing. She said that she was speaking in a rambling way, but the summary as it is presented in the *Times* is coherent and intelligible enough, clear and readily grasped.

The report of the afternoon session was more ironical, commenting that the Christian Scientists, for all their disbelief in matter, perspired like everybody else and were unable to deny the heat. It went on:

> Grammatically viewed, Christian Science is a noun in the feminine gender. A few men — a sort of job lot — in various stages of adolescence and decrepitude relieved the sea of bonnets that reached from the vestibule to the church platform. A remarkably nice lot of women, though, with pleasant, healthy, wholesome faces, good color, and plump, round figures. There must be money in metaphysics, and a good deal of it, for nearly all the "healers" had on new gowns, black satin prevailing; diamond ear-rings, gold watches and long chains were the rule rather than the exception. . . .

Although the preponderance of delegates were women, almost all of the speakers were men, and it was a man, the Reverend George B. Day, who presided over the afternoon session with what the *Times* reporter called

> . . . meager grace. He is a scholarly, dyspeptic-looking man, with an ecclesiastical air, a voice as big as an after-dinner coffee-cup, defective hearing, and a most treacherous pair of eyes. . . .

The descriptions might have come out of *Tom Sawyer*, and one imagines the reporter making the best use of what was for him an otherwise dreary day.

While these triumphs were proceeding in Chicago, the dissident group in Boston were able to obtain the records of the Christian Scientists' Association, the secretary having left them at home when he went with Mrs. Eddy to Chicago. These records were now given into the safekeeping of an attorney, and Mrs. Eddy was told that they would be kept as hostage until she directed the secretary to give each of the dissidents a letter of honorable dismissal. It is a tribute to the power of Mrs. Eddy's organization and standing in the mind-healing world that these dissident members preferred "honorable dismissal" to "expulsion," a public act often accompanied by the accusation of immorality.[29] An earlier group had not felt so much threatened. Mrs. Eddy tried to reconcile these people, but without success. There were thirty-six of them, finally, just under a fifth of the association membership, but most of them came from the Boston area and they represented only one of a number of problem groups among her followers. The next spring they received their letters of honorable dismissal and returned to Mrs. Eddy and her secretary the records of the association. There would undoubtedly have been more of them, but those who wavered on the border were influenced by the triumphs of Chicago to stay. Many of the people who left had undoubtedly also been influenced by the Dressers and those others who presented their evidence for the importance of Quimby's ideas in their own right. Some of them affiliated themselves with the New Thought movement, which was arising as an amalgam of mental healers with a moral rather than a religious philosophical foundation, the first significant, organized competitor to Mrs. Eddy and Christian Science.

This particular incident has been selected as a specific example of how Mrs. Eddy dealt with a challenge to Christian Science practice. The personality of Mrs. Corner was not an important factor in Mrs. Eddy's reaction. What was important was that Mrs. Corner had precipitated a threat to Christian Science, one that had to be met by whatever means Mrs. Eddy could improvise. She had shown that she could improvise quite effectively. However much it cost her, she rode out this storm with her signals intact, and if she lost three dozen followers, well, there had been others before and there would be others to come.

Some partial sense of what it cost her emotionally, however, can be surmised from the arrangements she made to attach herself now to yet another man, one Ebenezer J. Foster, a homeopathic physician who, impressed by the Christian Science cure of a friend, had called on Mrs. Eddy and entered her primary class in November of 1887. Just at that moment, her son George had invited himself with his whole family to visit. Mrs. Eddy had strongly opposed the visit. She lived, she said, in a schoolhouse, without room for guests, and all of her time was devoted to the fight against evil. Besides, George had refused her summons five years earlier when she had really needed him. She didn't need him now and didn't want him.

He came anyway, just after she had moved into a mansion at 385 Commonwealth Avenue, which, however large, did not contain enough room for the George Glover family of Lead City, in Dakota Territory. So they camped across the Mystic River in Chelsea, all through the winter and spring, through the upsetting times that Mrs. Corner's tragedy brought upon Christian Science, and then, finally, they left in May, just as Mrs. Eddy was busy making her plans for the trip to Chicago.

She was thus able to contrast her rough-hewn son with the more highly polished Dr. Foster, who was of about the same age. Mrs. Eddy was soon calling him "Bennie" and delighting in his courtly and admiring attentions. She took him in her entourage to Chicago; he took advantage of the trip to visit a brother in Wisconsin, whence he was summoned by the usual series of contradictory telegrams, and returned to Boston and Mrs. Eddy, who had by now learned of the kidnapping of the association records. She announced to him that she meant to make their relationship even closer. She meant to adopt him, she said, and make him her heir. He, relieved that her plans for him were limited to adoption, agreed to the arrangement, and the legal forms were drawn up in October of that year, 1888. Mrs. Eddy was not quite ready for the adoption to be completed, though. She felt that some gesture should be made toward formal instruction in obstetrics, for she did not want to expose again the vulnerability that had been revealed by Mrs. Corner's mishap. Foster was a physician and could earn his place in the family by helping out in the "college," so he taught pelvic anatomy in the obstetric class that month under the scrutiny of his prospective mother. That having been done to her satisfaction, the adoption proceedings were completed. He took the name Ebenezer J. Foster Eddy. His duties in the household were various, including playing the piano for Mrs. Eddy and accompanying her on drives. He served as her representative at meetings and in business affairs, and he assisted at the midnight crises that were once again intensified because of the struggles of that year. As appurtenances of his new position, he wore a grand, fur-lined coat and a diamond solitaire ring that his new mother had bought for him. It is to be expected that Foster Eddy's path was not strewn simply with rose petals. Mrs. Eddy's household included a good assortment of retainers, some of them more or less permanent, like Calvin Frye, others coming and going as their fortunes rose and fell in Mrs. Eddy's eyes, but all of them extremely jealous of their position.

Mrs. Eddy had the attitude that one finds so often in leaders of successful movements, that as the circle of her success grew, and as she attracted to herself more conventionally successful people, she began to feel that many of those from the old days were too humble in their talents and antecedents to suit her new position. Furthermore, the very same personal eccentricities that had made these people susceptible to the message of Christian Science now might become an embarrassment to a movement that, however revolutionary it might be in its theology, was meant to appeal to ordinary, prosperous, unadventurous folk.

Mrs. Eddy herself had always had a penchant for gentility,

affecting even in her school days a decorous opulence of dress and a formality of manner that the people around her then considered pretentious. But by now, in the mid to late 1880s, her normalization of the Church had progressed to the point that she retained the professional services of a Unitarian clergyman-turned-writer's assistant, who would regularize her syntax and her punctuation and organize her writings in an attempt to make them more easily understood by a wider audience and, at the same time, less provocative and less insistently subversive.

This engaging gentleman, the Reverend James Henry Wiggin, was born in Boston in 1836 and died there in 1900. He graduated from Meadville Theological School in 1861 and was ordained the next year, holding a pulpit until 1875, when he gave up the regular ministry and did some work as a writer's aide. He had some private means and was a raconteur and bon vivant and a member of Boston society. We have what purports to be his own description of his work for Mrs. Eddy, because about a year before he died he gave a long statement to a journalist, Livingston Wright, and entrusted to him some of the working papers that he had used in revisions of *Science and Health with Key to the Scriptures*. Wright published this story with his own additions in the New York *World* on the sixth anniversary of Wiggin's death.[30]

As Wiggin told the story, Mrs. Eddy had been referred to him by her publisher. Calvin Frye made the initial contact late in August of 1885, followed soon by Mrs. Eddy herself, who gave into his hands her proposed manuscript revision for the book. Wiggin said of it that in addition to problems of misspellings, capitalization, and punctuation, the thought and conception of the work were, to his mind, so inconsistent, historically inaccurate, and poorly integrated that nothing would do but a thorough revision. When he broached this diagnosis and recommendation to Mrs. Eddy, she accepted his proposals calmly and invited him to proceed.

Wiggin expatiated with a certain air of pomposity and self-satisfaction on Mrs. Eddy's lack of acquaintance with Sanskrit, Latin, or Greek, and on her unfamiliarity with the philosophers whom she was so fond of quoting. He was trying, undoubtedly, to refute her grand claims to a broad liberal education. One wonders if he also felt defensive, in retrospect, about the confrontation between the gentleman of the old school who had abandoned his calling and the woman of modest antecedents and education who was struggling her way to remarkable achievement.

What is most important from the story, though, is that Mrs. Eddy was willing to subject her writings to the kind of transformation that Wiggin could perform. That is, she was less interested in the specific form of her writing than she was in getting across her message to a broader audience. We have seen that she could rewrite her own poems and use them for different occasions. She did not consider her own writings sacrosanct. She would fight for a particular word or turn of phrase if she felt it expressed exactly what she wanted to say, but she often gave in to Wiggin's judgment on major renovations and emendations. Wiggin says that on one occasion, after he had convinced her to omit what he felt was a libelous attack on Kennedy, Spofford, and Arens, she said to him, "Mr. Wiggin, I often feel as if the Lord spoke to me through you."

Besides rewriting and rearranging *Science and Health with Key to the Scriptures*, beginning with the sixteenth edition of 1886 and concluding with a thorough revision in 1891, Wiggin edited the *Christian Science Journal*, pruned and altered Mrs. Eddy's poems, revised other of her published writings, and answered her critics either in her own name or, on occasion, under the pseudonym Phare Pleigh. He advised her on specific projects too and on one occasion dissuaded her from putting herself in a ridiculous position when she wanted to claim as an ancestress a poet whom Wiggin knew to have been a spinster. Only once, he said, did Mrs.

Eddy acknowledge to him a mercenary interest, and that was perhaps because she thought it a motive that might appeal to him:

> . . . she had one day made the usual expression of hope that I would join her Church and I had made my customary refusal. She thereupon declared with unusual earnestness: "Mr. Wiggin, Christian Science is a good thing. I make ten thousand a year at it."
>
> Those were her very words. In all those years, beginning with the fall of 1885, that I was associated with her as literary adviser that was the only time when Mrs. Eddy got right down to the practical phase of her enterprise.

Wiggin did sometimes tease his patroness, but she always, he said, would answer him with absolute seriousness:

> I had seen Mrs. Eddy wearing spectacles in those days. I had also, at her rooms, heard her complain of feeling chilled and heard her direct the servant thus: "Kindly step downstairs and stir up the furnace." In view of her doctrines, all this used to amuse me, and sometimes I would look over at her and smilingly ask her how it happened that she required spectacles or how it occurred that she was susceptible to cold. And many a time, in spite of the grin that Mrs. Eddy must have seen was on my countenance, I have heard her reply, without so much as the twitch of a muscle: "Mr. Wiggin, when I am in the mountains, among God's hills and God's grandeur, I have perfect eyesight and never wear spectacles. Nor do I feel the chill. But here in the city, surrounded as I am by mortal minds, I am not so free." And she would proceed with her work or conversation upon other topics with as much unconcern as though there could not be the slightest shadow of a question but that her reply about the spectacles and the chill had been absolutely the quintessence of rationalism.

It was clear, then, that Mrs. Eddy operated by a single standard: what was good for Christian Science. She could permit the adaptation of her own writings with the same readiness that she had used in borrowing from the writings of others. What was most important was the purpose to be served.

After Wright's articles were published, Mrs. Eddy issued at once a reply in the New York *American*.[31] She both acknowledged and deprecated the role that Mr. Wiggin had played on her behalf, but ended with a brief testimonial, remarkable in coming from one who had so often parted from her associates with acrimony:

> I hold the late Mr. Wiggin in loving grateful memory for his high-principled character and well-equipped scholarship.

These selected incidents from the years after Gilbert Eddy's death, the years of increasing success for Mrs. Eddy and for Christian Science, give only a limited picture of the complexity of her life at that time. There were other students with whom she was engaged in intense, prolonged personal struggles over domination and orthodoxy, there were other attacks to be answered or ignored, and there were plans to be made for the organization of Christian Science and for the construction of its first Church. But all of these many threads of purpose, enough to fill a life for a woman of fifty or sixty, were burdensome to a woman approaching seventy. Mrs. Eddy wanted to remove herself from the day-to-day demands of her movement. She set Foster Eddy to work to find a suitable retreat. His first solution, a house in Barre, Vermont, to which she moved in the spring of 1889, was a failure because she discoverd that the town band, whose summer concerts she could hear from her house, refused to give them up for her comfort. She returned to Boston until the next house was found in Concord, New Hampshire, to which she now moved but then again abandoned because of street noise. A third place, in Roslindale, now a part of Boston, a house that she actually purchased because she was so sure

that it would suit her, also was unsatisfactory because, once
she had moved in with all her furniture, she discovered that
she did not feel easy, either because Boston was too close or
because her neighbors were mesmerized, which was *her* explanation. She returned then to the house she had abandoned
in Concord, New Hampshire, and there, reconciled to the
noise of the town, she settled in to stay for three years until
the house outside of town would be found, the house that
was to be called Pleasant View.

Chapter Seven

Again, Mrs. Eddy tried to escape from misfortune by leaving the scene of disaster. Although she believed in the most literal sense that her enemies' hatred had poisoned the air, still, in each case she was able, once she survived the inner turmoil of her immediate disappointment, to set upon a course of action that would strengthen her cause.

It must have been clear to her now that the defection of a good third of her Boston followers in the aftermath of the Corner trial had revealed how tenuous was her hold on her own Church. An estimate of the loss can be derived from a count of healers' cards published in each monthly edition of the *Christian Science Journal*. In March of 1888 there were one hundred one cards, of which forty-two were from healers in Massachusetts. In September of that year, after the Corner incident and the convention, the number dropped to sixty-six, of which only twenty-one were from Massachusetts. By January of 1889, the number climbed back to ninety-five, but the number from Massachusetts rose only to twenty-eight. In that whole period, the percentage of healers from Massachusetts declined from 42 percent of the total to 29.

However reassuring it may have been to realize that she had a thriving movement elsewhere in the country, not even that part of her following could be counted on, for it had developed largely without her personal presence and was only partially subject to her control. And, as if to underline that lesson, several of the active organizers of the Chicago convention went off on tangents of their own almost immediately afterward and repudiated her. Mrs. Eddy was the leader of a dynamic, to be sure, but shifting and unstable group of individualistic, ambitious, enterprising, and, in part, eccentric, self-seeking people whose loyalty to her was of variable quantity and whose devotion to Christian Science was often based largely on immediate self-interest.

Christian Science attracted many practitioners by offering relief of their own pains and providing a means to a good livelihood for which but little preparation was required. But this very virtue, this accessibility, tended to ensure that practitioners might themselves be troubled people, impressionable, ready to live by their wits, and without that discipline which a more demanding period of training would require, one from which the flightier students might have dropped out in discouragement.

Early in a movement one seeks growth, availability, broad appeal: the quick, effective readiness to seize the moment. Later on, consolidation and stability might seem more attractive. The threat now was that groups of these quick, effective, convincing activist-converts might lead the Church off into new directions of their own contriving; even, perhaps, that they might move her Church right out from under Mrs. Eddy, who, as long as she got due acknowledgment, would have no control and little recourse.

One of Mrs. Eddy's staunchest long-term followers, Josephine Woodbury, provides a good example of the kinds of problems that a magnetic, energetic, and eccentric disciple could inflict on a religious leader struggling for stability and acceptance. Mrs. Woodbury and her husband had been attracted to Mrs. Eddy as early as 1879. He was one of the original charter founders of the Massachusetts Metaphysical College. The Woodburys had stood by Mrs. Eddy in those early years, Mrs. Woodbury being one of those who kept vigil for Gilbert Eddy and nursed him during his last illness.

She was eloquent and convincing, operating her own school, although, as she said in the book which she wrote about her experiences in Christian Science, careful to send the more affluent and important students to Mrs. Eddy herself for instruction.[1] She implied that it was she who had suggested James Henry Wiggin as Mrs. Eddy's literary adviser, and she was herself for a brief time the acting editor of the *Christian Science Journal*. She traveled at Mrs. Eddy's behest to far-distant places, to Denver, to Augusta, Maine, and to Montreal, preaching, trying to heal breaches and strengthen congregations. She had a flair for self-dramatization. She could transform a train ride in a western snowstorm into a confrontation with death, or an incident on a beach into an example of the resurrection of the drowned, all testimony to Mrs. Eddy and to Christian Science.

This enthusiasm and mystical conviction attracted to her a lively group of students and disciples who were by temperament and style very different from those who clustered about Mrs. Eddy. They were more romantic and sophisticated, sleeping in monkish cells, holding themselves open to revelation and to ecstasy, and pursuing the pre-Raphaelite aesthetic. They would follow Mrs. Woodbury to Maine for the summer each year, operating there a kind of peripatetic commune.[2]

These goings-on were not pleasing to Mrs. Eddy's household, and probably not to Mrs. Eddy herself either, although she was always reluctant to alienate a student directly, particularly an imposing one, for fear of the Malicious Animal Magnetism that disenchanted disciples could direct at *her*. However, shortly after a trip to Montreal in 1889, Mrs. Woodbury found herself to be pregnant, although she did not immediately acknowledge the fact.

There is some evidence that this pregnancy was engendered by one of Mrs. Woodbury's student-patients there who was infatuated with her. Mrs. Eddy apparently knew of the student's feeling for Mrs. Woodbury and had warned both of them of its danger, although it is not clear that she had expected it to go as far as it did.[3] To make matters even more embarrassing, Mrs. Woodbury had encouraged continence among her followers, even the married ones, and had let it be known that she and her husband abstained from sexual relations as an example of their renunciation of material phenomena. Furthermore, there was current a line of thought in Christian Science, encouraged by Mrs. Eddy, that in the perfect world, conception could occur without material intervention, much on the model of the conception of Jesus, although Mrs. Eddy maintained later that she meant it to be understood that such ideal happenings would be reserved for the end of days, when the mountain of the Lord's house would be established, and not for the Victorian present.

Here, then, is how Mrs. Woodbury described her first awareness of her own pregnancy and the events that followed:

> . . . On the morning of June 11, 1890, there was born to me a baby boy; though, till his sharp birth-cry saluted my ears, I had not realized that prospective maternity was the interpretation of preceding months of poignant physical discomfort, not unreasonably attributed to other physiological causes and changes, — growing out of my age,* and former reliance upon medical opinion, — pointing in the direction of some fungoid formation.

She named her son Prince Woodbury because "he came into our family as a veritable harbinger of peace" and described how she baptized her little Prince in a tidal pool in Maine, surrounded by a crowd of watchers who broke into a spontaneous hymn of praise at the moment he was drawn out from the waters for the third time.[4]

When the reports were brought to Mrs. Eddy of little Prince's baptism, she was furious. For once, the jealousy of her household was vindicated. It would be hard to know whether she was more bothered by the unfavorable publicity

---

* About forty.

that might accrue to Christian Science or by her envy of the drama of such a scene — one in which she herself did not occupy center stage. But her fear of Mrs. Woodbury's mental force deterred her from repudiating her disciple immediately and directly. It was a lesson to her of the need to construct an administrative machinery that would do the things she wanted without revealing her responsibility for them, that could disavow, for example, adherents who threatened her authority or who might bring embarrassment to Christian Science. Her apparent retirement to Concord provided a convenient pretext for this removal of herself from practical involvements, but the construction of such machinery would take time. For the moment Mrs. Eddy avoided direct rupture with Mrs. Woodbury, even when widely publicized lawsuits were initiated against her, in one case by a man who claimed that she had spirited his wife out of his home and into her own, and in another by a lady who claimed that her husband was devoting his entire income to the support of the Prince of Peace, having apparently been convinced that he was participating in the overture to the Second Coming. When finally Mrs. Woodbury *was* ejected from Christian Science, she formed her own church just as did, for example, Ursula Gestefeld, Sarah Crosse, Frank Mason, and Oliver Sabin, other disaffected Christian Scientists.[5] In all fairness to Mrs. Woodbury, at least some of her protestations of devotion to Mrs. Eddy must have been genuine; it could not have been mercenary interest alone that prompted her to attempt to continue her attachment to Mrs. Eddy long after it was clear that Christian Science no longer offered her a secure place in the movement. She seems honestly to have looked upon Mrs. Eddy as a representation of motherhood, firm, loving, high-principled, chastising her children the better to show them the right way. If the intense anger that she displayed when reconciliation finally was shown to be impossible was real, then at least part of that anger must have proceeded from the hurt feelings of a daughter disappointed in her mother's love.

As the events of these years must indicate, Mrs. Eddy's objectives were to free herself from the minutiae of day-to-day management of the movement, to assure herself of absolute control over the vital operations of the Church, and to displace from herself the appearance of responsibility for Church decisions. And all the time she was to give the impression of being an elderly, possibly immortal, religious leader who had gone up into Mount Sinai to commune and to receive continuing inspiration.

Her first act of disengagement was to relinquish responsibility for the *Christian Science Journal*. She announced in May of 1889 her intention to give the *Journal* to the Christian Scientists' Association, but she was still free to command the appointment of editors — as she did that July and at other times thereafter. Even her vagrant wishes were invariably honored, unless she herself countermanded them. At the time of her abdication of owner-editorship, she issued a set of Seven Fixed Rules, further to emphasize her apparent withdrawal:

1) I shall not be consulted verbally, or through letters, as to whose advertisement shall or shall not appear in the Christian Science Journal. [Refusal of advertising meant withdrawal of official recognition from a healer, for example.]

2) I shall not be consulted verbally, or through letters, as to the matter that should be published in the Journal and Christian Science Series.

3) I shall not be consulted verbally, or through letters, on marriage, divorce, or family affairs of any kind.

4) I shall not be consulted verbally, or through letters, on the choice of pastors for churches.

5) I shall not be consulted verbally, or through letters, on disaffections, if there should be any between students of Christian Scientists.

6) I shall not be consulted verbally, or through letters, on who shall be admitted as members, or dropped from the

membership of the Christian Science Churches or Asso-
ciations.

7) I am not to be consulted verbally, or through letters,
on disease and the treatment of the sick; but I shall love all
mankind — and work for their welfare.[6]

The *Journal* expressed her immediate pious intent:

As our dear Mother in God withdraws herself from our
midst, and goes up into the Mount for higher communings,
to show us and the generations to come the way to our
true consciousness in God, let us honor Him and keep
silence; let us keep from her and settle among ourselves,
or, with God for ourselves, the small concerns for which
we have looked to her. . . .[7]

Mrs. Eddy's critics have pointed out that although she
gave away the *Journal*, she never renounced her own freedom to intervene in its operations, and that although the
Journal had a thriving circulation, it was not yet very well
managed and was still heavily in debt; what Mrs. Eddy gave
up often became a burden to someone else. But her disciples
were willing to accept their burdens and, granting her the
legitimacy of her own claims, one can hardly fault her for
her objectives or for the single-mindedness and dexterity
with which she went about achieving them.

Her next disentanglement was from the Massachusetts
Metaphysical College. She had not originally intended to
make permanent her withdrawal to New Hampshire. She
had undertaken to have the walls of her personal quarters in
the Boston home lined with lead as a sound-deadening device,
for greater comfort when she would return. But the move,
once she made it, had demonstrable advantages and made it
impossible for her to continue active participation in the
college.

Still, it was *her* college; she had been sole faculty member,
except for Ebenezer Foster, who had given those few ob-

stetrics lectures the preceding fall. He was now delegated to replace her, but when he proved a lackluster substitute, she summoned in his stead an old soldier and recent convert, General Erastus Newton Bates, who moved from Cleveland with his wife and whose appointment was announced in the *Christian Science Journal* for October of 1889. His teaching was more inspiring, apparently, but this brought problems too, for Mrs. Eddy, always reluctant to be upstaged, found her disciple's success more troubling than her adopted son's failure. She closed the college, therefore, even though this meant giving up a substantial income.

Another motive for closing the college, it was said, was that the Attorney General of Massachusetts was at that very moment investigating institutions that granted medical degrees with insufficient training, and the Massachusetts Metaphysical College was vulnerable, as the Corner case of the preceding year had shown. Josephine Woodbury even proposed the theory, later, that Mrs. Eddy was subject to arrest in Massachusetts on that score, and that this was the reason for her flight to New Hampshire and for the infrequency of her subsequent visits to Massachusetts, and those only on weekends when presumably a summons couldn't be served.[8] Whatever the mixture of reasons, the college was closed and General Bates, recently enlisted, was discharged again to his own devices.

The resolution dissolving the corporation, adopted on October 29, 1889, was published in the *Christian Science Journal* for December of that year.[9] Part of it bears close reading because it established the argument and procedure that Mrs. Eddy was to use in accomplishing her second objective, obtaining and perpetuating her control of the body of her Church:

> Whereas, The Massachusetts Metaphysical College, chartered in January, 1881, . . . has fulfilled its high and noble destiny, and sent to all parts of our country and into

foreign lands, students instructed in Christian Science Mind-healing to meet the demand of the age for something higher than physic or drugging; and

Whereas, The material organization in the beginning was like the baptism of Jesus, a "suffer it to be so now," but the teaching was a purely spiritual and scientific impartation of Truth, whose Christly spirit has led to higher ways, means, and understanding, the President, Rev. Mary Baker G. Eddy, at the height of prosperity in the Institution which yields an extensive income, is willing to sacrifice it all for the cause, even the advancement of the world in Truth and Love; and

Whereas, Other Institutions for instruction in Christian Science that are working out their periods of organization will doubtless follow the example of the *Alma Mater* after having accomplished the worthy purpose for which they were organized, and the hour has come wherein the great need is for more of the Spirit instead of the letter, and SCIENCE AND HEALTH is better adapted to work this result than personal teaching: The fundamental principle for growth in Christian Science is spiritual formation first, last, and always, while in human growth material organization is first; but mortals must learn to lose their estimate of the powers that are not ordained of God, and attain the bliss of loving unselfishly, working patiently, and conquering all that is unlike Christ and the example he gave; therefore

Resolved, That an Institution for instruction in Christian Science, which is the highest, purest, and noblest of all teaching, should be of a spiritual formation wholly outside of material regulations, forms or customs.

Resolved, That we find no platform in Christ's teachings for such material methods of instruction in Christian Science, and we must come into the meekness of his methods as we rise in Christian experience; . . .

After due deliberation and earnest discussion it was unanimously voted: That as all debts of the Corporation have been paid, it is deemed best to dissolve this Corporation, and the same is hereby dissolved.

Thus the argument to be used was that Mrs. Eddy had come to the conclusion that Christian Science, depending as it did on *spiritual* truths, must guard itself from being too heavily invested in material phenomena, things like colleges, formal instruction, bureaucratic organizations, rules and regulations, charters, and the like, and that Mrs. Eddy, "at the height of prosperity in the Institution which yields an extensive income," was nevertheless "willing to sacrifice it all for the cause" as a demonstration that institutions must yield place to ideas.

Her next move, following the same rationale, was to send a letter to the Church of Christ (Scientist), Boston, on November 28, 1889, urging that the Church dissolve its material organization and continue only as an informal public meeting:

Dear Brethren:

The Church of Christ (Scientist) in Boston was my patient seven years. When I would think she was well nigh healed a relapse came and a large portion of her flock would forsake the better portion, and betake themselves to the world's various hospitals for the cure of mortal maladies. These straying sheep would either set up claims of improvements on Christian Science and oppose the mother Church, or sink out of sight in religious history. This state of the church has lasted ten years. . . .

As one who is treating patients without success remembers that they are depending on material hygiene, consulting their own organizations and thus leaning on matter instead of Spirit, saith to these relapsing patients, "Now quit your material props and leave all for Christ, spiritual power, and you will recover." So I admonish this Church after ten years of sad experience in material bonds to cast them off and cast her net on the spiritual side of Christianity. To drop all material rules whereby to regulate Christ, christianity, and adopt alone the golden rule for unification, progress, and a better example as the Mother Church.

194

THE MOTHER CHURCH,
The First Church of Christ, Scientist, Boston.
Deo juvante.

When this is done I have already caused to be deeded to those who shall build a Church edifice, the lot of land designed for the site of such an edifice, and which is now valued at $15,000.

This offer is made on condition that the question of disorganization shall be settled by affirmative vote at the annual meeting of this Church held December 2nd, 1889. . . .[10]

The members of the Church complied, abandoning their formal rules and guarantees of membership. The argument concerning the error of material organization was perhaps inconsistent with the offer Mrs. Eddy made to provide the land for a very material edifice and would seem to have been in some contrast to the encouragements from the *Christian Science Journal* for those in other places to continue organizing new churches and new classes.

A further source of incongruity must have been the history of that particular parcel of land that was offered in the letter as the site for the new church because, until the preceding year, that land had been owned by the Church itself, anyway, and not by Mrs. Eddy.[11] The *members* had purchased the lot in 1886, giving the seller a mortgage for part of the purchase price. Two years later, by a series of complex and dubious financial transactions conducted by a lawyer who was later disbarred, Mrs. Eddy bought up the mortgage and sold the land at a foreclosure sale to her lawyer's brother, who, for a price, transferred it to a representative of her own, Ira O. Knapp, thus assuring her control.

The Church was, at that time, a body that operated by its own bylaws, individual members having some formal say, as participants in a congregation, over its rules, administration, and leadership. It was this potential independence that Mrs. Eddy was determined to extirpate, having experienced the threat it posed to her own control and to the cohesiveness and coherence of *her* Church. An analogy might be made to a business whose founder realizes that the day-to-day operations have become too complex for him to manage all by himself and the needs of whose expansion require that he sell stock to the public. He will naturally feel that it is *his* business and will attempt so to arrange the organization of the new corporation that none of the stockholders, either individually or in concert, threatens to take real control out of his own hands. The analogy is particularly relevant to the period, for this was the time in American history that witnessed the rise of the large corporations. Mrs. Eddy, who used the best legal help she could get, had available to her men who had direct experience in business manipulations of this sort, and we will see how well they served her.

But the matter was not completely settled yet, for one of the trustees empowered with responsibility for erection of the new church felt that these transactions were not legal and saw to it that all of the contributions for construction of the church were returned to their donors before he and the other trustees resigned.[12] Mrs. Eddy protested that this was a legal quibble, saying that she had God's title to the land. The property devolved once again to Knapp, who now sold it to Mrs. Eddy for a dollar. She had, of course, really owned it all along. Her followers did not endorse the scruples of the former trustees and saw it very much from Mrs. Eddy's point of view, so a second attempt was now made. Four new trustees were chosen, receiving the property on September 2, 1892, on condition that they erect within five years a church building that was to cost at least fifty thousand dollars. These trustees, moreover, were to constitute a permanent and self-perpetuating body, a Board of Directors, who would conduct all of that church business that ordinarily concerns a congregation — for example, electing the pastor or leader, holding public worship services, and making all of the rules necessary to these functions. Furthermore, if the trustees neglected to fulfill Mrs. Eddy's conditions of the trust, then the property, church and all, would revert to Mrs. Eddy.

A temporary problem arose, in that the Massachusetts Commissioner of Corporations refused to grant a charter under these terms, saying that the original charter of the

Boston Church, granted in 1879, was still valid and that the congregation itself had rights to such matters as the ownership of church property. But an old statute was discovered which said that under certain conditions, officers and trustees of a church could constitute a corporation for the purpose of taking and holding grants of property made either to them or to their successors, or to their churches. This provided the legal foundation for the Board of Directors, bypassing the congregation's charter.

And so Mrs. Eddy had succeeded not only in controlling the Church but in disenfranchising the congregation, who now had no rights over their own Church operation. They did not even have rights of membership, for Mrs. Eddy now appointed twelve Charter Members who would ballot upon all candidates for admission, that is, anyone, including themselves, who wanted to be a member of the Mother Church. Since the original Church had disorganized itself three years earlier, each former member now found himself reduced in status to being a candidate. Mrs. Eddy then submitted a list of First Members of the Church, thirty-two in all, whom the Charter Members were to vote upon and who would have some special titular dignity but certainly no very special privilege. They were required, once elected, to subscribe to three Tenets, which were very general in content:

TENETS

1) As adherents of Truth, we take the Scriptures for our guide to eternal Life.

2) We acknowledge and adore one supreme God. We acknowledge His Son, the Holy Ghost, and man in His image and likeness. We acknowledge God's forgiveness of sin, in the destruction of sin, and His present and future punishment of "Whatever worketh abomination or maketh a lie." And the atonement of Christ, as the efficacy of Truth and Love. And the way of Salvation as demonstrated by Jesus casting out evils, healing the sick, and raising the dead, — resurrecting a dead faith to seize the great possibilities and living energy of the Divine Life.

3) We solemnly promise to strive, watch, and pray for that Mind to be in us which was also in Christ Jesus. To love the brethren, and, up to our highest capacity, to be meek, merciful, and just, and live peaceably with all men.[13]

Surely this was an unprovocative creed, a spirit less revolutionary than that which had infused the first editions of *Science and Health*; the way was being sweetened for new, more prosperous and conventional, and less adventuresome converts.

The mechanism for membership having been constructed, Mrs. Eddy now established that the Boston church was not simply a local congregation but was to be, rather, The Mother Church. The National Christian Scientists' Association, which up to that time might have been considered the central organization of Christian Science, had ceased to exist, dissolved by its own action in 1892 at Mrs. Eddy's behest, using the same rationale that had inspired the self-disenfranchisement of the Boston congregation three years earlier. This dissolution left as orphan the *Christian Science Journal*, which Mrs. Eddy had given over to the association in 1889, but ownership of which she now reassumed with the association's acquiescence. Just to quiet any doubts, she produced a document that she had had prepared at the time of the original gift, smoothing the way for the return of the *Journal*, now out of debt, to her own proprietorship. Christian Scientists from all over the world were exhorted to join The Mother Church in Boston, and they, having just dissolved their own national organization, transferred their allegiance to The Mother Church and became the passive members of an organization in which they, too, now no longer had any vested rights. At the same time, the broadening of the base of membership and its geographic dispersion made it unlikely that any one segment of the congregation could mount a successful revolution against the Board of Directors or, through them, against Mrs. Eddy herself, who, removed from day-to-day contact with her followers, would seem to have become increasingly idealized as an object of veneration, her remarkable and often difficult personal traits obscured by the haze of distance. She herself contributed to this process of idealization with all of the splendid vigor she was still able to command in her seventieth year.

She sent to press in 1891 a new edition of *Science and Health*, the last one for which she had available to her the editorial services of James Henry Wiggin. One could not assume that her increasing material security served to reduce her suspicions. Like the oceans whose saltiness continues undiminished whatever the weather on the surface, Mrs. Eddy's vulnerability to distrust was not to be ameliorated by good fortune or by the success of her own endeavors. This edition, coming from the Cambridge printshop of the University Press, and thus so close to the evil spirits that had driven Mrs. Eddy from Boston two years before, was supposed to be extraordinarily vulnerable to typographical errors. To eliminate these dangers, Mrs. Eddy organized a cohort of her followers under the leadership of Dr. Foster Eddy to give absent treatment to those responsible for the new edition. The Scientists, apparently not contented with *absent* treatment, intruded their presence into the workrooms and caused the very disruption they were supposed to have circumvented, but the volume was finally produced, its arrival having been anticipated with unusual fanfare in the *Journal*:

> . . . those who confine themselves to the reading and studying of SCIENCE and HEALTH and the Bible are likely to be and generally are further advanced than those given to reading promiscuously what is wrongly called by many persons "Christian Science literature."[14]

Subsequent exhortations to drop the Bible itself for a season and to concentrate on *Science and Health*, and burn all other Christian Science literature, were later repudiated as excessive but reflected Mrs. Eddy's wish to assure her position of prime and controlling influence in her followers' minds.

She considered this latest version "the marvel of my life."[15] Indeed, she considered each successive edition a marvel and an improvement on its predecessors, not for the novelty of its thought, certainly, for the thought was unchanging and eternal, representing the rediscovery of the perfection embodied in the mission of Jesus, but a marvel for the increasing clarity of its expression, for its pedagogical aptness, as it were. Christian Scientists were expected to retire previous editions and obtain fresh copies of each new edition to live with and to peruse for their increasing edification.

In that same year, 1891, Mrs. Eddy published her idealized autobiography, *Retrospection and Introspection*, which achieved a standing among Christian Scientists almost equal to that of *Science and Health*. It padded out an image of Mrs. Eddy so conventionally inspirational that nothing in it would ever joggle the soul of a good, upwardly striving, middle-class Victorian believer. Perhaps today, with the change of fashion in inspirational literature, a truer picture of Mrs. Eddy, showing some part of her shrewd, self-seeking, phantasmagoric energy, would be more attractive than the deified, mummified model of the genteel conventions that served a century ago. But Mrs. Eddy was buttressing her position of absent prophet.

The Church body having been reorganized along the lines of her program, she was in a position to give her attention to construction of the visible church building. Late in 1893 she made a personal request of fifty people that they each contribute a thousand dollars, the immortal fame of their generosity to be assured by the list of their names that would be placed in the cornerstone of the new building. Almost all of them complied, the cornerstone was laid on May 21, 1894, and by January 6 of the next year the building was finished and dedicated, completely paid for. The six thousand people who came to Boston to attend the four dedicatory services elicited those respectful tributes from the Boston newspapers that large, orderly groups of affluent citizens and expensive, imposing structures almost always seem to evoke.

We know of only one discordant note that marred this occasion. Among Mrs. Eddy's most successful disciples was Augusta E. Stetson, founder of the First Church of Christ, Scientist, in New York City, an attractive and forceful lady and much more stable and independent than Josephine Woodbury. Mrs. Stetson had been recruited by Mrs. Eddy herself for her Massachusetts Metaphysical College class of November 1884 and sent by her to New York, where she was soon appointed Pastor of the First Church. The music director of Mrs. Stetson's church had written an anthem for the dedication of The Mother Church. Mrs. Stetson sent Mrs. Eddy a copy of that anthem and received from her an invitation to bring her choir from New York to Boston to perform the anthem at the dedicatory services. When the choir members arrived, however, tuneful and eager, they were met with unaccountable hindrance from the Church officials on the spot, who told them that the program was too long as it was, that there was no place to rehearse anyway, and that unless they wanted to rehearse at 4:00 A.M., perhaps they might not sing at all or, at most, maybe a little hymn that Mrs. Eddy herself had created some years before. The choir and Mrs. Stetson agreed without demur. Mrs. Stetson later wrote:

. . . This thwarted the effort of impersonal evil (malicious animal magnetism) to make discord at that Dedicatory Service of The Mother Church . . .[16]

Mrs. Eddy, who had not herself attended the services, wrote Mrs. Stetson a week later disclaiming foreknowledge of the incident. Mrs. Stetson's account of her subsequent contradictory experiences with Mrs. Eddy and her entourage makes clear how hard it was to negotiate both Mrs. Eddy's mixed feelings toward ambitious, successful disciples and the jealousy of the household staff and the Board of Directors toward someone whom they perceived as competition.

Mrs. Eddy did not see the building itself until April 1,

1895, three months after the dedication, when she came without notice, slept overnight in the specially furnished "Mother's Room," and then left after making some brief remarks at the worship service the next morning. She preached in the building only once again, later on. One wonders at her absence from the dedication and at the paucity of her subsequent interest in the building itself. Perhaps she was ill at the time of the dedication. She was no more exempt from illnesses of a physical nature than from those of psychological origin, and a woman of seventy-four, however vigorous, is entitled to her indispositions. Perhaps, however, she viewed that edifice with mixed feelings, for it was both her monument and her memorial. Mrs. Eddy repeatedly promised her household that her ultimate demonstration would be against Death himself. She promised Calvin Frye that she would survive him and bear witness in future ages to his faithfulness. And yet, however much she was captivated by the enticement of her own myth, whatever her glorification of the spirit and of hope, she knew in her material flesh that time brings, inevitably, infirmity and death and that the solid foundations of The Mother Church were the visible sign that she would, in her turn, have a successor, an heir.

An heir and successor is an object of both hope and bitterness. For many people, children are precious in part at least because they preserve beyond the grave some part of their parents' lives, in the genetic continuity of their bodies, in the impress of their parents' love, ideals, and ambitions, and in the use and preservation of their parents' property. Anyone who has occasion to observe the ways in which property is transmitted, the conditions and restrictions attached to its inheritance, knows how ambivalent the experience of bequest really is, how intense the desire to grasp power from beyond the grave, to cheat mortality, and how keen the submerged resentment that many a parent feels toward his heirs. The sons will spend without effort what the father hoarded up with labor and tenacity. They will enjoy fruit the taste of which is fresher and more intense to the young than to those contemplating their own last days. Perhaps the love of one's children, the capacity to put oneself into the lives of others, one's ability to be disinterestedly generous, serves to soften the bitterness of these reflections and bring some contentment to old age. But Mary Baker Eddy was not able to invest herself in other people's lives in that way. Her investment was in herself, and her only true child was Christian Science, whatever the biological details of George Glover's parentage, whatever the legal details of Ebenezer J. Foster Eddy's adoption, and whatever the ritual and mythical implications of the title of *Mother* by which she was so widely known at this time. She could not bear the notion of a human successor and, consciously or not, began to set about to protect herself against the likelihood of such a disaster.

She had ceased to preach regularly when she moved to New Hampshire. A pastor had been appointed for the church in Boston, and she had become Pastor Emeritus. Shortly after her first visit on April 1, 1895, to the recently completed church building, she caused to have passed by the First Members of The Mother Church a bylaw that:

> . . . Ordained the Bible and *Science and Health with Key to the Scriptures*, as the pastor on this planet of all the churches of the Christian Science denomination.[17]

Since these bylaws of The Mother Church did not automatically apply to other Christian Science churches, the wording of this bylaw was modified to read:

> I, Mary Baker Eddy, ordain the BIBLE, and SCIENCE AND HEALTH WITH KEY TO THE SCRIPTURES, Pastor over The Mother Church, — The First Church of Christ, Scientist, in Boston, Mass., — and they will continue to preach for this Church and the world.[18]

This signal of her intent having been given, the pastors of all other Christian Science churches withdrew from their positions and ensured the adoption of similar ordinances in their own churches. This designation of her official successor was but the first step. The next month, on May 4, 1895, she arranged to have appointed four of her most devoted students to serve with her as a committee to codify the many bylaws that she had issued or caused to have issued by the Church administration, and to prepare a formal manual for the governance of The Mother Church. This manual, while it was designed for The First Church of Christ, Scientist, in Boston, actually defined the relationship of that institution to other Christian Science churches and specified very clearly what was expected of them. The manual, once completed, could be revised only with Mrs. Eddy's acquiescence. Since there was no acknowledgment of the possibility that she might die, and no provision for revision of the manual after that event, it has remained, unaltered, the code of governance for The Mother Church.[19] And since The Mother Church controls the publication of Christian Science books and has sole authority for granting bachelor's and doctor's degrees in Christian Science, degrees that are necessary qualifications for readers in other Christian Science churches, the manual has become, in fact, Mrs. Eddy's last word in the governance of Christian Science as a whole, another aspect of her function as Founder and Discoverer to which no human being has ever become successor.

It is only natural, considering her careful provision against succession, that her uneasy attention should now have turned to Dr. Ebenezer J. Foster Eddy, her adopted son. George Glover, her natural son, however unpresentable he might have been, was no real threat, for he occupied realms of being that didn't intersect with Mrs. Eddy's interests in any way. Dr. Foster Eddy, though, was her own creation, her own designated representative to Christian Scientists about the country, and he was also president of The Mother Church and chairman of the Publishing Committee. He derived a substantial income and generous deference from all of these activities. Mrs. Eddy knew at first hand, from her own treatment of Quimby's memory, that a disciple may begin by giving loving acknowledgment to his teacher and end by denying her entirely. This very denial that one builds on foundations laid by others has been practiced consistently by religious orders since before the time of recorded history. Saints' days and saints' legends record the observances and myths of their pagan predecessors, and not only have churches regularly been built upon the foundations of pagan temples, but even these have contained, buried beneath their floors and forgotten, the altars of their neolithic predecessors.

There were other irritating features to Dr. Foster Eddy, in addition to his possible threat as heir apparent. By temperament a dilettante, he was no more consistent and committed as a publisher than he had been as a homeopathic physician or as a musician. His management of the *Journal* was as uninspired as had been his brief tenure as teacher in the Massachusetts Metaphysical College. And he seemed without eagerness to enter upon the work of producing the new edition of *Science and Health* that appeared in 1894 and the still newer one that was scheduled to come forth two years later. Furthermore, even if he had been businesslike in his attention to practical matters, there were enough envious souls in the Church in Boston and in Mrs. Eddy's entourage in Concord to broadcast and magnify every possible criticism and suspicion of misconduct. He was accused of falsifying accounts, of philandering with the widow of a former friend, and of being less than absolute in his devotion to his "mother." She, only too vulnerable to these suspicions out of her own concerns about being supplanted, transformed them in her usual way into the certainty that Foster Eddy was addressing toward her a baleful hypnotic influence. His protests over each of these accusations, his attempts to document his honesty, probity, high moral conduct, and devotion, couldn't possibly overcome the very source of her distrust of him — that he was her adopted son. She tried to protect herself from his magnetic influence by ordering him to Philadelphia, at the same time begging him to disregard all requests that he move away from her. He elected to stay in Boston. Mrs. Eddy arranged that the First Members replace him with an-

other as president of The Mother Church and, shortly thereafter, that he be replaced as her publisher as well. The next
year he was offered a readership in the church in Philadelphia,
an exile that he was now willing to accept. But the awkward-
ness of his position there and his vulnerability to unfriendly
scrutiny led soon to his dismissal from that post as well. An
attempt to reconcile himself with Mrs. Eddy led to their final
decisive separation, and although she put the responsibility
for his fall and dismissal onto him and to those delegated with
the administration of Church affairs, she reiterated her own
accusation:

> . . . you were governed by hypnotism to work against me
> and yourself and to take me as your authority for so
> doing. . . .[20]

And so Dr. Ebenezer J. Foster Eddy retired to his home
in Vermont, living on his private means and on the savings
from his brief venture into the life center of Christian Science, nursing his wounds and remembering his grievances.
His mother put him out of mind and was already writing to
Edward Bates, the successful businessman who had succeeded
him as president of the Church:

> My beloved Son,
>   I must call you so at this time, but will try not to often,
> it would create such envy. . . .[21]

As other successful men were attracted to the Church administration, content to accept a limited place in an organization grown large enough to offer scope for their talents, the
leadership of the Church became more efficient and Mrs.
Eddy became more securely confirmed as the undisputed
leader of her organization. She had, entirely by her own
ingenuity, determination, and force of character, successfully
transformed an uneasy proprietorship into a successful
corporation.

Chapter Eight

By 1895, Christian Science had grown large enough, and its financial affairs had reached sufficient scale, to attract to its bureaucracy men who would find there enough scope for their own ambitions to justify leaving the world of business. With the fashioning of the Board of Directors and the whole organization of Church management, it could be said for the first time to have a life of its own apart from Mrs. Eddy's daily involvement. Most of the important members of the administrative hierarchy were men, while often the most effective and influential healers and leading spirits of churches outside of Boston were women. Although the Church has always refrained from releasing statistics of membership and details of its finances, some estimate of its relative growth can be gleaned by counting again the healers' cards in the *Journal*. By March of 1895 there were 553 of them, five and a half times the number just seven years earlier. A tally of the first quarter of the list shows that nine of the cards were for male healers, thirty-three were for couples, and ninety were for female healers, a dramatic preponderance.

This split reflected the predominance of men in business and financial positions generally, in contrast to the opportunities that Christian Science from its earliest days had offered to women for healing and for dynamic leadership. It was a dichotomy that sharpened the constant uneasiness and rivalry between dynamic and conservative elements in the Church, and represented as well different elements of Mrs. Eddy's own feelings: she liked to have men close to her, needed them there, but tended to see adventuresome women not only as necessary to the growth of Christian Science, but also as potential rivals and competitors, which indeed, inspired by her very example, they often were.

Although she had relinquished command of day-to-day operations, Mrs. Eddy continued to intervene as she pleased in the conduct of Church affairs. Because she had an intense personal conception of how she wanted her Church to be, her interventions, however fitful and episodic they might have seemed at any particular moment, acted together over time to make the whole Church a coherent operating organism. In this respect, she was much like her contemporaries, the automobile inventors, who, each working alone and putting together a functioning vehicle, continued to tinker with it, perfecting its performance each according to his own standards and achieving at length a very individual machine that worked the more smoothly for being the unified product of a single intelligence.

That is not to say that Christian Science does not have its weaknesses, but, as with Mrs. Eddy herself, its weaknesses are the obverse of its strengths. Since the qualities she now sought were stability, durability, conservatism, and freedom from the influence of particular individuals (other than herself, of course), then dynamism, spontaneity, ecstasy, and the powerful, attractive influence of individual leaders would have to be sacrificed and were, in fact, to be avoided. Even if the conservatism and superficial, matter-of-fact, day-to-day ordinariness of Christian Science limit its capacity to attract new members today, especially from among young people, it can be argued that this is true of most other long-organized religious groups too. Sheer survival ability must offer some advantage of its own.

The most useful tool that Mrs. Eddy employed for her increasing refinement of Church operations was the Church manual.[1] This was copyrighted in revision on at least eleven different occasions between 1895, when it was first presented, and 1908, two years before Mrs. Eddy's death.

She herself wrote that the rules and bylaws that are contained in the manual:

> . . . were written at different dates, and as the occasion required. They sprang from necessity, the logic of events, . . .[2]

She would constantly amend the bylaws to deal with new crises, especially those relating to what she felt to be unseemly personal leadership exercised by one or another of her disciples, or challenges to her dogmatic authority that might open the way to revisionistic influences in the Church, to schisms, and to conflicts. We have seen that one of her first moves in the direction of controlling the leadership of Christian Science churches had been to vest the pastorate in books rather than in people, ensuring that the worship service would be conducted by readers rather than by pastors or preachers.[3]

Over the next few years the functions of readers were carefully defined and circumscribed. There were to be two of them, a man and a woman. One of them, the Second Reader, was to read *Bible* texts and the other, the First Reader, was to read specified correlated texts from *Science and Health with Key to the Scriptures*. Readers were elected subject to Mrs. Eddy's disapproval for a term of three years. The reader was not a leader and could not be president of a church. Readers were forbidden to make remarks explanatory of the lesson-sermon, nor were they permitted, during their term of readership, to give any lectures at all.[4]

The expression of Mrs. Eddy's enduring control and final authority is the last paragraph of the Church manual:

> No new Tenet or By-Law shall be adopted, nor any Tenet or By-Law amended or annulled, without the written consent of Mary Baker Eddy, the author of our textbook, *Science and Health*.[5]

In fact, the Church manual has not been changed since Mrs. Eddy last took up her pen to change it.

All of these developments increased Mrs. Eddy's external security. Church operations became increasingly efficient and effective in combating threats to her authority. The enlarging membership guaranteed a market for successive editions of her books, the royalties from which increased her private fortune. She was becoming a national phenomenon. But these evidences of security did not free her from the consequences of her own conflicting passions, which remained young and lively despite her advanced age. For example, when the Board of Directors of The Mother Church was able to expel Mrs. Josephine Woodbury from membership in 1896, without any of the responsibility for that excommunication appearing to reside in Mrs. Eddy herself, she experienced the same fears that would have presented themselves twenty-five years before.

Mrs. Woodbury attempted at first to preserve the appearance of a good relationship with Mrs. Eddy, but when she failed to achieve reinstatement, she joined forces with the Quimbyites and attacked Mrs. Eddy in a magazine article published in *The Arena* in May 1899.[6] She challenged Mrs. Eddy's claim to have originated Christian Science, compared side by side the testimonial to Quimby that Mrs. Eddy had written for the newspapers in 1862 with the revised history Mrs. Eddy had published in the *Christian Science Journal* in 1887, and quoted the poem Mrs. Eddy had composed at the time of Quimby's death, together with the letter she had written to Julius Dresser asking him to take Quimby's place. She specified Mrs. Eddy's more obvious mercenary ventures, such as selling souvenir spoons and copyrighted photographs. She ridiculed Mrs. Eddy's literary failings and pretensions and described in detail how Mrs. Eddy had alienated those closest to her and manipulated the management of the Church so as to assure herself of control over it. She attacked Mrs. Eddy's claims to healing, suggested that many of the cases which Mrs. Eddy claimed as her own were really bor-

rowed from Quimby, and summarized her assault by sat-
irizing Mrs. Eddy's title of Discoverer and Founder of
Christian Science:

> . . . what she has really "discovered" are ways and means
> of perverting and prostituting the science of healing to her
> own ecclesiastical aggrandizement, and to the moral and
> physical depravity of her dupes. As she received this sci-
> ence from Dr. Quimby, it meant simply the healing of
> bodily ills through a lively reliance on the wholeness and
> order of the Infinite Mind as clearly perceived and prac-
> tically demonstrated by a simple and modest love of one's
> kind. What she has "founded" is a commercial system
> monumental in its proportions, but already tottering to
> its fall.[7]

At least no one could have accused Mrs. Woodbury of
ambiguity. Although Mrs. Eddy was frightened, she rose to
exact revenge and, in her annual communion message the
next month, she attacked Mrs. Woodbury with a fine piece of
theological invective but without mentioning her by name:

> . . . The doom of the Babylonish woman, referred to in
> *Revelation*, is being fulfilled. This woman, "drunken with
> the blood of the saints, and with the blood of the martyrs
> of Jesus", "drunk with the wine of her fornication," would
> enter even the church, — the body of Christ, Truth; and,
> retaining the heart of the harlot and the purpose of the
> destroying angel, would pour wormwood into the waters —
> the disturbed human mind — to drown the strong swimmer
> struggling for the shore, — aiming for Truth, — and if
> possible to poison such as drink of the living water. . . .[8]

Mrs. Woodbury brought suit for libel. Mrs. Eddy suffered a renewed intensity of her nightmares and physical
pains. She thought she could discern among the company
of her enemies once again the face of Richard Kennedy,
still alive in her thoughts. She instructed her administrators

in Boston to take up mental defense against both Mrs. Woodbury and Kennedy, but also to find the best lawyers they could. Her legal defense was based upon the assertion that her annual communion message had not referred to Mrs. Woodbury at all, either by name or by intent, but that Mrs. Woodbury had been trying to injure Mrs. Eddy for a long time and that this suit was simply the latest in a series of mischievous acts. Mrs. Eddy and her lawyers were able to convince a whole flotilla of witnesses to testify that they did not hear in Mrs. Eddy's message any allusion at all to Mrs. Woodbury. Only one man was willing to testify the opposite.[9] The case was decided against Mrs. Woodbury and she retired to England, where she outlived Mrs. Eddy by twenty years, a personal vindication, perhaps, but one of little significance to anyone else.[10]

One wonders, naturally, how much Mrs. Eddy herself believed her own official versions. Her conception of history was often more metaphorical than literal. She herself never acknowledged that her own legend was contrived, nor did she ever seem at all concerned about the distinction between the real facts and the emotionally charged fiction that passed for Church history. That distinction seemed to be a thorn that pricked her critics keenly, but herself not at all. She enjoyed the power she possessed and felt that she was honestly entitled to it. She expressed that conviction in a letter to her son:

. . . God has lifted me up to my work, and if it was not pure it would not bring forth good fruits. . . .[11]

That is, since she had been successful in founding her thriving Church, the means that she had used in achieving her goal must have been acceptable to God and needed no man's scrutiny. She herself saw no reason to question that she had been divinely elected and even, for a time, encouraged her followers to call her Mother Mary, issuing a bylaw to assure that title to herself. Her critics found the title a target worthy of satire, so she, with little taste for satire, changed her mind. But she did offer encouragement to one of her followers who chose to imagine that she could prove by genealogical research that Mrs. Eddy was connected to the British Royal Family and, by this connection, to the House of David and thereby to the Virgin Mary herself. When these researches were unavailing, Mrs. Eddy decided that the genealogists had been obstructed by Malicious Animal Magnetism and that her follower really harbored a desire to cause her harm.

This was, however, but a minor disturbance. She had been accustomed to worse and, for the moment, life was untroubled at Pleasant View, where she was honored, protected, and cared for. Like any woman in her mid-eighties, she no longer had the same resistance to minor illnesses, but she seemed always able to recover her physical integrity and her mental grasp and force of personality. The very routine predictability of her daily life helped her, for old people are vulnerable to uncertainty and to rapid changes.

She was protected not only by her native good physical constitution and by the admiring and fearful attention of her household, but also by the embarrassment that might accrue from any public acknowledgment of her indispositions. Her followers were discouraged from expecting her to appear at public gatherings by being told that she had more important things to do. They were told that their attention should be given to *Science and Health* and not to the particular person of Mrs. Eddy. The lesson was important. Interest in the person, whether proceeding from curiosity or from reverence, was a form of idolatry and not consistent with the Ideal of Truth.

She did not regularly attend the annual communion meeting in Boston; more often, she would send a message to the meeting, inviting those present to Concord, where, depending on her state of health, she would receive them or speak to them from her balcony or merely appear before them and wave her handkerchief. She observed the regular practice, though, of taking a carriage ride each day. The sight of the closed carriage containing a muffled, elderly figure, the pompous, portly person of Calvin Frye up front next to the driver, following its customary itinerary, was a familiar part of the daily life of the town.

But no one can be protected forever from the claims of mortality, and on May 3, 1903, she had her first attack of pain from kidney stones. The ordinary measures taken by her household to repel attacks of pain were insufficient to soothe her. Encouragement, exhortations, vigils, the concentrated thoughts that were supposed to repel Malicious Animal Magnetism — all were unavailing. Finally, the physicians were called in, the first one at two o'clock in the morning, then another, and then, after daybreak, a third, this one her own cousin. He gave her an injection of morphine to relieve the pain. As the days passed, it became clear that attacks were likely to come without warning. Morphine would have to be given repeatedly and at regular intervals during the attacks.

Mrs. Eddy was better later that month and invited those who came to Boston for the annual communion service in June to come to Pleasant View afterward. She greeted them from her veranda. But later that summer she caused to be created a "Board of Missionaries," an official body whose true function was to take instruction in the proper administration of hypodermic injections so that they could care for her safely at home without requiring so many potentially embarrassing visits from physicians.

A Christian Science church was built in Concord that year. Mrs. Eddy had contributed the largest part of the money for its construction; it was felt to be her own church, and some of her students gave generously to it in her honor. The communicants at the annual service in June of 1904 were invited to come to Concord to see it. Contrary to what they expected, though, Mrs. Eddy did not address them at that gathering, or even appear in public. She came in her closed carriage. The president of The Mother Church entered the carriage, spoke with her for a few moments, and then emerged to convey her message of welcome to those assembled. Many were disquieted by her failure to appear in person; some few attempted to watch for her in the neighborhood of her house and along the route of her daily drive. To protect herself from their anxious and curious gaze, she issued "The Golden Rule," Article VIII, Section 27, of the Church manual:

> A member of The Mother Church shall not haunt Mrs. Eddy's drive when she goes out, continually stroll by her house, or make a summer resort near her for such a purpose.

Since she was so often hidden now, sporadic speculations about her health and even rumors that she was no longer alive appeared in the press, but, for the time being, she was put under little pressure to show herself. In 1906, however, an event occurred that intensified curiosity about her state of being. The First Church of Christ, Scientist, in New York City had built a new edifice, at a cost of $1,185,000, that was dedicated on November 29, 1903. It was much more splendid than The Mother Church. When they heard of its planned construction, the Board of Directors decided to build their own enlarged Mother Church because they did not want to live in the shadow of a less important church in another city. Mrs. Eddy would not permit replacement of the original building and issued a bylaw to that effect:

> The edifice erected in 1894 for The First Church of Christ, Scientist, in Boston, Mass., shall neither be demolished, nor removed from the site where it was built, without the written consent of the Pastor Emeritus, Mary Baker Eddy.[12]

She specified that the new building was to be considered only an extension of the original building although, indeed, it might be called the "Excelsior Extension." She did not want anything pertaining to herself to be succeeded or replaced by anything, however grand. The Excelsior Extension was to occupy the large plot of land immediately adjacent to the small corner wedge that was the site of The Mother Church. The erection proceeded slowly. At one point, Mrs. Eddy decided that the delays were caused by Malicious Animal Magnetism exerting its effect on the architects and arranged for the Directors to have them treated. At last, on June 10, 1906, the day arrived for the dedication. The large, high-domed building was proudly proclaimed to be a foot higher than the Bunker Hill Monument.[13] The Mother Church now had about 40,000 members, twice the number of four years before, when the decision was originally made to build the extension. These members together had contributed the two million dollars that it cost, all of which was paid before the dedication. At least half the membership came to Boston that day. Six services were held. Two hundred ushers led the faithful to their seats. But Mrs. Eddy was unable to be present because, according to Calvin Frye's diary, she had not yet recovered her strength from the recurrent attacks of kidney stones that she had had that winter. In the midst of the glorious if restrained rejoicing of the dedication, her absence and her silence attracted marked attention.

Members of the press tried to obtain interviews, but were told that Mrs. Eddy didn't grant them, that her time was taken up with other things. She could be seen taking her daily carriage ride, they were told, and that ought to be proof enough of her existence. At the same time, Mrs. Georgine Milmine, the young writer from Rochester, New York, sold to *McClure's Magazine* her carefully researched manuscript biography of Mrs. Eddy's life, which included specific information about transactions in which legal ownership of her properties was passed from person to person, often coming to rest in the formal possession of Calvin Frye. (The transaction relating to the land on which the original Mother Church was built was an example.) Outsiders, un-

The Mother Church and the Extension

The original building, at the right, is in the form of a cross, and the immense "annex," with its dome, is supposed to represent a crown, the two buildings thus forming the Christian Science seal — the cross and the crown.

familiar with Mrs. Eddy's concerns, might very well suspect that she was either dead or so decrepit that she was no longer in command of her own affairs and that Frye was masterminding a hoax in order to preserve for himself the rich benefits of his position and, for the Christian Science Church, the rich promise of Mrs. Eddy's immortality. They were in no position to know that she was afraid that in the event of her death attempts might be made to break her will. Claims might be made on her estate by her son George, for example, or by others of her relatives, or even Foster Eddy. Such claims might jeopardize her own duly designated successors, *Science and Health* and Christian Science itself.

Information about the property transfers was conveyed by representatives of Joseph Pulitzer's New York *World* to two men with whom Mrs. Eddy had business dealings in Concord, the treasurer of the Concord church and a cousin of Mrs. Eddy's, the secretary of a Concord bank. These men knew that Mrs. Eddy was alive, and since they met with her only at her own initiative, when she was in good health, they saw no reason for her not to be interviewed. They were sure that she would either disprove or explain the property manipulations. They arranged for the reporters to meet with Frye, who didn't deny that he was the owner on paper of much of Mrs. Eddy's fortune. They accused Frye of malfeasance and threatened to expose him unless Mrs. Eddy herself would see them in the presence of a neighbor who could verify her identity. The neighbor they chose was one for whom Mrs. Eddy felt particularly cordial hatred. This made Frye's dilemma only slightly worse; Mrs. Eddy was at that very moment enduring another attack of kidney stones and was in no condition to see anyone. An interview was arranged nevertheless, but she was so ill and in pain, so clouded by the morphine she was taking, that she was barely able to remain standing for the few moments of the reporters' intrusion, and left them certain that although she was in fact alive, she must surely be senile, a puppet of her household staff.

When, the very day after this pathetic interview, she was seen to take her regular drive, the reporters were determined to find out if it was really she in the carriage. Surely the Mrs. Eddy they had seen the day before was in no condition to take carriage rides! Since the carriage was dim and the figure inside well wrapped and shielded from curious eyes by a parasol, they adopted a ruse whereby one of them on one side of the street made a great show of curiosity, causing the person inside the carriage to move the parasol to that side, giving the reporter on the other side of the street a relatively clear view of the person inside. He thought he identified Mrs. Pamela J. Leonard, a well-known Christian Scientist from New York who had recently become attached to Mrs. Eddy's household. Was it really Mrs. Leonard, or was the reporter mistaken and was it Mrs. Eddy herself, feeling better that day? No one knows, but the *World* had a good story and presented it several weeks later, on October 28, in sensational style.

The next day, a whole cloud of reporters descended on Concord and Mrs. Eddy's household. Alfred Farlow, president of The Mother Church and chief of the Boston Publication Committee, was summoned. He called upon H. Cornell Wilson, the Publication Committee person in New York. Together they set about collecting affidavits from prominent local citizens who could testify to Mrs. Eddy's good health. Such measures were not enough to satisfy the press, who demanded to meet with Mrs. Eddy herself. Farlow and Wilson were more worldly men than Frye and better able to negotiate. They arranged an interview with Mrs. Eddy for the next day at which eleven of the reporters might be present, but questions would be limited to Mrs. Eddy's state of health, whether she was under the care of a physician other than God, whether it was indeed she who took the daily drive, and whether she herself ran her own business affairs. The questions were to be asked by Sibyl Wilbur O'Brien, representing a little-known magazine called *Human Life* and, unbeknownst to the other reporters, already busy preparing an official authorized biography of Mrs. Eddy.

But Mrs. Eddy was little better now than she had been at the time of the earlier meeting and barely able to endure three minutes of interview. Each reporter wrote up the event in a different way, the descriptions ranging from commanding to pathetic. A curious reader would have obtained only a very unclear picture of the true state of affairs. *That* couldn't be revealed because an honest account of Mrs. Eddy's real state of health and of her medical care would have caused more harm to Christian Science than all of the unsubstantiated speculation, which only bred confusion and permitted each person to believe whatever he wished.

Pulitzer, having decided that Mrs. Eddy was being used by her associates, retained William E. Chandler, ex-Senator from New Hampshire, to file suit against those associates, presumably on Mrs. Eddy's behalf, to free her from their control. The suit was to be instigated at the behest of those most interested in the preservation of Mrs. Eddy's estate, her potential heirs, but she was to be the nominal petitioner, acting through what were to be called her "next friends." These next friends, however, had yet to make themselves known.

First on the list was George Glover. He had sought money from his mother from time to time, and although he usually received something from her, it was never as much as he would have liked. She had had a house built for him and contributed other small sums, but always reluctantly. In 1898 he had gone to see her to get money with which to pay debts and to invest in a quartz mill. She had given him a check for some of what he asked and promised to send the rest, but then sent him a letter saying that she couldn't give him any more because Frye, who made her account for every penny, wouldn't permit it. Frye was a convenient excuse for Mrs. Eddy's parsimony. She rarely could do something that would anger somebody without finding someone else to blame for it. But George was happy to believe that it was Frye's fault, not his mother's. In 1903 he reappeared, again to ask for money. Mrs. Eddy kept him waiting for days before she would see him and then accused him of having refused to accept aid *she* had offered. He thought she was out of her mind and was more sure than ever that Frye was in absolute control. Now, three years later, he was eager to believe the suppositions laid before him by the emissary of the New York *World*. He set out for Washington to consult with Senator Chandler, taking his daughter Mary and writing his mother that they were planning to visit her. At first, she asked him not to but thought better of it and invited him to come, but also to return to her all of the letters she had ever sent him:

> Pleasant View, Concord, N.H.
> Jan. 11, 1907
>
> My Dear Son: The enemy to Christian Science is by the wickedest powers of hypnotism trying to do me all the harm possible by acting on the minds of people to make them lie about me and my family. In view of all this I herein and hereby ask this favour of you. I have done for you what I could, and never to my recollection have I asked but once before this a favour of my only child. Will you send to me by express all the letters of mine that I have written to you? This will be a great comfort to your mother if you do it. Send all — ALL of them. Be sure of that. If you will do this for me I will make you and Mary some presents of value, I assure you. Let no one but Mary and your lawyer, Mr. Wilson, know what I herein write to Mary and you.
>
> > With love,
> > Mother, M.B.G. Eddy[14]

George refused to return her letters, full of accusations against others and substantial evidence for the lawsuit. When he and his daughter did appear at Pleasant View, Mrs. Eddy greeted him kindly but became confused over a detail of the conversation and, not able to acknowledge that she had made a mistake, argued herself deeper and deeper into uncertainty. She began to tell George of the plots that were being made against her, of people who tried to kill her. He was absolutely convinced that she was senile and incompetent. Since she was thought to have a private fortune of at least three million dollars, he must have felt that he had something to gain by protecting her estate.

She, on her side, became doubly suspicious because he asked about her will but didn't ask her for money. She knew he was in contact with Senator Chandler, and when he returned to Washington she sent him a telegram:

DONT LOSE ANY TIME HURRY HOME AND GET THE MONEY THAT I HAVE SENT TO LEAD CITY ENJOY IT[15]

Another "next friend" was Mrs. Eddy's nephew, George W. Baker, who had his own share of grievances because Mrs. Eddy had been ungenerous toward his mother, Martha Rand Baker, and toward him. His father, Mrs. Eddy's brother Sullivan, had inherited their father's entire estate except for the dollar left to each of the three Baker daughters; forty years later, Mrs. Eddy still resented her disinheritance and still laid responsibility for it at the door of her sister-in-law.

On March 1, 1907, a petition was filed in the Superior Court at Concord, in which "Mary Baker Eddy," acting through her "next friends," George W. Glover, Mary Baker Glover, and George W. Baker, asked the court to appoint a receiver to take control of her property out of the hands of ten of her associates, among them Frye, who were charged with depriving her of the proper use of it. "She," through these "next friends," asked the court to make whatever further disposition of this property the court would deem appropriate. Ten days later, Ebenezer J. Foster Eddy and Fred W. Baker, another nephew, joined the "next friends," and Foster Eddy revealed to the New York World's eager readers the next day his version of the events that had precipitated Mrs. Eddy's break with him, laying the blame directly on Frye.[16]

Mrs. Eddy's response to the petition was to arrange for all of her property to be put into a trust, wholly out of her own control and administered by three good men, upright and respectable, and only one of them a Christian Scientist. He was Archibald McLellan, who had been a lawyer and businessman before joining the Church and becoming editor of the Christian Science periodicals and a member of the Board of Directors of The Mother Church. The others were Henry M. Baker, Mrs. Eddy's cousin, a successful lawyer active in New Hampshire politics, a member of Congress, and a participant in many respectable organizations; and Josiah Fernald, president of the bank with which Mrs. Eddy did business. All of these men were well known and highly regarded in Mrs. Eddy's community. Opposition to the "next friends" petition was under the direction of Frank Sherwin Streeter, a distinguished lawyer and former partner of two justices of the New Hampshire Supreme Court. His list of affiliations, like those of Henry Baker and Josiah Fernald, made him a solid member of the Concord establishment. Streeter's first move after establishing the trusteeship was to request that the court replace the "next friends" with the trustees, that is, substitute them as the petitioners, since they were, as trustees, the people legally responsible for the preservation and proper administration of Mrs. Eddy's estate. That would have ended the whole matter at once. The court disallowed the request, but the creation of the trust and the appointment of the trustees had reduced the issue to the question of whether Mrs. Eddy was competent to create the trusteeship. Since the trustees were considered above reproach, and if Mrs. Eddy were competent, then the trust was valid and the ten defendants had no control over any of Mrs. Eddy's property at all. The solicitude of the "next friends" would be unnecessary. Mrs. Eddy herself wrote a letter to the presiding judge, Robert N. Chamberlain, in which she explained why she had executed the trust deed:

Pleasant View
Concord, N.H.
May 16, 1907

Hon. Judge Chamberlain
Concord, N.H.

Respected Sir:
It is over forty years that I have attended personally to my secular affairs, to my income, investments, deposits,

expenditures and to my employees. I have personally selected all my investments except in one or two instances and have paid for the same.

The increasing demands upon my time labors and thought and yearning for more peace and to have my property and affairs carefully taken care of for the persons and purposes I have designated by my last will influenced me to select a board of trustees to take charge of my property namely Hon. Henry M. Baker Mr. Archibald McLellan Mr. Josiah E. Fernald.

I had contemplated doing this before the present proceedings were brought or I knew aught about them and I had consulted Lawyer Streeter about the method.

I selected said trustees because I had implicit confidence in each one of them as to honesty and business capacity.

No person influenced me to make this selection I find myself able to select the trustees I need without the help of others.

I gave them my property to take care of because I wanted it protected and myself relieved of the burden of doing this.

They have agreed with me to take care of my property and I consider this agreement a great benefit to me already.

This suit was brought without my knowledge and is being carried on contrary to my wishes. I feel that it is not for my benefit in any way but for my injury and I know it was not needed to protect my person or property.

The present proceedings test my trust in divine Love.

My personal reputation is assailed and some of my students and trusted personal friends are cruelly unjustly and wrongfully accused.

Mr. Calvin A. Frye and other students often ask me to receive persons whom I desire to see but decline to receive solely [because] I find that I cannot "serve two masters" — I cannot be a Christian Scientist except I leave all for Christ.

Trusting that I have not exceeded the bounds of propriety in the statements herein made by me

I remain Most Respectfully Yours
Mary Baker G. Eddy.[17]

225

This letter was notarized and filed before the court. Senator Chandler raised doubt that Mrs. Eddy had written the letter herself. It was known, he said, that Calvin Frye was able to reproduce her signature; perhaps Frye had forged the entire document. Mrs. Eddy's competence still remained to be proved. The defense engaged two well-known alienists, what we would today call forensic psychiatrists, to examine Mrs. Eddy and testify to her mental capacity. In addition, the masters appointed by the court interviewed her in person at Pleasant View.

She was in good form and conducted herself magnificently. She admitted to some deafness, was slightly confused at times about details of history, and contradicted herself now and again, but she made it clear to all those assembled that she was an intelligent, shrewd, and forceful person, well able to manage her affairs, with a good grasp of the details of investment, with reasonable and definite ideas about the people she had chosen to administer her estate, and determined to provide for her audience an imaginative and idealized account of the origins of Christian Science.

They were charmed. Judge Edgar Aldrich, one of the masters, told Mrs. Eddy that he had an eighty-year-old mother. She responded in her noblest and most benign public manner, asking the judge to give his mother her blessings. The masters were impressed, as so often people are, by such lucidity in old age. Senator Chandler withdrew the suit after negotiating, it was rumored, a financial settlement for George Glover and Foster Eddy that was somewhat better than that provided for them earlier.[18] This settlement was to be in lieu of inheritance, so that Mrs. Eddy could be reassured that they would not contest her will.

The defense had taken advantage of Mrs. Eddy's fortunate good health that summer to arrange for her to be interviewed by reporters from a number of newspapers, among them the Hearst papers and the Boston *Globe*, which had shown a friendly attitude toward her and toward Christian Science. These reports read very much alike, all appreciative of the wit and charm and vivacity of this eighty-six-year-old woman. But respect and admiration were not universal. In that same year, 1907, Mark Twain's polemic *Christian Science* was published,[19] and Mrs. Milmine's series in *McClure's Magazine*, the introduction to which had appeared in 1906, continued. Subsequent chapters, each with fresh revelations meticulously detailed and buttressed by references, quotations, and affidavits, brought continuing embarrassment. When Mrs. Milmine had presented her original proposal to *McClure's Magazine*, the publisher had assigned to assist her on the project three of his own staff, Willa Cather, Burton Hendrick, and Will Irwin. In their task of preparing the series of articles for publication, they gathered vast amounts of detailed supporting documentation. They employed Frederick Peabody, the same attorney who had represented Josephine Woodbury, to obtain sworn accounts from those who had known Mrs. Eddy in earlier times and could report something at variance with her own official history. They pored through court records and registries of deeds. Dr. Ives Hendrick, sixty years later, remembered vividly the intense discussions at his father's Sunday dinner table in which newly discovered facts were laid side by side with Mrs. Eddy's version. He remembered Mrs. Eddy being quoted as having said:

> Never give up the religion. Religion is the sugar that attracts the flies.[20]

The writers of the *McClure's* series felt that Mrs. Eddy was a talented and impressive mistress of humbuggery, but they tried to make the prose of their series as measured, unexcited, and scrupulous as they could.

Mrs. Eddy was able to find only a few minor details in the first installment with which she could safely disagree. She withdrew into silence, preferring to discourage her flock from reading either *McClure's Magazine* itself or the *Literary Digest*, which carried excerpts. Sibyl Wilbur

O'Brien attempted to provide an antidote in her series published in 1907 in *Human Life* magazine and then later issued in one volume as *The Life of Mary Baker Eddy*. She was subsidized by John V. Dittemore, then a Director of The Mother Church. Mrs. Eddy wanted no publicity at all if she could help it and refused at first to give permission for the publication of Mrs. O'Brien's book, but Mrs. O'Brien had a contract with the promise of royalties and threatened a public suit. Mrs. Eddy relented and provided a most grudging authorization:

> I have not had sufficient interest in the matter to read or to note from others' reading what the enemies of Christian Science are said to be circulating regarding my history, but my friends have read Sibyl Wilbur's book, "Life of Mary Baker Eddy," and request the privilege of buying, circulating, and recommending it to the public. I briefly declare that nothing has occured in my life's experience which, if correctly narrated and understood, could injure me; and not a little is already reported of the good accomplished therein, the self-sacrifice, etc., that has distinguished all my working years.
>
> I thank Miss Wilbur and the Concord Publishing Company for their unselfed labors in placing this book before the public, and hereby say that they have my permission to publish and circulate this work.
>
> Mary Baker Eddy[21]

The book carried the author's maiden name, Sibyl Wilbur, because, Dittemore said, such being the petty prejudices of the day, O'Brien sounded too Catholic for the author of an authorized biography of Mrs. Eddy.[22]

These were not the only troubles of that painful year of 1907. Perhaps the most awkward was the death by suicide of someone very close to Mrs. Eddy herself, coming right at the time of the "next friends" suit and, in its way, intimately connected with it. Mrs. Eddy's "Committee on Business," whose function was to constitute a shield for

Mrs. Eddy's residence against Malicious Animal Magnetism, was then composed of Irving Tomlinson, reader of the Concord church, and his sister Mary. On April 20, shortly after the introduction of the lawsuit, Mary Tomlinson, who was suffering from an acute agitated depression, threw herself from the window of a fourth-floor room in the Parker House hotel in Boston and died. Frederick Peabody wrote that she had become deranged because of her horror at being asked to "treat" Mrs. Eddy's son George and his lawyer by putting metaphysical arsenical poison into their veins, or by killing them by any other means at her imagination.[23] Christian Science was denying officially that it used absent treatment to harm anyone, and Miss Tomlinson was, Peabody said, so disillusioned by the recrudescence of the old practices that she repudiated Mrs. Eddy, became depressed, and killed herself. Another of her brothers, Vincent Tomlinson, a Universalist minister, accused Mrs. Eddy of ultimate responsibility in the matter and accused his brother Irving of complicity. The publicity was distinctly unfavorable.

There were other deaths, too — on December 7, 1907, Joseph Armstrong, a Director of The Mother Church, and only a month later, Pamela Leonard, the woman who had been attached to Mrs. Eddy's own household the year before and whom the reporter had accused of impersonating Mrs. Eddy in her daily carriage ride.

Were these warnings directed against Mrs. Eddy herself? She wondered whether Malicious Animal Magnetism was poisoning the atmosphere of New Hampshire. Besides, the state itself was at fault, she said, because if the laws had been different, she wouldn't have had to experience the unpleasantness of the lawsuit or the interviews, or the revelations of her private fortune, her property manipulations, her dearth of charitable contributions, and the fact that she vastly understated her net worth for tax purposes. She might not have been subjected to the danger that her intermittent poor health could become public knowledge. So she prepared to move again, for the last time now, and ordered a thirty-four-room stone mansion on twelve acres of grounds to be purchased near Boston in Chestnut Hill. Her living quarters on the second floor were commanded to be re-modeled so as to reproduce exactly the arrangement of rooms with which she was familiar at Pleasant View. Work proceeded by day and by night. The identity of the new owner was kept hidden from neighbors. Even the furniture was moved by night. And when the day came for Mrs. Eddy's journey to her new home on January 26, 1908, three locomotives were engaged for the journey, one before, to test the track, a second to pull the special train with Mrs. Eddy aboard under the care of her physician cousin, Dr. Alpheus Morrill, and a third behind, guarding the rear.

She settled into her house and resumed the pattern of her life in Concord, with the same arrangement of rooms, the same household staff, now somewhat enlarged, and the same daily drive. Soon she was feeling better, well enough to write to the New York *Herald*:

> Permit me to say, the report that I am sick (and I trust the desire thereof) is dead, and should be buried. Whereas the fact that I am well and keenly alive to the truth of being — the Love that is Life — is sure and steadfast. . . .[24]

and for the *Christian Science Sentinel*:

> To Whom It May Concern:
> Since Mrs. Eddy is watched, as one watches a criminal or sick person, she begs to say, in her own behalf, that she is neither; therefore to be criticized or judged by either a daily drive or a stay at home, is superfluous. When accumu-lating work requires it, or because of a preference to remain within doors she omits her drive, do not strain at gnats or swallow camels over it, but try to be composed and resigned to the shocking fact that she is minding her own business and recommends this surprising privilege to all her dear friends and enemies.[25]

The attacks of renal colic came and went, and in the space between periods of pain she felt very much her old self. But the unpleasant publicity of the *McClure's Magazine* series seemed endless; she wanted to respond as she had in the past by mounting boycotts against the periodicals that offended her. The Board of Directors felt, however, that a boycott might arouse lively attention from the news media, already sensitive to stories about Christian Science.

A bylaw in the Church manual states:

> A member of this Church shall not patronize a publishing house or bookstore that has for sale obnoxious books.[26]

Furthermore, the manual also had established Committees on Publication, whose purpose was (and is) to correct "false impressions" that appear in the press.[27] These committees were quite effective in suppressing articles and books they didn't like and in discouraging book dealers from displaying, and magazine and newspaper publishers from printing, such material. This was essentially a negative approach.

In March of 1908, however, Mrs. Eddy received a suggestion from a Christian Scientist who was also a newspaperman, John L. Wright, of Chelsea, Massachusetts, which pointed the way to a more positive approach — the establishment of a daily newspaper

> . . . owned by Christian Scientists and conducted by experienced newspaper men who are Christian Scientists. . . . I think many would like to read a paper that takes less notice of crime, etc., and gives attention especially to the positive side of life, to the activities that work for the good of man and to the things really worth doing. . . .[28]

On August 8, in the clear space between two painful attacks, Mrs. Eddy sent her decision to the Board of Trustees of the Christian Science Publishing Society:

Beloved Students: —

It is my request that you start a daily newspaper at once, and call it the *Christian Science Monitor*. Let there be no delay. The Cause demands that it be issued now.

You may consult with the Board of Directors. I have notified them of my intention.

Lovingly yours,
Mary B.G. Eddy[29]

Just three months later, on November 25, 1908, the first issue of the *Monitor* appeared, motivated by an ambition for excellence and guided by a high moral intention. From its very beginning, however, one of its most important functions was to assure that a loyal Christian Scientist who read that one newspaper alone need never be subjected to information or ideas that did not pass Mrs. Eddy's standard of acceptability or that of the Board of Directors, the Committees on Publications, and the Board of Trustees of the Christian Science Publishing Society.

In all of this corral of protective security, there yet remained one single danger, the threat that someone might take over the direction of the Church, supplant Mrs. Eddy by filling the space she occupied in the hearts of her followers, challenge the conservative authority of the Directors and committees and boards of the Church, and lead off the flock to new pastures. That has been a pattern of religious history; it was, in effect, what Mrs. Eddy had done to Quimby. The living embodiment of this predatory threat was Mrs. Augusta E. Stetson, founder and leader of the First Church of Christ, Scientist, in New York City and Mrs. Eddy's most attractive and effective field lieutenant. It was she who had brought the choir from New York to sing at the dedication of The Mother Church in 1895. She had a strong, loyal following among her own students and patients but aroused jealousy in the Christian Science workers already in New York, who broke away from the First Church to found Second, Third, Fourth, and even Fifth Churches there. In addition to her enormous success as a healer, teacher, and administrator, Mrs. Stetson had a most remarkable talent for raising money. The First Church moved into a succession of ever-larger buildings until it built its own in 1903, the act that prompted the determination of the Boston Directors to build the Excelsior Extension.

Mrs. Eddy had mixed feelings about Mrs. Stetson's success. She valued the advantages that accrued to Christian Science, especially since Mrs. Stetson was irreproachable in her devotion to her Leader and Teacher. The First Church was dedicated to Mrs. Eddy with an inscription large enough to be seen from a great distance. Mrs. Stetson showered her with valuable, well-chosen presents: ermine wraps, diamond brooches, winter and summer garments, anything a mother could want. Although Mrs. Eddy theorized against excessive interest in material things, she liked to live well and look good and be surrounded by impressive possessions. Mrs. Stetson's gifts set a useful example to Mrs. Eddy's other students, who exerted themselves to do as well and earn similar appreciation.

On the other hand, her success also aroused resentment because she profited from her accomplishments at least as much as Mrs. Eddy did. The generous gifts she gave Mrs. Eddy came from coffers already overflowing, most of whose contents were set to work in *Mrs. Stetson*'s interest. So much admired, might she not eclipse Mrs. Eddy herself? Mrs. Stetson seemed to fear the possibility of envy; she would at times deliberately suppress praise and publicity favorable to herself lest it detract from Christian Science and Mrs. Eddy. She was always publicly humble toward her leader, careful never to cast abroad her own private ambitions, whatever they might have been.

Mrs. Eddy tested her devotion with one restriction after another, to each of which Mrs. Stetson responded with the most good-natured acquiescence. When The Mother Church was completed and Mrs. Eddy ordained *Science and Health* and the Bible as pastors, Mrs. Stetson resigned at once from her own pastorate, of which she was very proud, to become only a reader. But Mrs. Eddy restricted the term of readership, and Mrs. Stetson became simply a trustee of her own church. When Mrs. Eddy learned that the new First Church building contained offices for perhaps forty healers, she decreed that church buildings should not be contaminated with healing facilities; immediately, Mrs. Stetson and her healers abandoned their offices and set up their healing practice elsewhere. The great new church building was insufficiently large to hold the congregations her services attracted. When Mrs. Stetson instituted overflow and then branch services, Mrs. Eddy made bylaws forbidding each of these in succession. A successful leader in Christian Science had to choose a path carefully calculated to avoid the appearance of personal ambition, but how could one be successful like Mrs. Stetson without also being ambitious?

Mrs. Stetson's greatest safeguard was that Mrs. Eddy was afraid of her. She wanted to be rid of her but was also afraid to offend her lest her resentment take the form of Malicious Animal Magnetism. Whatever was to be done had to be done through the Church, without any apparent responsibility being attributed to Mrs. Eddy herself.

The Directors were at least as determined as she. They knew that Mrs. Eddy was gradually failing, albeit with great reserves for recovery from individual bouts of illness. Their power resided as much in the confidence Mrs. Eddy placed in them as it did in the bylaws and the bureaucratic machinery of The Mother Church. If Mrs. Stetson were to remain the most impressive, dynamic, and successful leader in Christian Science, then she might take Mrs. Eddy's place once she died. Both the Directors and Mrs. Eddy wanted to preside over an organization without formal corporeal leadership, not merely an organization in which leadership was dispersed among its component churches. Strong leaders in individual churches might become organizers of schism and rebellion and threats to the authority of the Directors of The Mother Church. The way it was put was that Personality should be considered inessential before the message embodied in *Science and Health*.

The match was laid to Mrs. Eddy's resentment when in July of 1909, Mrs. Stetson's congregation, on the occasion of their annual communion service and in commemoration of her quarter century in Christian Science, gave Mrs. Stetson a letter of praise that described her as the vessel of the Father-Mother God and as the manifestation of Truth, the "bread of Heaven and the water of Life." They accompanied this idolatrous tribute with a great gift of gold. Mrs. Stetson sent both the letter and the gold to Mrs. Eddy, saying that it was really *she* who deserved them. Mrs. Eddy was furious. She sent the letter on to the Board of Directors, admonishing them to deal with it as a serious administrative problem, and sent Mrs. Stetson a cool letter of thanks with the information that from that time on, their correspondence would be handled through her secretary, Mr. Adam Dickey.

At about the same time, a former disciple of Mrs. Stetson's accused her of having attacked her and her husband with a particularly virulent form of Malicious Animal Magnetism. Mrs. Stetson was summoned before the Board of Directors to answer the charge, but Mrs. Eddy was so frightened by the story that she decided to leave Mrs. Stetson alone lest she herself become the victim of that terrible, distant wrath. Another member of Mrs. Stetson's church, however, the First Reader, brought to the Board of Directors clear evidence that Mrs. Stetson had practiced absent treatment on her enemies, not simply to shield herself from them but actually to injure them. Among these enemies she numbered her competitors in Christian Science and even directors of The Mother Church. Of course, Mrs. Eddy and her entourage had done the same thing, perhaps even as recently as two years before, at the time of the "next friends" suit, although such practice was officially forbidden and considered a grave failing. Mrs. Eddy herself had used it only secretly, as a last resort and under most unusual circumstances.

Mrs. Stetson was prepared to deny these accusations by an argument of curious theological subtlety. She would say that when she did such things, she was in her human form, that is, in her material form, not in the form of her true, real, absolute self. So she could honestly deny that (in her real self) she had ever done the things of which she was accused. She had used this kind of rationalization on another occasion to justify lying in court and had influenced some of her students to do the same.

Practitioners from her congregation were called to Boston and interrogated carefully. The Directors withdrew her license, removed her practitioner's card from the *Christian Science Journal*, and served her with a notice of their findings, which she submitted to her own board of trustees. Mrs. Eddy issued a statement denying that she had any personal interest in the matter, that it was all a question of the "written and published rules."

When Mrs. Stetson's own board of trustees exonerated her, the Board of Directors of The Mother Church demanded that she appear before them, formally charged. Mrs. Eddy wrote a letter to the trustees of Mrs. Stetson's church, asking them to support The Mother Church. After three days of careful examination, Mrs. Stetson was found guilty of the charges raised against her and was dropped from membership in The Mother Church. According to the bylaws, this meant that she could not practice or hold office in her own church. She resigned and her board of trustees accepted her resignation. A new board was elected, composed of her opponents. They upheld the decision, and she ceased to exist as a serious influence.

Mrs. Eddy had made her last contribution to Christian Science. The removal of Mrs. Stetson and the acknowledgment by the board of trustees of the First Church in New York had demonstrated the supremacy of The Mother

Church. Christian Science churches were formally "autonomous" and "democratic," that is, unfederated, lest federation serve as a nucleus for revolt. But now it was even more clear than before that the Board of Directors of The Mother Church had, in fact, the most far-reaching authority; their position was now as secure as they and Mrs. Eddy could make it.

Her life at Chestnut Hill went on as before, but it was evident to her household that she was ebbing. The struggles for position among the staff became even more intense, sharpened perhaps by the presence of Adam Dickey, her new secretary, who had arrived shortly after the move from Concord. He had been recruited by a committee whose purpose was to search the country over for suitable Church members who would be willing to come for a time to serve in Mrs. Eddy's household. They had to be examined as carefully as sheep chosen for sacrifice in Solomon's Temple; no blemishes were permitted, no physical defects, and no history of illness because illness was belief in mortal mind and might contaminate the atmosphere and distract Mrs. Eddy from her work. Dickey, who had been chosen to be Mrs. Eddy's secretary, was a strong, vigorous man. Shortly after his arrival at Chestnut Hill, Mrs. Eddy's coachman was found in his quarters one morning, dead. The uproar in the household was centered on two concerns, perhaps of equal importance: what were the spiritual consequences of a death inside the walls, and how would a replacement be found in time for Mrs. Eddy's daily drive? Dickey showed himself the perfect resource, in this as in every other circumstance, for he was ready to drive the carriage himself, tenderly, with Mrs. Eddy inside and Frye beside him on the box.

The custom was that Mrs. Eddy's rooms would be cleaned while she was on her daily drive. When she would return, she would become irate if each piece of furniture was not replaced in its exact customary position, and the maids seemed never able to put things just so. Dickey saved the day again by driving small tacks into the floor to designate the precise

MRS. EDDY AT THE HEIGHT OF HER CAREER

location of each table and chair leg. Mrs. Eddy in her eighty-ninth year was no less susceptible to strong arms than she had been fifty years before, and much to Frye's dismay Dickey became in many respects master of the household, subject only to Mrs. Eddy's countermand. It is true that when he moved his *wife* into the house, the others rebelled and made formal complaint to Mrs. Eddy. In this instance, the interest of the household was allied to Mrs. Eddy's own, for she did not like her subjects to have divided loyalties. She examined the lady in enough detail to discover that she had once been ill, once had suffered a belief in illness, and she had to be sent away. But aside from this modest defeat, Dickey carried all his campaigns to victory.

As a mark of her greatest favor, at a crucial time in her last year, Mrs. Eddy made Dickey promise that if she died, he would write a history of her last days to show that she had not died of natural causes but had been mentally murdered.[30] Frye was furious, for she had asked him to do the same, and it seems that each man had the feeling that he alone was chosen for this special mission. Mrs. Eddy was still expert at giving each person the feeling that what she was asking him to do was a special favor for him alone and a great private pledge.

During that last year of her life, 1910, she made some concession to her increasing vulnerability. She reproached the Benevolent Committee, which she had created a year earlier, for failing in its appointed task, which was to provide for "scientific weather," that is, weather that was not stressful to her. At one point in the fall of that year, when she was in great pain, she offered a thousand dollars to any member of her household who could heal her. Frye said how sad he was not to be more helpful. Dickey, not to be outdone, said that *he* would be glad to offer a thousand dollars himself to anyone who could do it. Mrs. Eddy, in a fine expression of Shakespearean resignation, replied, "Has it come to this! If you all feel like that, turn your minds away from me and know that I am well."[31]

But she was not well. Her pains returned, compounded by

Dickey's and Frye's fear that she was addicted to the morphine that relieved her, and they restricted the dosage. In late November she caught a cold. She feared the end. Calvin Frye records that she asked him again to testify that if she died, it was because of Malicious Animal Magnetism rather than from natural causes. Finally, pneumonia, the friend of the very feeble, came in the night and released her from the weakness and pain that had assailed her pride. On December 3, 1910, in the evening, she died.

The medical examiner was called next morning, which was a Sunday, to certify her death. At the close of the service that day, the First Reader informed the congregation simply that Mrs. Eddy had passed from earthly sight.

A modest funeral was held. There were no official precedents for funerals in Christian Science. Final burial in the Mount Auburn Cemetery had to await construction of a suitable tomb. During the interim, the coffin was guarded night and day. In the room with the watchers and the dead woman was a telephone, whose fame has had a surprising longevity. Even today, almost three quarters of a century later, people who know very little about Mrs. Eddy will know about that telephone and wonder whether it is in her tomb, connected and functional, should she awaken and have need of it!

Her death solved some problems and created others. She could no longer subject the Directors to her apparently arbitrary and capricious orders. She would no longer awaken her household to repel the evil wishes of her enemies and to comfort her in her pain and loneliness.

On the other hand, why had she not demonstrated over death, as she had promised? It was because, the Directors said, this is an imperfect world and the evil of material beliefs still stalks among us. That was what had caused her death, not aging or the natural course of life. It must have been a particularly difficult issue for the Directors, for two of their closest associates also had died, just before, and they must have wondered if Malicious Animal Magnetism had marked others for death as well.

True to its duty, the *Monitor* published very little of its own about Mrs. Eddy, no eulogy and nothing about her death as such. It reprinted without comment eulogies that appeared in other newspapers and provided a description of her funeral, including the list in detail of official mourners. More space was given to the publication in full of her very important last will and testament. Since Mrs. Eddy owned the Church, both materially and in spirit, it was of the most material and spiritual importance to know who would inherit it. To the same point, the *Monitor* carried, day after day, column upon column of messages of loyalty and acknowledgment from Christian Science churches all over the country and abroad, testifying that The First Church of Christ, Scientist, in Boston, and her Board of Directors occupied the central place of undisputed authority in the implicit organization of Christian Science.

One would have imagined that the mourners could go about their business of grief and recollection undisturbed once the rites were over, the will published, the household's sleep freed from disturbance, and the testimonials of fealty gathered in. It was discovered, though, that an unanticipated complication had been created because the Trustees of the Christian Science Publishing Society were not identical with the Board of Directors of The Mother Church, and a protracted struggle began between these two groups of ambitious men to decide where the real power and authority resided, a struggle that was to occupy many years and pursue its slow course through the courts.[32]

Who remained to mourn Mrs. Eddy herself? Among her household, there must have been some few devoted people accustomed to serve without question, whose lives were made the poorer by her departure and who could treasure up some crumbs of kindness given and kindness received. For others, Mrs. Eddy offered a way to career and power; for them the arena was moved now to within the bureaucracy of the Church. Still others, those to whom she had felt close in the years past, had been pushed aside because of her fear that loving brought helplessness, vulnerability, and disappointment. For her there had been no comfort in intimacy.

The only exception, her faithful Calvin Frye, the one person whose ambition was most wholly satisfied by his place in her life, was given a place in her house in Boston. He assured himself of a generous pension by allowing it to be known that if he were treated parsimoniously, he would tell what he knew about this thirty years as Mrs. Eddy's secretary. The important people begrudged him his crotchets but dared not affront him directly. He kept his vow of silence for the few years remaining to him but disinherited the Church on his deathbed.

Afterword

How then are we to understand the phenomenon of Mrs. Eddy herself? Four different kinds of influences could be considered: her endowment of talent and temperament; her psychological development and character structure; the external life events and social changes that affected her and that she mobilized for her own purposes; finally, the role of Divine Inspiration.

Here immediately we come to our first problem, Divine Inspiration, an unmeasurable factor that each person will weigh differently. It has not been addressed here and yet, to the believer, it would be the important guiding and determining element, beside which all other matters would be trivial. Mrs. Eddy herself would have said that God is All and that there should be no need to consider more mundane and material influences.

Talent and temperament present problems, too, because although they must certainly exist as particular influences in every person's life, they are not easily distinguished as separate strands in the complex tangle that every person comes to be. Nor can they ever be explained, but merely observed and admired. Intelligence, creative talent, and energy must all be identified as Mrs. Eddy's particular and inexplicable qualities. Intelligence and drive can be discerned among members of her immediate family. Her father was a widely capable man, although not focused in his efforts or particularly successful in either a worldly or a spiritual way. Her sister

Abigail and her brother Albert, too, were both capable people, Abigail successful to the limit permitted by her conventional life, and Albert cut down early from a promising career. George Sullivan, the youngest of her brothers, gave hint of an enterprising nature, but with an absence of focus and just a bit of the suggestion that, for him, the easy way out was best. Among her Baker and Morrill cousins there were a number of successful lawyers and doctors, evidence that the family genetic endowment included at least enough intelligence and drive to permit those modest achievements. But for Mrs. Eddy's particular talent there is no accounting, for her unusual ability to pick up from the life around her those special needs and the circumstances of her time that she could weave together into the strong ladder that so many others could climb toward hope.

We *can* have some understanding of what drove her on, and of the shifting balance of psychological forces that made possible her unusual career, of how it could be that a woman who would have seemed only helpless, eccentric, and inconsequential suddenly, in mid-life, experienced such a dramatic change and became so focused, forceful, and innovative.

As a child she was faced with parents of sharply opposed temperaments, her father driving, suspicious, legalistic, but deeply religious, loving, and capable; her mother unassertive, acquiescent, sentimental, but certainly caring for and idolizing her children. Mary, the spoiled youngest, learned very early that she could get what she wanted by being helpless, appealing, and imaginative, on condition that she not express openly anything significant in the way of drive, ambition, or direct anger. The struggle of conflicting urges that such a split of capacities engendered caused her to have a wide range of bodily discomforts and spells, which she perceived as confirmed ill health. She learned to utilize her symptoms to control others and to arrange circumstances for her own comfort and protection. Her pains and trances thus came to serve two kinds of purposes: first, those that give expression to inner conflicts, and second, those that could be used as a means to accomplish certain personal goals.

Many people in every age experience bodily disturbances as expressions of inner conflict. Perhaps everyone does at one time or other. But people vary in the creative use that they make of their illnesses, in the way in which, as a secondary purpose, they may harness them to achieve other life goals. Mary Baker, in the first half of her life, used her weaknesses in fairly conventional ways, to legitimize her claim that others should care for her. If there was, buried within her, more of the speculative thinker and ambitious leader, those capacities remained hidden behind her apparent helplessness and lack of independent purpose.

But her attempts at such a conventional life arrangement were repeatedly frustrated, first by the premature death of her husband George Glover, next by the inadequacy of Daniel Patterson, and then, just when she thought that she had finally found her ideal healer and mentor, by his death as well. Her first impulse was to attempt to continue the same pattern by finding someone to take Quimby's place; that failing, she was forced to acknowledge her loss and take whatever comfort she could from what Quimby himself had given her.

Her identification was only partly with Quimby. Her father too had just died. Although he left her only a dollar of his material goods, his talents and his drive and his harsh independence already resided latent within her character, struggling with the contrary tendencies that, up to that point, had dominated her conscious life. This hidden aspect of herself now took ascendency, given strength by her mourning for what she had gotten from Quimby — and perhaps in her earlier years from her father himself — and became the vehicle by which she carried on Quimby's work. But it was necessary for her to be beholden to no one, to make it all her very own, and to deny anyone on whom she depended, reassuring herself always that she was self-sufficient and in charge, however much the struggle of diverse personalities within her still persisted.

Her conflicts and symptoms now came to be harnessed and integrated into the creation of her Church. Here was a field for the exercise of her creative genius! She was able to use her own inner struggles, integrated with her finely tuned intuitive sense of the struggles of the Victorian world around her, to discover a solution that would offer hope for the amelioration of the everyday problems that burdened so many of her contemporaries. God is Good, she said, and evil and illness are illusions, engendered by the false beliefs of those not in harmony with the forces of God's healing. Her own pains now became explained in one of two ways: either her students and disciples were yearning for her to heal them, which would cause her to feel their pains; or her enemies were wishing illness upon her by thinking evil thoughts and feeling evil feelings, Malicious Animal Magnetism, which served to explain failures of Christian Science Healing as well. Either way, pain did not come from what was inside of her, which was in tune with Spirit, but from the material thoughts of others who turned away from belief in Principle and who thus introduced the illusion of evil in a world in which it had no real existence.

Another symptom that was particularly troublesome to Mrs. Eddy in this latter half of her life was her nightmares, in which her enemies, particularly men toward whom she had felt attraction and the danger of surrender, taunted her in obscene and lascivious ways. She was able to master and to integrate even this symptom into a mechanism useful to her calling. She would interpret her dreams as intuitive guides to the solution of problems that arose in the conduct of her church affairs. Here too she showed her remarkable creative ability to reach into her unconscious perceptions and to feel her way through to the domination of external circumstances.

Many religious sects have been founded by troubled visionaries who brought the inspiration of the moment but left to others the task of organizing, giving structure, writing the books, establishing the ceremonies and rules for membership, struggling with the rebels, and preserving the memory of the founder. Mary Baker Eddy did all of it by herself, working purposefully into her eighty-ninth year, and at a time when a woman was supposed to be decorative, attentive to the needs of the household, and grateful for what a man could give her. She brought the promise of good health and opportunities for successful careers to many women who could not reconcile themselves to the restrictions imposed upon them by their times, but who yet did not have the ingenuity and the strength and good fortune to be able to do it all by themselves; for many men she offered an alternative to the expectation that one should have to be so strong and so independent and so alone that success could bring neither happiness nor well-being nor a sense of personal satisfaction.

She believed in her science of health and she conveyed her certainty to others. Her followers believed that in discovering the cure for her own illnesses, she had given them hope for a better life for themselves, one in which right belief would bring freedom from all the things they regretted about this imperfect world: the evil, the misery, the prevalence of ordinary human unhappiness, the risks of being in love, the fear of death itself.

Whatever Mrs. Patterson had gotten from anyone else, Mary Baker Eddy was truly the discoverer and founder of Christian Science. She built it, stone by stone, plotting the design, laying the foundation, raising the pillars, and putting into place every keystone in every arch. She made her Church and her place in it. But by her strength, determination, and ingenuity, by her example and by the way she seized and molded the circumstances of her era, she made for herself a place in American history beyond the sectarian interests of Christian Science. The example of Mrs. Eddy tells us more about what we were, and more about what we might become.

Short Titles

For the convenience of the reader, the following short titles are used in the notes. Most of these sources are discussed in the Introduction.

Bates and Dittemore, *Mary Baker Eddy*	Ernest Sutherland Bates and John V. Dittemore, *Mary Baker Eddy: The Truth and the Tradition* (New York: Alfred A. Knopf, 1932).
C.S.J.	*The Christian Science Journal*
Dakin, *Mrs. Eddy*	Edwin Franden Dakin, *Mrs. Eddy: The Biography of a Virginal Mind* (New York: Charles Scribner's Sons, 1929; republished 1930, 1970).
Milmine, "Mary Baker G. Eddy" *Life of Mary Baker G. Eddy*	Georgine Milmine, "Mary Baker G. Eddy: The Story of Her Life and the History of Christian Science," *McClure's Magazine*, fourteen articles, announced in vol. 28, no. 2 (December 1906) and concluding in vol. 31, no. 2 (June 1908). Published as *The Life of Mary Baker G. Eddy and the History of Christian Science*, revised and with additional information, by Doubleday, Page and Co., New York, 1909;

reprinted with a new introduction in 1971 by Baker Book House, Grand Rapids, Michigan. In the notes, "Mary Baker G. Eddy" refers to the *McClure's* series; *Life of Mary Baker G. Eddy* refers to the book.

Peel, *Years of Discovery* *Years of Trial* *Years of Authority*

Robert Peel, *Mary Baker Eddy*, 3 vols. vol. I, *Years of Discovery*; vol. II, *Years of Trial*; vol. III, *Years of Authority* (New York: Holt, Rinehart and Winston, 1966, 1971, 1977).

Quimby Papers

Phineas Parkhurst Quimby, *Papers, 1859–66* (Washington, D.C.: Library of Congress Photoduplication Service, 1969; three reels, microfilm positive).

Wilbur, *Life of Mary Baker Eddy*

Sibyl Wilbur [O'Brien], *The Life of Mary Baker Eddy* (New York: Concord Publishing Co., 1908). The references in the notes are to the edition printed in Boston by the Christian Science Publishing Co. in 1913.

Notes

Introduction

1. Mark Twain, *Christian Science* (New York and London: Harper and Brothers, 1907), p. 49.
2. Richard C. Cabot, M.D., "One Hundred Christian Science Cures," *McClure's Magazine* 31, no. 4 (August 1908): 472–476.
3. Two books valuable as eyewitness descriptions of Mrs. Eddy at important periods of her life suffered this fate: Samuel Putnam Bancroft, *Mrs. Eddy as I Knew Her in 1870* (Boston: Press of Geo. H. Ellis Co., 1923), and Adam Dickey, C.S.D., *Memoirs of Mary Baker Eddy* (Boston: Lillian S. Dickey, C.S.B., 1927).
4. Horatio W. Dresser, ed., *The Quimby Manuscripts: Showing the Discovery of Spiritual Healing and the Origin of Christian Science* (New York: Thomas Y. Crowell Co., 1921).
5. Milmine, "Mary Baker G. Eddy: The Story of Her Life and the History of Christian Science," was published as fourteen articles in *McClure's Magazine*, announced in vol. 28, no. 2 (December 1906) and concluding in vol. 31, no. 2 (June 1908). The book, revised and with additional information, was published as *The Life of Mary Baker G. Eddy and the History of Christian Science* by Doubleday, Page and Co. in 1909 and reprinted with a new introduction in 1971 by Baker Book House, Grand Rapids, Michigan.

6. Published by the Concord Publishing Co., New York, in 1908.

7. Published by the Hancock Press, Boston, in 1910.

8. See note 4 above.

9. George A. Quimby, "Phineas Parkhurst Quimby," *The New England Magazine* 6 (1888): 267–276.

10. See Charles S. Braden, *Christian Science Today: Power, Policy, Practice* (Dallas: Southern Methodist University Press, 1958), especially chap. 4, for a description of events in the Church following Mrs. Eddy's death.

11. Published by Charles Scribner's Sons, New York; republished in 1930 and 1970.

12. Dakin, *Mrs. Eddy*. See the publisher's and author's introductions to the editions of 1930 and 1970.

13. Published by Alfred A. Knopf, New York, in 1932.

14. Dakin, in his introduction to the 1970 reprint of the second edition of *Mrs. Eddy*.

15. Robert Peel, *Years of Authority*, note 59, pp. 509–510. Dittemore died on May 10, 1937.

16. Letter from Mary Baker Eddy to Augusta Stetson, 1891, quoted in Dakin, *Mrs. Eddy*, p. 278, and used by Stefan Zweig as the introduction to his section on Mrs. Eddy in *Mental Healers: Franz Anton Mesmer, Mary Baker Eddy, Sigmund Freud* (New York: The Viking Press, 1934). Note that in this passage, Mrs. Eddy was referring to her most recent edition of *Science and Health with Key to the Scriptures*. Her words, however, could just as well be taken for an observation on her life itself.

Chapter One

1. Mary Baker Eddy, *Retrospection and Introspection*, Third Thousand (Boston: W. G. Nixon, 1891), p. 12.

2. Milmine, *Life of Mary Baker G. Eddy*, p. 8.

3. George W. Baker in the Lewiston, Maine, *Evening Journal*,

March 4, 1907, quoted in Peel, *Years of Discovery*, p. 5. Baker's article was written in rejoinder to Milmine's first article in *McClure's Magazine*.

4. Eddy, *Retrospection and Introspection*, p. 12.

5. The original of these letters and of many other early letters of Mrs. Eddy and her family members are to be found in the archives of the Longyear Foundation, Brookline, Mass.

6. Adam Dickey, C.S.D., *Memoirs of Mary Baker Eddy* (Boston: Lillian S. Dickey, C.S.B., 1927), pp. 133–134. This book is very rare. The copy that I used is in the Houghton Library of Harvard University. Dickey is also quoted by Bates and Dittemore, *Mary Baker Eddy*, p. 6.

7. Bates and Dittemore, *Mary Baker Eddy*, p. 32. This is also quoted in Peel, *Years of Discovery*, p. 76.

8. Isaac F. Marcosson, "The Girlhood of Mary Baker Eddy," *Munsey's Magazine* 45 (April 1911): 7, letter of September 7, 1835.

9. Ibid., p. 10, letter of April 17, 1837.

10. Wilbur, *Life of Mary Baker Eddy*, pp. 28–30.

11. Milmine, "Mary Baker G. Eddy," *McClure's Magazine* 28 (1907): 236.

12. Peel, *Years of Discovery*, pp. 49–50.

13. Wilbur, *Life of Mary Baker Eddy*, p. 27. Her reference is to Edward Young, *The Complaint, and the Consolation; or, Night Thoughts*. This meditation on the end of all things, composed in blank verse and published during the years 1742–1745, was enormously popular during the eighteenth and early nineteenth centuries. It is divided into meditations of nine nights. The first four were illustrated by William Blake, published in London in 1797 by Richard Edwards, and republished unabridged by Dover Publications, Inc., New York, 1975.

14. Quoted in Bates and Dittemore, *Mary Baker Eddy*, pp. 28–29.

15. Ibid., p. 30.

16. Mrs. Sigourney, 1791–1865, was a prolific composer of uplifting verse and prose, very popular among genteel folk

in the first half of the nineteenth century. I haven't been able to find this particular poem but can offer, as an example of her style, the first verse of one tuned to a similar subject, "Widow at her Daughter's Bridal":

> Deal gently thou, whose hand hath won
> The young bird from its nest away,
> Where careless, 'neath a vernal sun,
> She sweetly carol'd day by day.
> The haunt is lone, the heart must grieve,
> From whence her timid wing doth soar;
> They pensive list at hush of eve,
> Yet hear her gushing song no more.

Chapter Two

1. Bates and Dittemore, *Mary Baker Eddy*, p. 38.
2. Joseph I. Waring, *A History of Medicine in South Carolina, 1825–1900* (Columbia: South Carolina Medical Association, 1967), pp. 30, 35.
3. Wilbur, *Life of Mary Baker Eddy*, p. 43; Milmine, *Life of Mary Baker G. Eddy*, p. 27; Mary Baker Eddy, *The First Church of Christ, Scientist, and Miscellany* (Boston: Christian Science Publishing Society, 1913), p. 313.
4. Mary Glover to Daniel Patterson, April 29, 1853, quoted in Bates and Dittemore, *Mary Baker Eddy*, p. 64.
5. Gordon S. Haight, *Mrs. Sigourney: The Sweet Singer of Hartford* (New Haven: Yale University Press, 1930).
6. Marjorie Worthington, *Miss Alcott of Concord* (Garden City, N.Y.: Doubleday and Co., Inc., 1958).
7. Louisa M. Alcott, *Work: A Story of Experience* (Boston: Roberts Brothers, 1875).
8. Thomas H. Johnson, *Emily Dickinson: An Interpretive Biography* (Cambridge, Mass.: The Belknap Press of Har-

vard University Press, 1955); John Cody, *After Great Pain: The Inner Life of Emily Dickinson* (Cambridge, Mass.: The Belknap Press of Harvard University Press, 1971).

9. Mary Glover to Martha Rand, March 20, 1848, quoted in Dakin, *Mrs. Eddy*, p. 21.
10. Milmine, *Life of Mary Baker G. Eddy*, p. 29.
11. Dakin, *Mrs. Eddy*, p. 21.
12. Bates and Dittemore, *Mary Baker Eddy*, p. 48.
13. Mary Glover to George Sullivan Baker, November 22, 1849, quoted in Lyman P. Powell, *Mary Baker Eddy: A Life Size Portrait* (New York: The Macmillan Co., 1930).
14. Quoted in Bates and Dittemore, *Mary Baker Eddy*, p. 49.
15. Quoted in Peel, *Years of Discovery*, p. 94.
16. Bates and Dittemore, *Mary Baker Eddy*, p. 50.
17. Mary Glover to George Sullivan Baker, Thanksgiving Day, 1850, quoted in Peel, *Years of Discovery*, p. 96. The portion beginning "in the spring . . ." can also be found in Bates and Dittemore, *Mary Baker Eddy*, p. 50.
18. Mary Baker Eddy, *Retrospection and Introspection*, Third Thousand (Boston: W. G. Nixon, 1891), pp. 26–27.
19. Ibid., 17th Thousand (1900), pp. 32, 33.
20. Mary Glover to Mr. and Mrs. Andrew J. Glover, her husband's brother and his wife, with whom George was visiting, Peel, *Years of Discovery*, pp. 97, 98.
21. Wilbur, *Life of Mary Baker Eddy*, p. 53.
22. Quoted in Bates and Dittemore, *Mary Baker Eddy*, p. 57.
23. Mary Glover to Daniel Patterson, April 29, 1853, ibid., p. 64.
24. Daniel Patterson to Mary Glover, March 31, 1853, ibid., pp. 59, 60.
25. Daniel Patterson to Mary Patterson, February 1857 or 1859, ibid., p. 69.
26. Ibid., p. 73.
27. New Hampshire *Patriot*, June 9, 1848, ibid., p. 46.
28. New Hampshire *Patriot*, October 20, 1852, ibid., pp. 54–55.
29. New Hampshire *Independent Democrat*, ibid., p. 74.
30. From a local newspaper, June 26, 1862, ibid., p. 76.

Chapter Three

1. Daniel Patterson to Phineas Parkhurst Quimby, October 14, 1861, in *Quimby Papers*, reel 3, frame 1374. These letters, the correspondence of Daniel and Mary Patterson with Quimby, and other writings and newspaper clippings relating to Quimby's career can also be found in Horatio W. Dresser, ed., *The Quimby Manuscripts* (New York: Thomas Y. Crowell Co., 1921). Mrs. Eddy's trustees sued the publisher to suppress publication of her letters to Quimby, and a second edition of this book was published from which those letters were omitted.

2. Mary M. Patterson to P. P. Quimby, May 29, 1862, *Quimby Papers*, letter no. 1, frames 1379–80.

3. Mary M. Patterson to P. P. Quimby, August 1862, ibid., letter no. 2, frames 1382–83.

4. Quoted in Bates and Dittemore, *Mary Baker Eddy*, p. 88.

5. Mary M. Patterson, "What I do not Know, and what I do Know," article in the Portland, Maine, *Courier*, November 7, 1862, in *Quimby Papers*, frames 1478–79. This newspaper article was also published in Milmine, *Life of Mary Baker G. Eddy*, pp. 58–59.

6. Article in the Portland, Maine, *Advertiser*, November 8, 1862, in *Quimby Papers*, frame 1479.

7. Mary M. Patterson to the Portland, Maine, *Courier*, November 1862, in *Quimby Papers*, frames 1479–80.

8. George A. Quimby, "Phineas Parkhurst Quimby," *The New England Magazine* 6 (1888): 267–276.

9. Charles Poyen, *Progress of Animal Magnetism in New England* (Boston: Weeks, Jordan and Co., 1837).

10. Horatio W. Dresser, ed., *The Quimby Manuscripts*, pp. 27, 28.

11. *Quimby Papers*, frames 1435–37.

12. Ibid., frames 1442–43.

13. John Bovee Dods, *The Philosophy of Electrical Psychology*, stereotyped edition (New York and Boston: Fowlers and Wells, 1852).

14. Article in the Portland, Maine, *Advertiser*, February 14, 1862, in *Quimby Papers*, frame 1471.
15. George A. Quimby, "Phineas Parkhurst Quimby," p. 272.
16. *Quimby Papers*, frame 1484.
17. See note 7 above.
18. Bates and Dittemore, *Mary Baker Eddy*, p. 77.
19. Mary M. Patterson to P. P. Quimby, January 12, 1863, in *Quimby Papers*, letter no. 3, frames 1385–87.
20. Mary M. Patterson to P. P. Quimby, January 31, 1863, ibid., letter no. 4, frames 1388–90.
21. Mary M. Patterson to P. P. Quimby, March 10, 1863, ibid., letter no. 5, frames 1397–98.
22. Mary M. Patterson to Mrs. Williams, March 8, 1863, ibid., frames 1394–96.
23. Mary M. Patterson to P. P. Quimby, Saco, September 14, 1863, ibid., letter no. 6, frames 1400–01.
24. Mary M. Patterson to P. P. Quimby, Warren, Maine, March 31, 1864, ibid., letter no. 7, frames 1391–93.
25. Mary M. Patterson to P. P. Quimby, Warren, Maine, April 10, 1864, ibid., letter no. 9, frames 1376–78.
26. Mary M. Patterson to P. P. Quimby, Warren, Maine, May 1864, ibid., letter no. 12, frames 1411–13.
27. Milmine, *Life of Mary Baker G. Eddy*, pp. 66 ff.
28. Ibid., p. 68.
29. Bates and Dittemore, *Mary Baker Eddy*, p. 101, quoting a letter by Mrs. Crosby to the Waterville, Maine, *Morning Sentinel*, February 1907.
30. Mary M. Patterson to P. P. Quimby, Lynn, July 29, 1865, in *Quimby Papers*, letter no. 14, frames 1422–23.

Chapter Four

1. Quoted in Milmine, *Life of Mary Baker G. Eddy*, p. 70.
2. Paragraph in the Lynn, Mass., *Reporter*, February 3, 1866, quoted in Bates and Dittemore, *Mary Baker Eddy*, p. 108.

3. Milmine, *Life of Mary Baker G. Eddy*, pp. 84–86, affidavit sworn by Alvin G. Cushing on January 2, 1907.

4. Mary M. Patterson to Julius Dresser, Lynn, February 14, 1866, first quoted by Dresser himself in a letter to the Boston *Post*, February 23, 1883; later by Josephine Woodbury in Woodbury and Horatio Dresser, "Christian Science and Its Prophetess," *The Arena* 21, no. 5 (May 1899): 536–570, pp. 556–557.

5. Julius Dresser to Mary M. Patterson, March 2, 1866, quoted in Bates and Dittemore, *Mary Baker Eddy*, p. 110.

6. Wilbur, *Life of Mary Baker Eddy*, pp. 130–132.

7. Milmine, *Life of Mary Baker G. Eddy*, pp. 84–86.

8. Ibid., p. 113.

9. Advertisement by Hiram Crafts reproduced in Milmine, *Life of Mary Baker G. Eddy*, p. 112.

10. Advertisement appearing June 20, 27, and July 4, 1868, in *Banner of Light: A Weekly Journal of Romance, Literature, General Intelligence* (New York and Boston: Berry, Colby & Co., Publishers). This weekly newspaper appeared in 100 volumes, from 1857 to 1907. The subtitle changed to reflect changes in publisher, but the topics of the articles and advertisements reflected interest in spiritualism, mesmerism, phrenology, and related occult and quasi-scientific subjects. Mrs. Glover also advertised on December 4 and 11, 1869, with more confidence:

    > Mary M B Glover
    > Is prepared to take students at her residence, Stoughton, Mass., and teach them a SCIENCE by which all diseases are healed. Those who learn it are the greatest healers of the age. No medicine is used. All can learn it. No charges unless they can heal. Terms for payment settled one week after taking lessons.

11. Milmine, *Life of Mary Baker G. Eddy*, p. 123.

12. Ibid., p. 125. Affidavit by Horace T. Wentworth.

13. The terms of the first agreement are quoted in Peel, *Years of Discovery*, p. 239. The second arrangement is described in Bates and Dittemore, *Mary Baker Eddy*, p. 138.

Chapter Five

1. Lynn *Semi-Weekly Reporter*, August 13, 1870, quoted in Peel, *Years of Discovery*, p. 246.
2. Horatio W. Dresser, ed., *The Quimby Manuscripts* (New York: Thomas Y. Crowell Co., 1921), chap. XIII, pp. 165–178.
3. Samuel Putnam Bancroft, *Mrs. Eddy as I Knew Her in 1870* (Boston: Press of Geo. H. Ellis Co., 1923). In this charming and devoted memoir, Bancroft describes Mrs. Eddy as she was in those early years. The Longyear Foundation in Brookline, Mass., holds the copyright. Copies have always been very scarce.
4. Ibid., p. 10.
5. Mary Baker Eddy, *Science and Health*, 1st ed. (Boston: Christian Science Publishing Co., 1875). A copy of this rare edition was published in Jerusalem by W. W. Gatling in 1924. See Micah 4:2: "For out of Zion shall go forth the law and the word of the Lord from Jerusalem."
6. Eddy, *Science and Health*, 1st ed., p. 329.
7. Ibid., pp. 371, 375–376, 378.
8. Ibid., pp. 373–374.
9. Bancroft, *Mrs. Eddy*, p. 32.
10. Bates and Dittemore, *Mary Baker Eddy*, p. 157.
11. Eddy, *Science and Health*, 1st ed., pp. 166–167.
12. A photograph of this house may be found in Bancroft, *Mrs. Eddy*, facing p. 31.
13. Quoted in Bates and Dittemore, *Mary Baker Eddy*, p. 166.
14. Quoted in Milmine, *Life of Mary Baker G. Eddy*, p. 173.
15. Eddy, *Science and Health*, 1st ed., p. 193.
16. Milmine, *Life of Mary Baker G. Eddy*, p. 174.
17. Bates and Dittemore, *Mary Baker Eddy*, p. 177.
18. Quoted in Milmine, *Life of Mary Baker G. Eddy*, p. 161.
19. Quoted in Bates and Dittemore, *Mary Baker Eddy*, p. 185.
20. Mary Baker Glover Eddy, *Science and Health, Volume II* (Lynn, Mass., No. 8 Broad Street, published by Dr. Asa

G. Eddy, 1878, reproduced by the Rare Book Co., 99 Nassau Street, New York, 1935).

21. Ibid., pp. 136–137.
22. Milmine, *Life of Mary Baker G. Eddy*, pp. 240–241.
23. Quoted in Bates and Dittemore, *Mary Baker Eddy*, pp. 191 ff.
24. Milmine, *Life of Mary Baker G. Eddy*, p. 242.
25. Bancroft, *Mrs. Eddy*, pp. 42–43.
26. Glover described these events in an interview published in the New York *World*, March 3, 1907.
27. Bancroft, *Mrs. Eddy*, p. 13.
28. Quoted in Milmine, *Life of Mary Baker G. Eddy*, p. 276.
29. Quoted in Bates and Dittemore, *Mary Baker Eddy*, p. 214.
30. Quoted ibid., p. 217.
31. Boston *Post*, June 5, 1882.

Chapter Six

1. "The Meeting of Two Spirits," in Bates and Dittemore, *Mary Baker Eddy*, p. 50.
2. "Meeting of My Departed Mother and Husband," in Milmine, *Life of Mary Baker G. Eddy*, p. 290.
3. Ernest Sutherland Bates, "Mrs. Eddy's Right-Hand Man," *Harper's Magazine* 162 (February 1931): 256–268.
4. Bates and Dittemore, *Mary Baker Eddy*, shows a photograph of a page of Frye's diary facing p. 230.
5. Quoted in Dakin, *Mrs. Eddy*, p. 527.
6. Peel, *Years of Trial*, p. 144.
7. Milmine, *Life of Mary Baker G. Eddy*, p. 304.
8. Dakin, *Mrs. Eddy*, pp. 525–530.
9. Bates and Dittemore, *Mary Baker Eddy*, pp. 231–232.
10. Ibid., pp. 274–275.
11. This is a reference to the Oneida Community, whose founder, John Humphrey Noyes, had practiced faith heal-

ing at an earlier period and believed that perfect health was the natural concomitant to Primitive Christianity. See Robert David Thomas, *The Man Who Would Be Perfect: John Humphrey Noyes and the Utopian Impulse* (Philadelphia: University of Pennsylvania Press, 1977).

12. Henry James, *The Bostonians* (New York: Dial Press ed., 1945), pp. 48, 60, and 63.

13. George M. Beard, *American Nervousness: Its Causes and Consequences* (New York: G. P. Putnam's Sons, 1881).

14. Barbara Sicherman, "The Uses of a Diagnosis: Doctors, Patients, and Neurasthenia," *Journal of the History of Medicine and Allied Sciences* 32, no. 1 (January 1977): 33–54.

15. See Nathan G. Hale, Jr., *Freud and the Americans: The Beginnings of Psychoanalysis in the United States, 1876–1917* (New York: Oxford University Press, 1971), especially pp. 24–68. During this period abortion became much more generally used, both to delay parenthood and to limit family size. See James C. Mohr, *Abortion in America: The Origins and Evolution of a National Policy, 1800–1900* (New York: Oxford University Press, 1978).

Two recent review articles by Willie Lee Rose discuss the changing place of women in American society during this period and refer to extensive social and historical research being done today. See Willie Lee Rose, "American Women in Their Place," *The New York Review of Books* (July 14, 1977), and "The Emergence of American Women," *The New York Review of Books* (September 15, 1977). For an earlier, comprehensive presentation of this problem see Donald Meyer, *The Positive Thinkers: A Study of the American Quest for Health, Wealth and Personal Power from Mary Baker Eddy to Norman Vincent Peale* (Garden City, N.Y.: Doubleday and Co., Inc., 1965), especially pp. 46–59.

John Demos, "Oedipus and America: Historical Perspectives on the Reception of Psychoanalysis in the United States," *The Annual of Psychoanalysis*, vol. 6 (New York:

International Universities Press, 1978), pp. 23–39, discusses changes in the atmosphere of the American family during the latter half of the nineteenth century.

16. This opening quote is adapted from Eddy, *Science and Health*, 1st ed., pp. 60–61: ". . . The Chaldean shepherd saw in a comet the fate of empires, and read the fortunes of man in a star; no higher revelations than the horoscope hung out upon empyrean . . ."

17. *C.S.J.* 5 (October 1887): 369. Also found in Milmine, *Life of Mary Baker G. Eddy*, p. 320.

18. *C.S.J.* 3 (August 1885): 97.

19. *C.S.J.* 5 (January 1888): 526.

20. *C.S.J.* 6 (March 1889): 637–639. Also found in Milmine, *Life of Mary Baker G. Eddy*, pp. 324–326.

21. For an enlightened Christian Science view of the following issues, see Peel, *Years of Trial*, pp. 133 ff. Mr. Peel naturally emphasizes the differences between Mrs. Eddy and Quimby, just as I emphasize the psychological importance of the *similarities* between them. He takes a more doubting attitude toward the authenticity of the Quimby manuscripts.

22. Letters in the Boston *Post* of February 8, 19, 23, and March 9, 1883. In the letter of February 23, Dresser first publishes the excerpt from the letter Mrs. Patterson wrote him after Quimby died, quoted in Chapter 3 above.

23. Milmine, *Life of Mary Baker G. Eddy*, pp. 99–101.

24. Julius A. Dresser, *The True History of Mental Science* (Boston: A. Mudge & Son, 1887).

25. *C.S.J.* 5 (June 1887): 109–118.

26. See the announcement in *C.S.J.* 4 (September 1886): 156.

27. Milmine, *Life of Mary Baker G. Eddy*, p. 353.

28. Chicago *Times*, June 15, 1888.

29. Bates and Dittemore, *Mary Baker Eddy*, p. 289, reports that two bylaws of the association at that time read:
    Resolved, that everyone who wishes to withdraw without reason shall be considered to have broken his oath

and

Resolved, that breaking the Christian Scientists' oath is immorality.

I have been unable to verify that wording. A Constitution and By-Laws of the Christian Scientists' Association dating from about 1885 contains the following article:

Article V: Offences: Sec. 1. If a member violates the Constitution or the By-Laws, or if he or she departs from strict morality and rectitude of character, thus forsaking the foundations of Christian Science, that member shall be expelled from this association. It is not necessary that the individual be notified to appear at the meeting at which this expulsion takes place, if any member of the association furnish evidence of one or more of the aforesaid offences. Any member can withdraw from this association who is dissatisfied with the demands of Christian Science.

30. Livingston Wright's articles appeared in the New York *World*, November 4 and 5, 1906.

31. New York *American*, November 22, 1906; also published in *The Christian Science Sentinel*, December 1, 1906.

Chapter Seven

1. Josephine Curtis Woodbury, *War in Heaven* (Boston: Press of Samuel Usher, 1897).
2. Milmine, *Life of Mary Baker G. Eddy*, pp. 428–429.
3. Peel, *Years of Trial*, pp. 268–269.
4. Woodbury, *War in Heaven*, pp. 50–57.
5. Milmine, *Life of Mary Baker G. Eddy*, p. 435.
6. *C.S.J.* 8 (September 1890): 249.
7. *C.S.J.* 7 (May 1889): 55.
8. Josephine Curtis Woodbury, "Christian Science and Its Prophetess: Part II, The Book and the Woman," *The Arena* 21, no. 5 (May 1899): 550–570.
9. *C.S.J.* 7 (December 1889): 454–455.

10. Quoted in Bates and Dittemore, *Mary Baker Eddy*, pp. 301–302.
11. Milmine, *Life of Mary Baker G. Eddy*, p. 399.
12. This trustee, William G. Nixon, had published previous editions of *Science and Health* in addition to his other duties. His defection forced Mrs. Eddy to find a new publisher; see below.
13. Bates and Dittemore, *Mary Baker Eddy*, p. 313.
14. *C.S.J.* 8 (April 1890): 43.
15. Mary Baker Eddy to Augusta Stetson, 1891, quoted in part in Dakin, *Mrs. Eddy*, p. 278.
16. Augusta E. Stetson, C.S.D., *Reminiscences, Sermons, and Correspondence: 1884–1913* (New York and London: G. P. Putnam's Sons, 1913), p. 29.
17. Bates and Dittemore, *Mary Baker Eddy*, p. 334.
18. So it stands today in Mary Baker Eddy, *Manual of The Mother Church: The First Church of Christ, Scientist, in Boston, Massachusetts* (Boston: The First Church of Christ, Scientist, 89th ed., latest copyright 1908), Article XIV, Section 1, p. 58.
19. The latest copyright of this 89th edition, the most recently revised and current one, is Mrs. Eddy's own, dated 1908, two years before her death. The use of the term "edition" apparently refers to successive printings rather than to special revised versions of the original text.
20. Milmine, *Life of Mary Baker G. Eddy*, p. 423.
21. Bates and Dittemore, *Mary Baker Eddy*, p. 339.

Chapter Eight

1. Mary Baker Eddy, *Manual of The Mother Church: The First Church of Christ, Scientist, in Boston, Massachusetts* (Boston: The First Church of Christ, Scientist, 89th ed., latest copyright 1908).
2. Extract from a letter in Mary Baker Eddy, *Miscellaneous*

Writings 1883–1896 (Boston: Allison V. Stewart, 1917), p. 148, copyright 1896; quoted on p. 3 of Eddy, *Manual*.

3. Eddy, *Manual*, Article XIV, Section 1, p. 58.

4. The relevant passages in the *Manual* are: Article II, Section 1, p. 29; Article III, Section 4, p. 32; Article I, Section 4, p. 26; Article III, Section 8, p. 33; Article III, Section 6, p. 32; Article XXXII, Section 5, p. 95.

5. *Manual*, Article XXXV, Section 3, p. 105.

6. "Christian Science and Its Prophetess," *The Arena* 21, no. 5 (May 1899), in two parts: "Part I, The Facts in the Case," pp. 537–550, by Horatio W. Dresser, son of Julius and Annetta Dresser, described Quimby's history and particularly Mrs. Eddy's relation to him. "Part II, The Book and the Woman," pp. 550–570, was by Josephine Curtis Woodbury.

7. Ibid., p. 570.

8. Mary Baker Eddy, *The First Church of Christ, Scientist, and Miscellany* (Boston: Christian Science Publishing Society, 1913), from the communion speech of June 4, 1899, pp. 125–126. Beginning in the late 1880s or early 1890s, a Christian Scientists' "communion," or meeting, was held on June 5 or 6 of each year.

9. William Nixon, a former associate, the same man who had challenged sixteen years earlier the circumstances of Mrs. Eddy's manipulation of the property on which The Mother Church was built.

10. Mrs. Woodbury withdrew from the scene, but her attorney, Frederick W. Peabody, had become so outraged by his experience at the trial that he became a specialist in litigation relating to Christian Science and finally, in 1910, published *The Religio-Medical Masquerade: A Complete Exposure of Christian Science* (Boston: The Hancock Press, 1910), in which he told of his experiences and set forth specific evidence to support his contention "that Christian science was a deliberate fraud foisted upon mankind by Mrs. Eddy in the name of religion for the mere purpose of extorting money from credulous people" (p. 14).

He was to discover, as those who attack religions so often do, that believers are not dissuaded by appeals to their reason, nor religious movements substantially harmed by attacks that purport to reveal the opportunistic motives of their founders.

11. Mary Baker Eddy to George Glover, April 27, 1898, published in the New York *World*, March 11, 1907, in an abbreviated form that left out some references to Frye's scrupulous honesty. This was a piece of deviousness on the part of the newspaper publisher, Joseph Pulitzer (see below). This letter is published in full in Milmine, *Life of Mary Baker G. Eddy*, pp. 449–450.

12. Eddy, *Manual*, Article XXXIV, Section 3, p. 103.

13. Bates and Dittemore, *Mary Baker Eddy*, p. 391.

14. Mary Baker Eddy to George Glover, January 11, 1907, published in the New York *World*, March 10, 1907. Their subsequent visit is described in the same newspaper account.

15. Quoted in Dakin, *Mrs. Eddy*, p. 429.

16. New York *World*, March 12, 1907.

17. Mary Baker Eddy to Judge Chamberlain, May 16, 1907. This letter is reproduced in facsimile in Michael Meehan, *Mrs. Eddy and the Late Suit in Equity*, authorized edition (Concord, N.H.: Michael Meehan, 1908). Meehan, editor of the Concord *Patriot*, whom Mrs. Eddy addressed as "Beloved Student" (p. 168), had written Pulitzer on her behalf in an attempt to dissuade him from involving his newspaper in an attack on Mrs. Eddy. He published an extensive record of the case, including emended transcripts that omitted matters about which Christian Scientists were not supposed to know, such as Mrs. Eddy's references to her poor hearing and other infirmities, letters to her son, and complex property transactions.

18. In order to avoid litigation, Glover had been offered a last-minute settlement of $125,000, but had refused. Two years later, on November 10, 1909, it was finally arranged to pay $250,000 to Glover and $50,000 to Foster Eddy (Bates and Dittemore, *Mary Baker Eddy*, pp. 407, 418).

19. Mark Twain, *Christian Science* (New York and London: Harper and Brothers, 1907).

20. Personal communication from Dr. Hendrick. The statement is more likely to reflect the attitude of the collaborators than to be a true account of something Mrs. Eddy actually said.

21. Wilbur, *Life of Mary Baker Eddy*. Mrs. Eddy's acknowledgment appeared in 1910.

22. Bates and Dittemore, *Mary Baker Eddy*, p. 402.

23. Peabody, *Religio-Medical Masquerade*, pp. 192 ff.

24. Letter to the New York *Herald*, May 15, 1908.

25. Quoted in Dakin, *Mrs. Eddy*, pp. 471–472. It also appears in Eddy, *The First Church of Christ, Scientist, and Miscellany*, p. 276.

26. Eddy, *Manual*, Article VIII, Section 12, Obnoxious Books, p. 44.

27. Ibid., Article XXXIII, pp. 97–101.

28. Bates and Dittemore, *Mary Baker Eddy*, pp. 421–423.

29. Ibid., p. 422.

30. Adam Dickey, C.S.D., *Memoirs of Mary Baker Eddy* (Boston: Lillian S. Dickey, C.S.B., 1927). This description of Mrs. Eddy's last years was published by Mr. Dickey's widow after he died. When the Directors of The Mother Church read it, they ordered all copies returned and withdrawn from circulation because of the detail with which it presented Mrs. Eddy's true condition in those last years. Only a few copies remain in circulation today. The one I consulted is in the Houghton Library of Harvard University. The Directors' reasoning in ordering the book sequestered is quite sophisticated. Mrs. Eddy asked Dickey to *write* a memoir of her last days, they said, but she didn't ask him to *publish* it.

31. Quoted from Calvin Frye's diary, Monday, September 26, 1910, in Dakin, *Mrs. Eddy*, p. 530.

32. Charles S. Braden, *Christian Science Today: Power, Policy, Practice* (Dallas: Southern Methodist University Press, 1958), chap. 4, pp. 61–95.

Index

Eddy, Mary Baker (*cont.*)
39, 49, 51, 54; use of morphine, 39, 50, 93, 215, 219, 240; accommodates to widowhood, 39–41; death of mother, 43–45; and father's remarriage, 45–47; second marriage, *see* Patterson, Daniel; and plagiarism, *see* plagiarism; refurbishes old poems, 58–59, 147; relationship to Quimby, *see* Quimby, Phineas Parkhurst; healing others causes her to develop their symptoms, 81, 84, 85, 86, 95; lectures on Quimby's method, 86; practices spiritualism, 87–88; burgeoning capacities, 88; fall on ice, 92; conflicting versions of fall, 92–99; restructuring of life, 99–101; and Hiram Crafts, 103; and Mrs. Webster, 103–106; biblical commentary, 104–105, 107; advertises to teach healing, 106, 111, 257; and Sally Wentworth, 106–108; relies on Quimby's method, 107, 111, 124; and Richard Kennedy, *see* Kennedy, Richard; lectures (1870), 111–112; redefines debt to Quimby, 116–118, 120, 122; struggles with malicious mesmerism, *see* malicious mesmerism; *Science and Health* published, 119–123; chooses name of Christian Science, 119, 123; buys first house, 124; and Gilbert Eddy, *see* Eddy, Asa Gilbert; and Spofford, *see* Spofford, Daniel H.; and Arens, *see* Arens, Edward J.; dreams, 129, 146, 151–153, 246; preoccupation with evil, 133–135; regular preaching begins, 136; followers revolt, 139–141; ordained pastor, 141; advertises to teach obstetrics, 141, 171; resides in Boston, 135, 137, 138, 142; explains Eddy's death, 143–144; and Frye, *see* Frye, Calvin; whole involvement in Christian Science, 153, 159, 170, 204; Christian Science as separate from mental healing, 158, 161; establishes *Christian Science Journal*, 159–161; and Arens suit, 166–169; revises history of Quimby years, 169; and Mrs. Corner's failure, 170–174, 177; at Chicago convention, 174–176; healers defect, 177–178, 185; adopts new son, *see* Eddy, Ebenezer J. Foster; employs J. H. Wiggin, 180–183, 187, 200; moves to Concord, N.H., 183–184, 189; and Woodbury, *see* Woodbury, Josephine; fear of alienating followers, 187, 189; freed from routine duties, 190–192; issues Seven Fixed Rules, 190–191; closes college, 191–193; dissolves Church, 194–196; gives land for new church, 196–197; establishes The Mother Church, 199; autobiography, 201; collects money for church building, 201; visits The Mother Church, 203; Pastor Emeritus, 204; uses bylaws to shape Church, 205, 209–211, 234; concept of history, 213–214; life at Pleasant View, 214–215; kidney stones, 215, 217, 219, 231; reclusiveness, 216, 217–220; and Excelsior Extension, 216–217; interviewed, 220, 226–227; "next friends" suit, 221–226; property put in trust, 223–225; and articles about her, 227–228; at Chestnut Hill, 230, 237–238; founds *Christian Science Monitor*, 231; and Stetson, *see* Stetson, Augusta E.; asks Frye and Dickey to write her story, 239; "know that I am well," 239; last illness and death, 240; last will and testament, 241; divine inspiration, 243; talent and temperament, 243–244; integration of psychological and social forces, 244–

Stetson, Augusta E. (*cont.*)
Church, 202; perceived as
threat, 232–236; success as leader,
232–233; devotion to MBE, 233;
accepts restrictions, 233–234;
tribute from congregation, 235;
angers MBE, 235; accused of malicious mesmerism, 235; expelled
from The Mother Church, 236
Stoughton, Mass., 106
Straw, Jane L., 139
Streeter, Frank Sherwin, 224
Stuart, Elizabeth G., 139

Taunton, Mass., 103
Tilton, Abigail Baker, 21, 23, 32,
38, 48, 49, 56, 62, 80, 81, 99, 104,
244
Tilton, Albert, 58, 81
Tilton, Alexander Hamilton, 21, 22
Tilton, N.H., *see* Sanbornton
Bridge, N.H.
Tomlinson, Irving, 229
Tomlinson, Mary, 229
Tomlinson, Vincent, 229
touch (manipulation), 76, 82, 110,
112–114, 121–122
Twain, Mark, 23, 227

urbanization, changing mores and
religious values, 31–32, 156–157,
260–261

Vail, William T., 61, 62, 64
Vinci, Leonardo da, 99–100

Ware, J., 70
Ware, Emma and Sarah, 166–167
Warren, Me., 83
Washington, D.C., 58, 60, 79, 141

water cure (hydrotherapy), 61, 62,
64, 137
Webster, J. W., 70
Webster, Nathaniel, 104
Webster, Mrs. Nathaniel, 103–106
Wentworth, Alanson, 107, 108
Wentworth, Horace, 107–108
Wentworth, Sally, 106–108, 117
West Medford, Mass., 170, 172
West Newton, Mass., 151
Wheelock, A. T., 73
Wheet family, 55–56
Wiggin, James Henry, 187, 200; as
MBE's editorial writer, 180–183;
MBE appeals to mercenary in-
terests, 182; teases MBE about
using spectacles, 182; kindly re-
membered by her, 183
Wilbur, Sibyl, *see* O'Brien, Sibyl
Wilbur
Wilmington, N.C., 34, 35, 36
Wilson, H. Cornell, 220
women, nineteenth-century: chang-
ing family roles, 31–32, 157;
authors encounter obstacles, 40–
41; career opportunities offered
in Christian Science, 142, 155,
176, 208–209; changing place in
society, 260
Woodbury, Josephine, 8, 192, 202,
227; important place in Christian
Science, 186–187; romantic manner and following, 187; unexpected pregnancy, 187; describes
birth of Prince, 188; ejected from
Christian Science, 189; attacks
MBE, 211–212; MBE's revenge,
212–213
Woodbury, Prince, 188–189
Wright, John L., 231
Wright, Livingston, 180, 183

yellow fever, 35, 36
Young, Edward, 30, 252